Theology and Ethics
for the Public Church

Theology and Ethics for the Public Church

Mission in the 21st Century World

Edited By

Samuel Yonas Deressa
Mary Sue Dreier

LEXINGTON BOOKS/FORTRESS ACADEMIC
Lanham • Boulder • New York • London

Published by Lexington Books/Fortress Academic
Lexington Books is an imprint of The Rowman & Littlefield Publishing Group, Inc.
4501 Forbes Boulevard, Suite 200, Lanham, Maryland 20706
www.rowman.com

86-90 Paul Street, London EC2A 4NE, United Kingdom

Copyright © 2023 by The Rowman & Littlefield Publishing Group, Inc.

All rights reserved. No part of this book may be reproduced in any form or by any electronic or mechanical means, including information storage and retrieval systems, without written permission from the publisher, except by a reviewer who may quote passages in a review.

British Library Cataloguing in Publication Information Available

Library of Congress Cataloging-in-Publication Data Available

ISBN 9781978713239 (cloth) | ISBN 9781978713246 (electronic)

Contents

List of Figures   ix

Foreword   xi
    Hak Joon Lee

Introduction   1
    Samuel Yonas Deressa and Mary Sue Dreier

PART I: PUBLIC THEOLOGY IN SPECIFIC GLOBAL CONTEXTS   5

Chapter 1: Public Theology of Abundance: Reclaiming Africa's Abundance in Public Theological Discourse   7
    Ibrahim S. Bitrus

Chapter 2: Leadership Solution to Africa's Enigma: Redefining Missional Leadership in African Context   25
    Samuel Yonas Deressa

Chapter 3: We Can't Breathe: The Role of Public Theology in the Midst of Social, Political, and Institutional Unrest   43
    David L. Everett

Chapter 4: Native Christian Mission in Burma   55
    Pum Za Mang

Chapter 5: Diakonia and Justice in an African Context: Highlights from the Kenya Evangelical Lutheran Church   71
    Margaret Kemunto Obaga

Chapter 6: Global Public Theologians in Rural Contexts: Malawi and Wisconsin:

Equipping Prophetic Public Companions for God's Mission in
Rural Communities — 87
Laurie Skow-Anderson

PART II: IMPLICATIONS FOR ETHICS AND SOCIAL RESPONSIBILITY — 107

Chapter 7: The Polis in Luther's Theology — 109
Robert Kolb

Chapter 8: Lesslie Newbigin's Idea of a Christian Society — 123
George R. Hunsberger

Chapter 9: Love in Luther: Beyond Thesis 28 — 141
John R. Stumme

Chapter 10: Citizenship as Co-Creation: Theological Foundations for Democratic Renewal — 157
Marie-Louise Ström

Chapter 11: Pandemic Politics: Critical Social Theory and Societal Chaplaincy — 171
Robert O. Smith

PART III: FAITH AND RELIGION IN CONTEMPORARY SOCIETY — 187

Chapter 12: Problems of a Theology of the Cross — 189
Gregory Walter

Chapter 13: Stunned: — 205
David E. Fredrickson

Chapter 14: The Sutures of Reason and the Short-Circuit of Faith: Belief in the Light of Contemporary Cognitive Theories — 219
Guillermo Hansen

Chapter 15: A Stranger God: Sketch of a Religionless Theology — 237
Josh de Keijzer

Epilogue I: Reflection about Professor Gary Simpson — 251
Marie Y. Hayes

Epilogue II: Gary M. Simpson: A Fruitful Vocation — 253
David L. Tiede

Afterword *Gary M. Simpson*	257
Select Bibliography	267
Index	271
About the Contributors	277

List of Figures

Figure 2.1. Three Dimensions of a Missional Church. *Image by Samuel Deressa.*   32

Figure 11.1. Civil Society between Lifeworld and Political State/Market Economy. *Critical Social Theory: Prophetic Reason, Civil Society, and Christian Imagination, Guides to Theological Inquiry (Fortress Press, 2002), p. 121.*   175

Figure 11.2. Colonization of the Lifeworld. *Critical Social Theory: Prophetic Reason, Civil Society, and Christian Imagination, Guides to Theological Inquiry (Fortress Press, 2002), p. 114.*   176

Foreword

Hak Joon Lee

This volume presents a collection of essays celebrating Gary Simpson's life-long achievements as a theologian, teacher, and public intellectual. It indisputably demonstrates the deep appreciation of Simpson's profound impact on the minds of many scholars and clergypersons now serving churches across the globe.

My first encounter with Gary happened at the annual meeting of the Society of Christian Ethics (SCE) in 1994. Thanks to our shared interest in critical social theory (especially Jürgen Habermas), public theology, Christian ethics, and globalization, and to no lesser degree thanks to his friendliness and down-to-earth openness, we immediately connected with each other despite our differences in denominations, nationalities, and racial-cultural backgrounds. It was a fresh encouragement for me to find a friend whose mind is quintessentially interdisciplinary. Our fellowship continued for over two decades, and I have been continuously impressed by Gary's ecumenical spirit, passion for social justice, inquisitive mind, and rootedness in the Lutheran tradition. He, in fact, helped me to correct my Reformed bias about Lutheranism.

Simpson's scholarship is distinctive in its interdisciplinary nature; as a professor who teaches systematic theology at the seminary, he seeks to build his theological framework in the intersectionality with public theology, congregational study/missional church, and Christian ethics, with a deep Lutheran root. Furthermore, his interdisciplinary theological framework is supported by his rigorous social analysis that pays close attention to particular cultural contexts, institutional dynamics, and civil society where a concrete form of congregational ministry takes place. This integrative approach, which I believe is the expression of Simpson's love of God, love of the church, and relentless pursuit of truth, is his unique and valuable contribution to Christian scholarship and global churches.

Apart from its celebratory intent, this volume has its distinctive scholarly merits. The contributors from the Global South and North apply rich insights that were learned from Simpson toward their own distinctive social contexts in a critical and constructive way. The editors of this volume do a skillful job in coherently organizing highly diverse essays around the three key themes: public theology in diverse global contexts, public theology for ethics and social responsibility, and the theology of the cross and public mission of the church. The topics are attractive, the scope is global, and the intellectual engagements are stimulating in demonstrating how Simpson's theological framework that interweaves public theology, missional church, Christian ethics, and the Lutheran tradition can competently address the challenges and opportunities that global churches face in their unique contexts.

Importantly, Simpson's legacy in this volume compellingly reminds us that higher education is far more than the accumulation of knowledge, the transmission of information, and professional training; in the final analysis, it is for the character formation of students with a public mind who are willing to speak the truth to the powers and authorities as they serve humanity for the common good.

When churches' moral authority is discredited and its social relevance is questioned, Simpson's faithful, balanced interdisciplinary approach deserves broad attention. This volume, along with the first one, is proof that his approach is not an empty speculative intellectual exercise happening in the ivory tower but a practical effective methodology of Christian praxis for civil society and pedagogy for global Christians.

I congratulate Gary Simpson for his impressive achievement as a scholar and teacher and his outstanding service to God's kingdom.

Introduction

Samuel Yonas Deressa and Mary Sue Dreier

The editors of this volume are pleased to make available this collection of works by theologians from both Global South and Global North demonstrating various ways in which the public Christian church is involved in mission globally. This book and its companion volume, *Forming Leaders for the Public Church*, are published in honor of Rev. Dr. Gary M. Simpson, Emeritus Professor of Systematic Theology at Luther Seminary, St. Paul, Minnesota, USA. Simpson is a prolific writer whose scholarship has influenced theologians and church leaders globally. The editors of this book consider Simpson "a public theologian *par excellence*" who deserves to be read globally.

A book such as this has been needed for some time, a book that brings together theologians from Global North and South to reflect on the public church and Christian missional vocation in the twenty-first century. All of these contributors have gained insights from Simpson's class lectures, learned from his numerous writings and presentations, and benefited from various interactions with him, including both formal and informal conversations. One can tell that Simpson has been generous with his time and energy to support his students and colleagues.

During over forty years as a theologian of the church, Simpson has been engaged in the important questions and debates within the larger Christian society regarding the role of the church in shaping the moral fabrics of a given society. It is his clear and compelling articulation of the public ministry of the church and the role of the church as public companion that became appealing to global theologians and church leaders who have continued to use his theological framework in dealing with issues related to Christian mission in their own contexts.

For Simpson, one of the reasons why congregations should consider engaging the public is because "the multiplicity of struggling and often isolated institutions native to civil society are beginning to cry out to one another for help."[1] He emphasizes that congregations in America and the global Christian community are becoming aware of their "renewed calling, a public moral vocation" because they have begun to give "ear to these cries for help from civil society."[2] As a theologian, he argues, one needs to engage in public discourse since the theologian is part of the social reality in which they are situated.

According to Simpson, "Congregations participate in the moral life of the community in two ways at once, one more internal and the other more external."[3] Internally, congregations are dedicated to the moral formation of their members. Focusing on discipleship and developing ministries that assist families in the upbringing or "moral formation" of their children, congregations prepare men and women for the public environment. Simpson emphasizes that the church's ministry is always public, and "its public character is rooted in its most basic identity constituted through public worship's proclamation of the gospel, distribution of the sacraments, and outcries of prayer as it anticipatorily groans and rejoices in communion with the Holy Spirit and with all creation."[4] Through internal ministries Christians are formed for public ministry striving for justice and peace as Christian citizens.

Externally, congregations live out their faith in public with integrity as public moral companions, and Simpson refers to this as the "external moral vocation" of congregations.[5] For him, the public—the *res publica*—encompasses all of "civil society." It includes "the vast and pluralistic, interlocking network of spontaneously emerging associations and institutions 'located' between the lifeworld and the two great systems" of political state and market economy.[6] This "lifeworld," according to Simpson, includes a larger space than the realms of the state, politics, and the economy.

Quoting Simpson:

> Civil society is that great plurality of different kinds of associations, affiliations, networks, movements, and institutions for the prevention and promotion of this, that, and the other thing. This teeming plurality is regularly attuned to how societal and cultural problems and injustices resonate in the private life spheres. Its core medium is social solidarity. It researches causative factors, distills critical issues, gives them a moral language and cultural energy, and transmits them in amplified forms to the political public spheres for democratic processing.[7]

As Simpson contends, it is in this civil society that the church is invited to play a role, a role in which it can be engaged in modeling the "background assumptions of a culture, society and personality that shape the defining and interpretation of a given situation."[8] On a larger scale, according to Simpson, the church is also invited not only to participate but to have a positive influence on the economic and political systems of society.

What makes Simpson's work on public theology an important contribution for the global Christian community? There are many reasons, two of which are particularly important to this book. First, as a Lutheran theologian, Simpson emphasizes that the starting point of public theology should be the Word of God, which strongly impels the church toward social, economic, and political analysis and involvement. During his class lectures and presentations and in his writings, he argues that just as the prophets in the Old Testament analyzed and criticized all forms of social and economic injustices in their prophetic task, theologians and leaders of the church today should stand against the systemic forces that are operative behind all forms of social maladies. Second, one unique characteristic of Simpson is that he consistently makes use of studies by social theorists, political scientists, economists, and other theologians to delineate the role of a church in a given society. He is an interdisciplinary and global thinker. His approach is interdisciplinary in that he, for example, utilizes critical social theory, which involves critical reflection on the actual social situations that impact humanity and the whole creation.[9] His global approach is readily apparent in the essays in this volume, as writers from the Global South and Global North reflect on its relevance and implications for diverse contexts.

This volume is divided into four sections. The first section articulates how public theology is emerging to address the challenges in specific contexts around the world. The second section focuses on the implications of public theology for ethics and social responsibility. The third section explores how the theology of the cross influences new thinking about the public role of faith and religion in contemporary society. The fourth section provides an afterword by Simpson and personal reflections by two of his Luther Seminary colleagues.

The editors would like to thank each of the authors for their valuable contributions and Lexington Books/Fortress Academic Press for their willingness to publish this volume. We trust these essays will enhance the reader's understanding of public theology and the role of the church in a given society. We hope that the insights shared in each chapter will spark a deeper conversation on how the church can better publicly serve the kingdom of God through faithful theology and ethics.

Samuel Deressa and Mary Sue Dreier, Co-Editors
St. Paul, Minnesota

NOTES

1. Gary M. Simpson, "Civil Society and Congregations as Public Moral Companions," *Word & World* 15, no. 4 (Fall 1995): 243.
2. Simpson, "Civil Society," 243.
3. Simpson, "Civil Society," 426. For more details on Simpson's public theology, see his other writings: *Critical Social Theory: Prophetic Reason, Civil Society, and Christian Imagination* (Minneapolis: Augsburg Fortress, 2002); "Civil Society and Congregations as Public Moral Companions," *Word & World* 15, no. 4 (Fall 1995): 420–27; "Toward a Lutheran 'Delight in the Law of the Lord': Church and State in the Context of Civil Society," in *Church and State: Lutheran Perspectives*, eds. John R. Stumme and Robert W. Tuttle (Minneapolis: Augsburg Fortress: 2003), 20–50; "Congregational Strategies for Invigorating Lutheranism's Just Peacemaking Tradition," *Journal of Lutheran Ethics* 3, no. 7 (July 2003); "Puckering Up for Postmodern Kissing: Civil Society and the Lutheran Entwinement of Just Peace/Just War," *Journal of Lutheran Ethics* 2, no. 11 (November 2002); "God against Empire: Implicit Imperialism, Deliberative Democracy and Global Civil Society, *Consensus* 29, no. 2 (2004): 9–60; "Our Pacific Mandate: Orienting Just Peacemaking as Lutherans," *Journal of Lutheran Ethics* 5, no. 7 (June 2005); "'God is a God Who Bears': Bonhoeffer for a Flat World," *Word and World* 26, no. 4 (Fall 2006): 419–28; and "God, Civil Society, and Congregations as Public Moral Companions," in *Testing the Spirits*, ed. Patrick R. Keifert (Grand Rapids, MI: Eerdmans, 2009), 67–88.
4. Gary M. Simpson, "Missional Congregations as Public Companions with God in Global Civil Society: Vocational Imagination and Spiritual Presence," *Dialog: A Journal of Theology* 54, no. 2 (Summer 2015): 141.
5. Simpson, "Civil Society," 426.
6. Simpson, *Critical Social Theory*, 169–70.
7. Gary M. Simpson, "Puckering Up for Postmodern Kissing: Civil Society and the Lutheran Entwinement of Just Peace/Just War," *Journal of Lutheran Ethics* 2, no. 12 (December 2002), para. [26], https://learn.elca.org/jle/puckering-up-for-postmodern-kissing-civil-society-and-the-lutheran-entwinement-of-just-peace-just-war/ (accessed August 29, 2022).
8. Simpson, "Puckering Up."

PART I

Public Theology in Specific Global Contexts

Ibrahim S. Bitrus maintains that Africa lacks an imaginative public theology of abundance despite its enormous political, human, and material resources. He disavows the gloomy neocolonial characterization of Africa as a continent of woes and asserts that its challenges are surmountable and not defining. He develops an African Christian public theology of abundance rooted in the abundant perichoretic being of the Triune God and reflected in Africa's own rich abundance. He argues that this is the key to the faithful harnessing of the continent's copious resources and opportunities.

Viewing Africa from a different angle, Samuel Yonas Deressa analyzes its current challenges as fundamentally a crisis of leadership. He observes that his native continent is in need of change and that the Christian church, despite rapid growth, has not positively addressed significant African needs. He defines transformational leadership, outlines the dimensions of the missional church, and suggests that Christians exercise transformational missional leadership grounded in a Trinitarian understanding of God. He proposes that such transformational missional leadership, exercised not only in the church but at all levels of African society, would positively impact the common good.

David L. Everett provides a challenging view of public theology through the eyes of a Black man in the USA today. He makes visible the fight and plight of Black people in the USA and outlines practical, inclusive ways for public theology to address the reality of racism. He suggests that the current situation has created a tension of opportunity for fostering change, and he offers a vision of trust and shared power. He issues an impassioned call to become "*public*ans" who move from passive to active citizenship through equitable leadership, ownership, and partnership.

Whereas the illustrious history of foreign missionaries to Burma has been well documented, Pum Za Mang narrates the mostly neglected but fascinating history of native Christian missionaries in Burma who worked with amazing success and enduring consequence. He clearly demonstrates how the Chin, Kachin, and Karen Christians played a key role in spreading Christianity among their own people and among diverse ethnic minorities. Mang relates their stories of strong zeal, resolve, and perseverance. In addition, the witness of these native missionaries bolstered religious, ethnic, and social ties between races and has served the Burmese well to protect their ethnic identity and keep their distance from their powerful lowland neighbors.

Margaret Kemunto Obaga draws insights from the Kenya Evangelical Lutheran Church (KELC) in exploring a contextual diakonia, which she defines as a response to the needs experienced by individuals and communities in their particular situations and changing social milieus. She uses her recent research among current leaders in the KELC to propose five common diaconal themes for the public church. She observes that contextual diakonia addresses needs and injustices, provides creative interventions, and demonstrates solidarity with the poor. It therefore offers a promising avenue of progress and justice as well as a rejection of fatalism among Africans.

Laurie Skow-Anderson reveals how practical public theology, lived out in rural faith communities, is relational, risky, and revolutionary. As a bishop in the Northwest Synod of Wisconsin (ELCA), she has observed rural congregations in the synod grow as public churches by holding missional theology and public praxis together. She identifies how three pathways—global, rural, and leadership—have led to that growth. A twenty-year partnership between the Northwest Synod of Wisconsin and the Evangelical Lutheran Church of Malawi, both in predominantly rural contexts, has significantly strengthened congregations and leaders in both places as they have shared their journeys along these three pathways.

Chapter 1

Public Theology of Abundance

Reclaiming Africa's Abundance in Public Theological Discourse

Ibrahim S. Bitrus

Abundance is the natural consequence of the revelation of God's immanent abundant being in creation. Africa is impacted by this natural consequence of divine revelation. But instead of critically and diligently discerning and engaging the question of abundance in its public discourse, the mainstream African public theology preoccupies itself with the human-made scarcity and other challenges of Africa. In this chapter I propose a new path for public theological discourse, which places Africa's abundance at the center of its public discourse rather than its challenges.

I start off with reviewing the current state of African public theology to properly situate my contribution. I also recast the meaning, nature, and task of Christian public theology. I analytically describe the being of God as abundance in the economy of salvation and in his immanent life as it is also reflected in Africa's abundant human and material resources. I argue for an African Christian public theology of abundance, which not only is rooted in the being of the Triune God as abundance but also reclaims Africa's abundance as the center of Christian public theological discourse on God in Africa.

CURRENT STATE OF PUBLIC THEOLOGY IN AFRICA

The dominant African public theology is too obsessed with discourse about the sickness of Africa. The contemporary Africa is rejected in its discourse for not being the Africa of our dream. The sickness of Africa is underscored to justify the fundamental need for developing public theology in Africa. In the most recent celebrated book, *African Public Theology*, Sunday Bobai Agang succinctly makes this claim: "Almost everyone in Africa acknowledges that we are currently living in Africa we do not want. It is not that we do not love Africa—we do, passionately and deeply. . . . But when we look around us, we see abundant evidence that all is not well in Africa."[1]

There is no doubt that the dominant discourse of African public theology is loaded with evidences marshaled to prove that Africa is not well socially, economically, politically, religiously, or environmentally. The maladies of Africa are chronicled in the African public theological discourse to demonstrate that Africa is a "shithole" continent, which needs urgent liberation and development. Although this derogative description of the continent is a racial slur made by President Donald J. Trump to belittle Africa, H. Jurgens Hendriks takes it and runs with it. Hendriks affirms the racial slur and discusses abundant evidences to show not only that Africans are responsible for President Trump's derogatory racial remark but also, more importantly, they have contributed enormously to making Africa a "shithole."[2]

African public theologians claim that constructing relevant African public theology must be undertaken in the complex context of the African challenges, which undermine the cherished dream of the Africa that everyone wants. The exponents of the public theology of African maladies believe that the redemption of the international reputation of Africa lies in unpacking, engaging, and addressing its challenges from the standpoint of the Triune God. According to them, the challenges plaguing Africa are not hard to perceive. Economically, insufficient basic infrastructures, monolithic economy, unstable national currency, and low Gross Domestic Product (GDP) characterize Africa. They point out the increasingly worsening income disparity between the haves and the have-nots, who live on less than two dollars per day. Politically, they claim that Africa is unstable. There is massive corruption in government, insecurity, dictatorship, and abuse of the rule of law. There is also massive electoral fraud and the Big Man Syndrome.[3]

Socially, African public theologians claim that many Africans are internally displaced persons and refugees due to civil unrest, terrorism, and banditry. Poverty and unemployment are the order of the day. The continent also experiences gross shortages of healthcare facilities and workers. Thus, a lot of the people, many of whom are women and children, suffer untimely death daily from preventable diseases such as malaria, tuberculosis, cholera, and typhoid. Again, they claim that social evils of xenophobia, sexism, religious conflict, racism, crimes, environmental issues, abusive cultural practices, and hopelessness are endemic in Africa.[4]

African public theologians do not just lay bare the African woes in their public theological discourse; they also make incredible proposals for engaging them. Hendriks proposes that Africa can be transformed from its retrogressive status into the Africa God wants via Spirit-led movement of the African people who act justly, love mercy, and walk humbly before God and in every public sector of African society. These Spirit-led African people will not only bear public witness to the truth, bind up the broken victims of systems of injustice, and live out the kingdom values but also live an alternative lifestyle that contradicts systemic evil that destroys humanity and our world and, thus, replace evil with good in Africa.[5]

Koopman claims that the multifaceted social, political, economic, ecological, sexual, medical, cultural, and personal challenges of Africa must be engaged from the Trinitarian perspective. The deployment of the Trinitarian approach, he believes, enables us to perceive the maladies as moral and theological challenges, both of which are related to God. The Trinitarian approach engages the challenges according to the famous Christian triad of faith, hope, and love:

> Faith expresses the foundation and anchor of our lives in something that happened in the past; hope articulates the joyous future, *telos*, purposes and ends of our lives because of what is yet to come; love reflects the present life of service and compassion on the basis of our past and future realities via remembrance of the past and expectation for the future.[6]

Koopman believes that public theology in Africa should critically reflect on the Christian faith that remembers what the Triune God has done in the past, is doing now, and will do in the future. The Trinitarian public theology provides a rational framework for an inclusive and faithful discourse about public life rooted in God, who not only creates, liberates, sustains, and renews but also actualizes flourishing life.

For Agang, public theology can overcome the immense evil of Africa. The key to this is massive theological education for the clergy and the laity. He believes theological education has the capability to teach them to realize that every department of human life is created and sustained by God. For this reason, it inspires everyone not only to live their life in every public sphere to the glory of God but also to proclaim the word, live out the way of Christ, and work for the healing of the nations.[7]

REIMAGINING CHRISTIAN PUBLIC THEOLOGY

Public theology is relatively a new field of theology in Africa. As a novel distinct branch of Christian theology, Christian public theology is yet to find a sound footing in the higher theological and secular educational institutions in Africa. The growing interest in public theology among scholars, students, and pastors clearly shows that public theology has a promising prospect of becoming one of the leading fields of theology in Africa. But what exactly public theology means is ambiguous and imprecise. Nevertheless, its ambiguity and imprecision do not defy any further attempt to reimagine it.

Public theology is a Christian theology that repudiates the practice of private discourse about God. It rejects modern forces that relegate the Christian faith to the private domain. Public theology doesn't obliterate the distinction between private and public departments of life, but it transcends the division. Public theology argues that the Christian faith is not just a personal relationship with God but also a relationship that impacts the public order of God's creation. It insists that academic discourse about God has public consequences. An academic discourse, public theology relates the Christian faith and life to public matters of importance in society. Ronell Bezuidenhout and Piet Naudé are right to submit that public theology "is an attempt to understand the relation between Christian convictions and the broader social and cultural context within which the Christian community lives."[8] The Christian faith does not teach one to abandon the good world that God has made and "flee to the desert, to isolate oneself from human society, to live in stillness and silence; for it was impossible to serve God in the world."[9] Indeed, it teaches that we are not of the world, but it insists that we are in the world to engage with its socio-economic and political affairs as its light and salt.

The Triune God, who is the author of the world and humanity, is the proper subject of this public theological discourse. Therefore, there is no public space in society where God is not directly or indirectly involved in shaping and impacting it. The public matters of significance, which affect the world and humanity that God so loved, are at the heart and soul of public theology. Contributing to discourse on public issues, public theology should not be influenced by any political ideology, whether right or left, but by scriptural convictions that transcend any political-ideological divides. Public theology should construct and reconstruct from rational and scriptural perspectives an informed and objective discourse on God about public matters that checks and balances the excesses of any political ideology. Public theology loses its credibility and integrity whenever it identifies itself outright with or promotes one political ideology over against the other in a democratic society. It must vehemently resist the temptation to be hijacked by any political ideology to serve as its mouthpiece.

Public theology seeks to influence public policy, law, value systems, and decisions, not only without forceful imposition of the Christian faith on society, but also without losing or compromising the substance and uniqueness of the Christian faith. Public theology accomplishes this through mass theological education, public persuasion, advocacy, and debate on public issues of significance. Thus, to publicize Christian theology is by no means to secularize and pluralize the Christian faith. In other words, public theology "secularizes" and "pluralizes" academic discourse on God about temporal public matters without secularizing and pluralizing the Christian faith, which remains true, unique, and unalterable no matter what through the ebb and flow of human history.

Even when it engages in public inter-religious dialogue with other religions in a multi-religious society, public theology insists on maintaining rather than undermining the particularity of the Christian faith. The publicness of Christian theology does not destroy but affirms and defends the sacredness and distinctness of the Christian faith. In the public discourse of the Christian faith, its divine sacredness and uniqueness remain sacrosanct! This explains why public theology appeals to scripturally grounded sacred symbols and articles of the Christian faith, apart from human reason and experience, in its task of engaging and illuminating urgent public matters of significance. It preserves the peculiarity of the Christian faith while engaging public issues in a responsible, delightful, and effective way for the good of the temporal order of God's creation and the neighbor in particular.

Constructing public theology is the public vocation of a theologian. The public vocation of a theologian is to bring academic discourse about God to bear on the art and process of capturing and exercising state power and allocating public resources. The public theologian believes that the wise exercise of state power and sharing of public resources by temporal authorities not only secures life and property but also provides for the common welfare of the people. As Bezuidenhout and Naudé put it, "The public theologian should function as a social critic, seeking to address contextual, public issues from a theological perspective. The task of a public theology is to contribute to the up-building and the critical transformation of our public life."[10]

Through critical engagement with fundamental issues in the public domain, public theologians concretize the academic discourse about God and make it intelligible to a public audience devoid of any technical and jaw-breaking theological jargon that is otherwise comprehensible only to their professional group. The sacred doctrines are discussed not merely as an abstract academic exercise but as a down-to-earth divine discourse in light of crucial issues of the time. In doing so the academic obtuseness, which Christian theology is often accused of, is obviated and circumvented, hence putting the abstract academic discourse on God within the reach of a public audience. By and large, public theology is the imaginative prophetic engagement of public issues with God's word to positively transform public minds and structures of society through the Spirit for the common good of the world God so loved.

THE THRUST OF THIS ESSAY

I disavow the characterization of Africa mainly as a continent of woes. Although Africa has its maladies like any continent of the world does,[11] the maladies by no means ultimately define its social, economic, cultural, and political substance. There is more to Africa than its woes unless the Africa we all envision is a perfect one, which I contend is not a temporal but an eschatological reality. Not only does Africa have good things of life, but it also thrives in virtually every public sphere of life, which public African theologians have either ignored or deliberately de-emphasized. Instead, they have overblown African challenges out of proportion, which has thereby created a global terrible misconception about Africa—that there is virtually nothing good about Africa but misery.

This gloomy characterization of the continent in African public theological discourse is arguably the offshoot of the European scholars' racist and savage portrayal of Africa during the colonial period. We need an urgent liberation from this neocolonial mindset. I argue that Africa is a continent of abundance. Thus, the thrust of this essay is that there is abundance in Africa, and this abundance is rooted in the abundant being of the Triune God. The African public theology must be communitarian theology,[12] not only because it correlates with the abundant communal character of the African community, but also because it captures the African abundant human and material resources. There is no more suitable and relevant theology to Africa than this public communitarian theology.

ECONOMIC BEING OF GOD AS ABUNDANCE: THE BASIS OF ABUNDANCE

The divine economy of creation is the epistemological basis for recognizing the immanent being of God as abundance. Though the Triune God's being is abundant in God's inner life, it is in the economy of creation, salvation, and sustenance of the world and humanity that God reveals and shares God's immanent abundant being. The divine economy reveals that God's being is the abundant communion of three divine persons. God created an abundant world through Christ in the Spirit. The abundant sharing of functions among the three divine persons in the economy of salvation is indescribable. Their abundant cooperative and functional relationships create, redeem, and sustain the world. The Father abundantly creates the world; the Son abundantly redeems it; and the Spirit abundantly sustains it not individually but collectively through and with the abundant collaboration and participation of all of them. The economic being of God[13] is the abundant free sharing of all good things among the divine persons of the Trinity with the world. As an abundant God, the Triune God creates and endows the world with abundant human and material resources.

Hence there is a correlation between God's abundant being and the abundance of his creation. According to the biblical account of creation, God created an abundant world. God made humans not only to prosper in every way and to enjoy the abundant resources but also to deploy the means that God has provided for them to flourish. Thus, the Triune God made humanity in not a sparse but a rich abundant world. Abundance is part of God's divine economy of creation. Scarcity is a human-made phenomenon that undermines God's will for his creation. In fact, borrowing from Gary Simpson, "It contradicts the perichoretic life and abundance of the triune God promised and made present by the Holy Spirit in the justifying word for the sake of the entire world."[14] Abundance is a shared gift of God to humanity. Our role is simply to grasp it and manage it faithfully and judiciously as God's stewards. As a gift, humans do not have any "divine right" to abundance; neither do they have any grounds to boast about it. As a common grace rather than human achievement, they're simply indebted to God for his abundant provision. Thus, humanity doesn't create abundance; humanity is only to responsibly contribute to it.

The Triune God made humanity with innate capacity and ingenuity to work, improve, and distribute justly and fairly God's created abundance for the benefit of all people. The Triune God's provision is abundant enough to go around unless it is deliberately thwarted by human greed and materialism. A certain powerful group of people has often accumulated and hoarded God's abundance for their own greed, pride, and pleasure. But, cooperating with God, humans can creatively manage God's created abundant resources by sustaining and improving them even to exceed their original provision for all to enjoy. God's intent is that all people should not merely exist but truly live having a fair access to and enjoying good things of life in abundance. But God does not give his abundance to humans on a silver platter to enjoy. If this were the case, then God would be the author of laziness! God didn't make Adam and Eve and put them in the garden to laze around and enjoy the fruits of the garden. No, the Triune God put them in the garden to work, even though the fall made work laborious and drudgery activity. The Triune God's gift of abundance is always grasped by collaboration between God and humanity through the means of labor. Luther expounds the cooperative relationship between divine and human agency in grasping God's temporal blessings in the world under the rubric of "masks of God."

> God could easily give you grain and fruit without your plowing and planting. But God does not want to do so. Neither does he want your plowing and planting alone to give you grain and fruit; but you are to plow and plant and then ask His blessing and pray. . . . What else is all our work to God—whether in the fields, in the garden, in the city, in the house, in war, or in government—but just such a child's performance, by which He wants to give His gifts in the fields, at home, and everywhere else? These are masks of God, behind which He wants to remain concealed and do all things. . . . We have the saying: "God gives every good thing, but not just by waving a wand." God gives all good gifts; but you must lend a hand and take the bull by the horns; that is, you must work and thus give God good cause and a mask.[15]

God designed humans to access and enjoy his created abundance through the exercise of their God-given ability to "till and keep the earth" (Gen 2:15). The abundant provisions of God cannot be grasped and enjoyed by people who are lazy and indolent. Neither can we grasp God's enormous material provisions by simply praying, "sowing seed," and naming and claiming them as prosperity gospel preachers teach! There is no shortcut to grasping God's abundant provision other than through vocation.

The incarnation of God in the economy also showcases the being of God as abundance. St. John minces no words in testifying it: "And the Word became flesh and lived among us, and we have seen his glory, the glory as of a father's only son, *full of grace and truth*. . . . From his *fullness* we have all received, grace upon grace" (John 1:14, emphasis added). The incarnation no doubt reveals abundant grace and truth of God to the world, which we wouldn't have known, accessed, or grasped without God's incarnation. God's grace and truth are no longer scarce "resources" in the world; they are revealed plentifully in Christ. As many as Christ may come to them will never lack God's full grace and truth, for Christ will grasp them in abundance.

In fact, here is God's irrevocable promise: even when lies and sin increase in the world, God's grace and truth will abound all the more! As St. Paul puts it, "Where sin increased, grace abounded all the more" (Romans 5:20). God's abundant grace and truth always overcome human sin and lies, no matter how pervasive and entrenched they are in the world. Unlike the devil who comes to steal, kill, and destroy human life, God became flesh in Christ to destroy the devil, sin, death, and lies that we "may have life, and have it *abundantly*" (John 10:10, emphasis added). The incarnation has let loose the superabundant life in the world. To have life abundantly is to delightfully grasp and enjoy God's promise of superabundant life that is characterized by superabundant love, superabundant forgiveness, superabundant freedom, and superabundant generosity in the world.

But proper distinction must be made between the grasping of God's provision of abundant human and material resources and his gifts of abundant spiritual grace, truth, and life. Making the distinction is quite necessary, lest we trash our incredible conversation on God's being as abundance. While we can grasp God's provision of abundant human and material resources by sheer hard work, or vocation, his gifts of abundant spiritual grace, truth, and life are grasped by faith alone in Christ as the word is preached and the sacraments are administered.

IMMANENT BEING OF GOD AS ABUNDANCE: THE SOURCE OF ABUNDANCE

The being of God as revealed in the Trinitarian economy invariably helps us recognize the immanent being of God as abundance. What this correlation affirms is that the economy being of God's abundance is indistinguishable from the immanent being of God as abundance. The economic being of God as abundance is the immanent being of God as abundance and vice versa. We can't get behind this abundant God in the economy and find a different immanent abundant God. Thus, God is not first and foremost abundant in his inner life before becoming abundant in the economy. God's being is abundant from his immanent life to his revelation in the economy. This abundance is not a quality or attribute of God. Abundance is constitutive of not just his personal relationships but also his unity. Abundance defines God as a communion of three divine persons without which God is not God. The Father, the Son, and the Holy Spirit are abundant in their personal relationships with one another and in their relational unity. As Simpson claims, "God's abundance resides in the three divine persons—Father, Jesus the Son, and the Holy Spirit—who freely and fully share in each other's open reality and who freely share their abundance in the creation of all things."[16] The abundance of their distinctive personal relationships does not threaten but affirms the abundance of their unity.

The immanent being of God as abundance is constant as well as dynamic in its trinity and unity. The immanent abundance of God as revealed in the economy incorporates humanity and the world without altering its constancy. The immanent being of God is the abundant sharing of unalterable inner life of the divine persons with the world and humanity. The being of God as abundance captures and emphasizes the relationality of God in the economy and in Godself. In other words, the being of God is characterized by abundant love and personal relationships *ad extra* (outwardly) and *ad intra* (inwardly) among the divine persons themselves and their creation. The immanent abundant being of God is the ultimate source, or origin, of all abundant life, abundant human relationships, and abundant material resources in the world.

Therefore, the abundant human and material resources in the world reflect the immanent abundant being of God. Though human and material resources in creation owe their origin to God, it would be a gross heresy to mistake their abundant nature for the abundant being of God. The Creator must not be identified as one and the same with the creature. God in Christ through the Spirit creates, redeems, and sustains abundant human and material resources in the world. This God is distinct from the world and humanity but is abundantly related to them in Christ through the Spirit. He provides all of these spiritual and material resources in the world, as Luther would put it, "out of pure, fatherly, and divine goodness and mercy, without any merit or worthiness of [ours] at all."[17] The knowledge that these resources are God's free provisions for human flourishing forces us to recognize them as God's gifts. Because of this, humans are duty-bound not only to love, praise, and thank God but also to devote these resources to his service and humanity.

AFRICA'S ABUNDANCE: THE GIFT OF THE TRIUNE GOD

Africa is arguably the biblical "promised land flowing with milk and honey" that contains every abundant resource needed for Africans to live abundantly according to God's design and mission. Simpson is right to say, "Africa is the Lord's and the Fullness Thereof. Praise Be the Lord."[18] As a gift of God, Africa is not a poor but an abundant continent. The reason for this is not far-fetched. According to Simpson, "Africa is an abundant continent [of human and material resources] precisely because the triune God is an abundant God. Yes, God is an abundant triune communion of three divine persons."[19] The abundant Triune God is he who creates and sustains Africa's abundance, without whom Africa is void and empty.

Africa is full not only of abundant communion of the Triune God but also of God's created abundant resources. The Triune God bestows these abundant resources unconditionally on Africa, not because of its righteousness or worthiness, but purely out of his abundant love and grace. Africa has reason not to boast about its God-given abundance but to gladly and humbly grasp it with gratitude to God. In the words of Simpson, "The triune God's created abundance is for the joy of all creation, for the joy of Africa."[20] The Africa we currently live in is the Africa of our joy, our delight, and our hope precisely because it is the Africa of abundance, which is grounded in the abundant being of God. That said, let's unpack the Triune God's created abundant resources in Africa.

Abundant Endowment of Natural Resources

God has blessed Africa with abundant natural resources, which have fostered socioeconomic and political development of the continent.[21] According to Innovation for Sustainable Development, "Africa is endowed with abundant natural resources, accounting for about 10 per cent of global freshwater resources, 17 per cent of global forest cover, a quarter of mammal species and a fifth of bird and plant species. Most rural households rely on these resources to meet their nutrition, health and energy needs."[22] Africa is also abundantly rich in the world's rare renewal and non-renewal minerals, which account for 70 percent of its exports. As the dominant elements of many African national economies, these natural resources constitute a major source of income and subsistence, not only for the large percent of their population but most importantly for their public revenue and national wealth. For example, Nigeria is Africa's largest exporter of crude oil, which accounts for over 90 percent of its foreign exchange earnings. The annual revenue accruing from the export of oil and gas runs into billions of dollars.

Surplus of Land

There's abundant land in Africa. Rosebud Kurwijila argues that Africa is home to an estimated 184,898 million hectares of arable land, which is equal to 13 percent of the world's arable land.[23] The abundance of "land lies at the heart of social, political and economic life in most of Africa, where agriculture, natural resources and other land-based activities are fundamental to livelihoods, food security, incomes and employment."[24] The abundant land of the continent employs the largest percent of its population. This population does not depend upon Western foreign aid and government jobs in Africa to make a living. They largely depend on the land for survival. Through engaging in agriculture, whether subsistent or mechanized, African people have been able to feed themselves and earn enough money to meet the basic human needs of life without external support. Kurwijila contends, "Agriculture still accounts for 70% of full-time employment, 33% of GDP and 40% of export earnings, more than 60–70% of the population live in rural areas and 80% of the rural population depend on agriculture for their sustenance."[25] As an important asset owned by most people in Africa, land serves as the ultimate form of social security for the people.

With the surplus of land in Africa, most African people, no matter how poor they are, own or have a secure access to individual or communal land not only for housing but for arable farming. The scarcity of land for human habitation, productive farming, and animal husbandry is arguably foreign to Africa. The abundant land of the continent is the basic asset for the majority African population, which supports their livelihoods through subsistent farming, small-scale mining, livestock farming, and timber and non-timber production. The practice of resorting to land to earn a living and income after losing government and company jobs is the last hope of most people in Africa. Cultivating the land and harnessing its resources have not only lifted many Africans out of poverty and improved their living standards but have also raised their socioeconomic and political statuses. In fact, even those who have gainful jobs still grow crops and keep animals to augment their salaries.

The social significance of land for bonding and perpetuating family and community relationships cannot be overstressed. "Land is a tool for perpetuating the family. Through it we subsist, and weave, maintain and consolidate links between different members of the family. It is the basis of all investment, economic expansion and development, safeguarding the family by providing security and material and spiritual refuge."[26]

Abundance of Human Resources

It is no longer news that Africa is one of the most densely populated continents in the world. According to the United Nations (UN) population projections, the population of the Sub-African area will grow from the current 901 million to 2.07 billion in 2050.[27] Nigeria is the most populous African nation with 200 million people, and it will more than double in size to 400 million people by 2050. Africa's enormous human population is not a threat to the socioeconomic and political development of the continent, as some scholars believe.[28] As a matter of fact, it is a *sine qua non* for a sustainable development. A greater percent of the population falls in the category of "working-age population," which is educated, healthy, and energetic. The population of the continent is not more than the capacity of its enormous economic resources to sustain. There is a significant correlation between population and economic growth and development. The potentials for reaping the demographic dividends of this human resource are huge for the continent. The population provides massive demographic opportunity for investment and sustainable development precisely because the working-age population enjoys relatively good health, quality education, decent employment, and a lower proportion of dependents.

Even the teeming population of unemployed young African people is not lazy. They are potentially productive and employable human resources precisely because they have acquired the knowledge, educational skills, and experience to compete favorably with their colleagues around the world in the global labor market. Some of them are creatively engaged in small and medium-scale enterprises, while others are searching for higher quality jobs to utilize their enormous gifts and knowledge to secure their economic future. The demographic of the African population of young people also provides titanic opportunity for investment in education, healthcare, and business. This investment will create jobs, reduce poverty, and turn around the economy of Africa.

Abundant Human Relationships

Africa is a continent of abundant human relationships. Western scholars often discuss scarcity in terms of material paucity without acknowledging that scarcity is not only material but also relational. The scarcest "commodity" in Western society is not insufficiency of material resources but an absence of abundant interconnected human relationships, which Africa possesses in abundance. Unlike in Western society, where a person is detached from the community and lives as an autonomous self, in Africa the reverse is true: a person is caught up in an inescapable matrix of human communal relationships from the family to the community. To be a person in Africa is to be in a network of relationships. As I claim:

> Communality is an essential part of an African's being and identity. There is no way a person cannot be communal in their interpersonal relation. Thus, freedom in African communal life is not *from* the other; rather, it is freedom *for* the other. To be a free person is not to pursue extreme personal liberty and privacy by avoiding the other, but to be in relationship with other members of the community.[29]

Living in communal relationship with other members of the community is prized over against possessing property or wealth, hence the African adage "Being in relationship with people is more important than being wealthy." He who has relationship with people is richer than he who has wealth. In Africa it is better for one to lose their property or wealth than to sever their relationship with their community. Even a personal problem is a shared problem of the community. There is no one who experiences any problems left alone to suffer or figure it out by themselves, as the saying goes in the West. The whole community delightfully stands in solidarity with the suffering person. Polycarp Ikuenobe clearly expresses it:

> The problem of an individual becomes other people's or the community's problem, and usually, the community's problem. . . . The communal structures in African cultures help to reduce the stress of dealing with many life problems by oneself alone, and they also provide structures of social responsibilities,

relationships, and expectations by constant reinforcement, chiding, ribbing or prodding. This is a sharp contrast from the practice or attitude in the West. ... Because of its extreme individualism and privacy, when one has a problem, one keeps it to oneself.[30]

This is also true of celebrating success and victory. When a person rejoices or celebrates success and victory, they don't do it alone. Every member of the community rejoices and celebrates with them. The success and victory of an individual is invariably the success and victory of the whole community! This life of shared relationships is in many ways the reflection of the shared relationships of the Trinitarian persons of the Triune God.

AFRICA IS THRIVING

Africa is thriving in various sectors of human life. This claim cannot be gainsaid without being unfair to the continent. The giant strides of Africa toward sustainable socioeconomic and political development need to be identified, acknowledged, and celebrated in African public theology. Politically, democracy, which is a government by elected representatives, is thriving in Africa. A good number of African countries have stable democracies with robust democratic institutions and civil society. Nigeria, for example, is the largest democracy in Africa. It has been practicing an uninterrupted democracy for more than two decades characterized by the conduct of periodic national and state elections, which are one of the hallmarks of modern democracy. Assessing the 2003 national and state elections in Nigeria, Peter Lewis and Etannibi Alemika write:

> The elections were held in a relatively peaceful, stable atmosphere, with less violence and political turmoil than was evident in previous civilian-administered elections in 1964 and 1983. The losing parties, though deeply aggrieved, pursued their complaints through the judicial system. This permitted a peaceful transition to a second civilian term of office, a watershed in Nigeria's political history.[31]

The democratic system of government has gained ground in Africa. Thus, military dictatorship is increasingly becoming repugnant to the majority of the African people. They have enjoyed the dividends of democracy in the form of good governance, freedom to vote and to be voted for, and freedom of speech and association so much that they would stake their lives to resist being ruled by any non-democratic government. Democratic leadership has transformed many African countries into cutting-edge socioeconomic and political pace-setting nations of the world. This is evident in large public investment in infrastructure and other growth-enhancing sectors in both urban and rural areas. As Emmanuel Nnadozie suggests, "Governance, public financing management, and transparency are improving [in Africa]. Governments have taken steps to provide the enabling environment, infrastructure, and regulatory framework to guide economies to fast growth trajectories."[32]

The economy of African countries is also not completely stagnant. There is evidence to support belief that the economy of the continent is experiencing significant growth. Nnadozie argues, "African economies have grown at least 5 percent in the last fifteen years. Confidence in and evidence for the sustainability of this growth is rising. . . . The economic growth is easing infrastructure constraints; increasing trade and investment ties with emerging and advanced economies."[33] The economy of Nigeria has grown impressively lately to be the largest economy in Africa. The country has an average GDP of $444.976 billion. The private sector investment in economy is huge. The small- and medium-scale businesses and companies, which have sprung up and flourished, have contributed enormously to economic growth in Africa.

Socially, Africa is not lagging behind. The social sector has witnessed incredible progress. There is massive public and private investment in the health, education, and entertainment industries. The establishment of public and private primary, secondary, and tertiary health and education institutions has dramatically increased in Africa. Public and private health and education institutions are found virtually everywhere on the continent. Nnadozie writes, "African countries have addressed enrollment and gender imbalances in primary education, which then extends to other education levels. For instance, the overall youth literacy rate for the population aged 15 to 24 years has improved in Africa through increased access to universal primary education, observed since 2000."[34] The investment in health and education has not only created jobs for the teaming youths but also led to a productive workforce, economic prosperity, healthier population, and social stability in Africa.

Again, the entertainment sector is doing exceedingly well. The entertainment sector in Nigeria led by Nollywood is experiencing monumental growth. Nollywood has grown impressively to overtake Hollywood to become not only the largest entertainment sector in Africa but also the world's second-largest film industry. Lately, the annual output of the industry has doubled to 2,500 films. According to Murilo Johas Menezes, "It's estimated to employ more than 1 million people and to generate more than $7 billion for the national economy, accounting for around 1.4% of Nigeria's gross domestic product."[35]

CONCLUSION

The Africa we all want is not some Africa of our human imagination but the Africa God has created for us, that is, Africa of abundance, which is realistic and graspable. The African public theology of abundance is grounded in the perichoretic being of God as abundance in the economy of salvation and in God's immanent life. The abundance in Africa is a gracious overflow of the abundant perichoretic being of God. The abundant human and material resources in Africa are purely God's gift, which God does not desire us to grasp without hard work, vocation. Though there are immense surmountable challenges threatening Africa, they do not ultimately define Africa. Public theology of abundance disavows any theological conversation that overemphasizes African challenges over against its abundance. The African public theology of abundance sees these woes as distractions from the reality of God's gift of enormous resources and abundant life on the continent.

Therefore, the African public theology of abundance not only liberates the African public from the neocolonial mindset and the shackles of unwarranted distractions but also empowers them to remain free, focused, determined, faithful, just, effective, creative, and innovative in their vocation of grasping and distributing Africa's God-given abundance. The African public theology of abundance does not do this, so to speak, but its subject, the Trinitarian God, does it when and where the Triune God wills to those people who hear the prophetic proclamation of the word and participate in the sacraments.

NOTES

1. Sunday B. Agang, "The Need for Public Theology in Africa," in *African Public Theology*, edited by Sunday B. Agang, H. Jurgens Hendriks, and Dion A. Forster (UK: Langham, 2020), 3.

2. See H. Jurgens Hendriks, "Public Theology and Identity," in *African Public Theology*, edited by Sunday B. Agang, H. Jurgens Hendriks and Dion A. Forster (UK: Langham, 2020),

3. For an in-depth analysis of the Big Man Syndrome, see Ibrahim S. Bitrus, *Community and Trinity in Africa* (New York: Routledge, 2018), 50–62.

4. See Nico Koopman, "Public Theology in (South) Africa: A Trinitarian Approach," in *International Journal of Public Theology* 1 (2007): 191–96.

5. Hendriks, "Public Theology and Identity," 381–98.

6. Koopman, "Public Theology in (South) Africa: A Trinitarian Approach," 205.

7. See Agang, "The Need for Public Theology in Africa," 4, 13.

8. Ronell Bezuidenhout and Piet Naudé, "Some Thoughts on 'Public Theology' and Its Relevance for the South African Context," in *Scriptura* 79 (2002): 8.

9. Martin Luther, "Notes on Ecclesiastes, Lectures on the Song of Solomon, Treaties on the Last Words of David," in *Luther's Works* vol. 15, edited by Jaroslav Pelikan and Hilton C. Onward (St. Louis, Missouri: Concordia Publishing House, 1972), 4.

10. Bezuidenhout and Naudé, "Some Thoughts on 'Public Theology' and Its Relevance for the South African Context," 11.

11. Having lived in the United States for almost a decade, I have come to the realization that no country is perfect. Every country, no matter how prosperous they are, has their own peculiar challenges to deal with, even though they wouldn't allow these challenges to define their global reputation.

12. This is a subset of Trinitarian theology that emphasizes the communal character of the Triune God.

13. This means the being of the Triune God as revealed in God's creative activity in the world, while the immanent being of God is the being of God in Godself—inner life. The two are indistinguishable, as we shall see in the next section.

14. Gary Simpson, "African Realities Today through Lutheran Lenses," https://crossings.org/african-realities-today-through-lutheran-lenses/?print=pdf (accessed September 22, 2021).

15. Martin Martin, "Selected Psalms III," in *Luther's Works,* vol. 14, edited by Jaroslav Pelikan and Daniel E. Poellot (St. Louis, Missouri: Concordia Publishing House, 1955–1958), 114–15.

16. Simpson, "African Realities Today."

17. Martin Luther, "The Small Catechism 1529," in *The Book of Concord: The Confessions of the Evangelical Lutheran Church,* edited by Robert Kolb and Timothy J. Wengert (Minneapolis: Fortress Press, 2000), 354.

18. Simpson, "African Realities Today."

19. Simpson.

20. Simpson.

21. I insist that the enormous blessings that Sub-Saharan Africa enjoys from its abundant natural resources outnumber their curses, which are, by the way, surmountable. Thus, I do not agree with Meaza Zerihun Demissie, who argues that Sub-Saharan Africa is experiencing a natural resource curse in the midst of its enormous natural resources. See Meaza Zerihun Demissie, "The Natural Resource Curse in Sub-Saharan Africa and Transparency and International Initiatives" (PhD Dissertation: The University of Southern Mississippi, 2014).

22. "Innovation for Sustainable Development: Local Case Studies from Africa," https://www.un.org/esa/sustdev/publications/africa_casestudies/ecosystems.pdf (accessed September 22, 2021).

23. Rosebud Kurwijila, "Securing Rights to Land: A Priority for Africa," in *African Union Commission: Commissioner for Rural Economy and Agriculture* (To be published), 15.

24. Julian Quan, Su Fei Tan, and Camilla Toulmin, eds., "Land in Africa: Market Asset or Livelihood Security?" in *Proceedings and Summary of Conclusions from the Land in Africa Conference Held in London November 8–9, 2004,* 1.

25. Kurwijila, "Securing Rights to Land: A Priority for Africa," 15.

26. Thiendou Niang & Salla Dior Dieng, "Land Tenure and Family Farming in Africa: With Special Reference to Senegal," in *LAND IN AFRICA Market Asset or Secure Livelihood?* (2004): 66.

27. See David E. Bloom, et al., "A Demographic Dividend for Sub-Saharan Africa: Source, Magnitude, and Realization," in *IZA Discussion Paper* No. 7855 (2013), https://ftp.iza.org/dp7855.pdf (accessed September 18, 2021).

28. See specifically Patrick O. Ohadike, "The African Population Growth and Development Conundrum," in *Health Transition Review* 6 (1996): 325–44, https://www.jstor.org/stable/40652267 (accessed October 22, 2021); and Sidney B. Wesley, ed., "Population Change and Economic Growth in Africa," in *National Transfer Accounts Bulletin*, 6 (2013), https://www.ntaccounts.org/doc/repository/NTAbulletin6.pdf (accessed September 22, 2021).

29. Bitrus, *Community and Trinity in Africa*, 27.

30. Polycarp Ikuenobe, *Philosophical Perspectives on Communalism and Morality in African Traditions* (Lanham, MD: Lexington Books, 2006), 294.

31. Peter Lewis and Etannibi Alemika, "Seeking the Democratic Dividend: Public Attitudes and Attempted Reform in Nigeria," in *Afro Barometer* (2005): 3, https://www.files.ethz.ch/isn/92613/AfropaperNo52_SEEKING%20THE%20DEMOCRATIC.pdf (accessed September 21, 2021).

32. Emmanuel Nnadozie, "Drivers of Economic Growth in Africa: Opportunities, Financing, and Capacity Issues," in *The African Capacity Building Foundation*, Occasional Paper No. 29 (2017): 7, https://media.africaportal.org/documents/Occasional_Paper_29_En.pdf (accessed September 21, 2018).

33. Nnadozie, "Drivers of Economic Growth in Africa," 5.

34. Nnadozie, "Drivers of Economic Growth in Africa," 7.

35. Murilo Johas Menezes, "5 Facts to Know about Africa's Powerhouse—Nigeria," *The European Sting*, August 12, 2019, https://europeansting.com/2019/08/12/5-facts-to-know-about-africas-powerhouse-nigeria/ (accessed September 24, 2021).

Chapter 2

Leadership Solution to Africa's Enigma

Redefining Missional Leadership in African Context

Samuel Yonas Deressa

INTRODUCTION

In Europe and America, one faces "the constant portrayal of Africa as a place beset by famine, drought, and civil war, or as an open-air ethnographic museum for the West."[1] As part of an African diaspora, I have come to witness that it is this image of Africa that is portrayed in Western media to describe the continent's place in the world. Is this a true image of Africa? I would say that they may have some elements of truth in them, even though some are blown out of proportion.[2] Africa is always ravaged by abject poverty and disease outbreaks as other continents continue to progress and grow economically.

What is Africa's problem? According to Emeka Xris Obeizu, Africa's main problem is "bad administration of economy and politics that have left Africa grappling with the vicious circle of poverty, socio-political conflict, and underdevelopment."[3] The famous Nigerian writer Chinua Achebe also combines all of Africa's problems into one—failure of leadership.[4] According to Achebe, "The Nigerian [African] problems is the unwillingness or inability of its leaders to rise to the responsibility and the challenge of personal example which are the hallmarks of true leadership."[5]

Africa is also a continent where Christianity has been growing rapidly. One out of four Christians presently lives in Africa. According to Pew Research

Center, African Christianity will grow by 40 percent by 2030.[6] It was for this reason that many scholars predicted Africa to be the next demographic and cultural base of the Christian faith. As Christian mission movements mainly moved to the global South, particularly Africa, many suggested that theological reflections will also follow the same trend. As Joel Carpenter observed, "Christian theology eventually reflects the most compelling issues from the front lines of mission, so we can expect that Christian theology will be dominated by these issues rising from the global South."[7]

It is because of the growth of Christianity in Africa that many are hoping to see a prosperous and strong continent. How is this growth in Christian faith reflected in good leadership, a leadership in which Christians could show it by example and change the image of Africa? How is the church enabled to embody Christ-like leadership embracing virtues such as love, peace, moral uprightness, and respect for human rights? What is the role of Christian leaders in bringing social and economic transformation in African communities?

With the growth of Christianity in Africa, the church is currently presented with an opportunity to positively influence, and even change, this reality with far-reaching impact. However, as George Kinoti rightly notes, even though "Christianity is growing faster in Africa than on any other continent, people are rapidly becoming poor and moral and the social fabrics of the society are disintegrating."[8] According to Kinoti, "Christianity is not making a significant difference to African nations."[9]

Christian churches in Africa have failed miserably to engage in public leadership, arguing that politics is a "dirty game" meant only for others. By creating a dichotomy between faith and politics, they continued to withdraw from the public life of their communities. For the Christian church to impact the continent positively, it must be prepared to reevaluate itself and its God-given mission in light of the Scripture and to equip and prepare effective, moral, and transformative leaders that can positively influence and alter the African situations by taking leadership roles in government structures. What Africa needs at present are Christian leaders that can be described in the Judeo-Christian shepherding tradition: "He pastured them with unblemished heart, with a sensitive hand he led them" (Ps. 78:72).

AFRICAN LEADERSHIP CRISIS

As rightly noted by Tokunboh Adeyemo, "There is hardly any other continent in the world that is as blessed with natural resources as Africa is. If developed wisely and managed properly, Africa could become a bread basket for the world."[10] Gary Simpson also affirms this by noting that "Africa is an abundant continent precisely because the triune God is an abundant God. Yes, God is an abundant triune communion of three divine persons."[11] The statistics are overwhelmingly impressive. Africa owns most of the minerals of the world such as fossil fuels, coal, petroleum, and natural gas.[12] Africa also has some of the world's reserves of diamonds, gold, copper, nickel, platinum, radium, bauxite, manganese, lithium, titanium, and phosphates.[13] However, for too long Africa's mineral fortune has mainly been the cause for conflict rather than development for much of the continent.

What I miss the most living in America for the last eleven years is the climate in Africa, yes! The climate is conducive to human existence, and the land is great for farming. Africa is also blessed with energy and human sources.[14] Yet, in this global village of the twenty-first century, Africans are faced with numerous challenges. Most Africans are struggling for survival when some of the basic needs such as food, shelter, healthcare, and education should have been met a long time ago. In many African countries, there exists a wide gap between the rich and the poor, and millions are suffering due to lack of enough resources in their communities. The wealth of the continent is controlled by a few groups, and this is occasioned by systems that encourage tribalism, nepotism, and favoritism.[15]

Africa's economic growth has been slow compared to other continents in the global South, such as Asia and Latin America. Some countries in the global South, such as Taiwan, Malaysia, and others, have shown tremendous growth in the past decades. When it comes to Africa, as stated in the publication of the Organization for Economic Cooperation and Development, "Africa's participation in the world economy has declined alarmingly over the past 50 years in terms of GDP, exports, and foreign investment. Only the continent's share of global population grew as its birth rate accelerated during the 20th century."[16]

For many years African leaders have put the blame on external factors such as Western colonialism followed by cultural imperialism and unjust international economic trade. Even the only country in Africa that had never been colonized by European countries, Ethiopia, has put the blame on inadequate foreign aid and the unwillingness of international financial organizations such as the World Bank and International Monetary Fund to help the country grow economically.

What is the cause of Africa's problems? Arguably, the widespread poverty in Africa can be attributed to lack of moral and responsible political leadership. According to Obeizu, African leadership is "often characterized by unequal distribution of power and resources between groups that are so divided by ethnicity, religion, or language."[17] African leaders are known for corruption and selfish lifestyles, and yet their own citizens are suffering under their leadership. Enigmatically, rather than working for the development of their own people, they elevate their own interest at the expense of others.

They are also known for breaches of human rights and lawlessness. In many aspects African leaders have failed their own people, not by the Western standards, but by Africa's own indigenous standards.

In his famous book entitled *What is Africa's Problem?* the president of Uganda, Yoweri Museveni, reiterated that "one of the biggest weakening factors in Africa is tribalism and other forms of sectarianism."[18] He then identifies five other root causes of Africa's problems: bad politics and politicians, communication difficulties, cultures that encourage idleness, lack of motivation for aggressive completion in business, and foreign interference and domination in economy.[19] All of these problems that he identifies are related to a leadership crisis in Africa.

Emerging African Christian scholars such as Jacinta Ahiambo, Felix E. Enegho, and George Kinoti also identify an African leadership crisis as the main cause of Africa's problems.[20] It is for this reason that I argue in this article that what Africa needs at present is transformational leaders, leaders that can bring transformation in the continent by introducing change so that essential services are available to people to change their situation. If Christians adopt transformational leadership and make themselves available for public ministry, some of the socioeconomic and sociopolitical challenges facing Africa could be a thing of the past. In other words, transformational leadership could be a solution to the endless problems facing Africa.

As a Congolese Lutheran theologian, Kå Mana, rightly argued, "Africa is yet to chart a dynamic [of leadership structures] for herself that would enable her to construct a future with a profound ability to change on an ethic of responsible creativity and inventiveness."[21] I believe that the Christian church in Africa has a big role to play in this. Christianity is growing in Africa. With the exception of the seven strongly Islamic countries mostly in the North, new churches are being established every day. More than 50 percent of the population is Christian. One can see that young men and women are rising up as full-time ministers in the church, and they are even impacting the global Christian movements. These days churches throughout the continent are declaring "Africa for Jesus, Jesus for Africa." How can Christianity be the means through which African leadership changes? What are the meaningful ways that African churches can restructure themselves and serve their communities better?

TRANSFORMATIONAL LEADERSHIP

As noted above, Africa has become the center of Christianity, which, according to many scholars, implies that it will take the lead in shaping the future of Christianity.[22] As I once heard from leaders while I was serving in Ethiopia, however, African Christianity is one mile long but one inch deep. To both shape the future of Christianity and make a positive impact on the continent, the Christian church in Africa needs more than numbers. The numerical growth (quantity) needs to be reflected in the church's health (quality of their service) and how the church is making an impact in the larger African community. For this to happen, they need transformational leaders, leaders that can bring transformative change both within the church and in the continent.

What is transformational leadership? Peter Northouse defines transformational leadership as "the process whereby a person engages with others and creates a connection that raises the level of motivation and morality in both the leader and the followers."[23] He also calls transformational leadership "a socialized leadership, which is concerned with the collective good" of followers.[24] As Burns argues, "Such leadership occurs when one or more persons engage with others in such a way that leaders and followers raise one another to higher levels of motivation and morality."[25]

Such an understanding of transformational leadership leads us, according to Burns, to a definition of leadership as a relationship of power for a specific purpose that is consistent with the motives, needs, and values of both the leader and the led. He states, "We must see power—and leadership—as not things but as *relationships*. We must analyze power in a context of human motives and physical constraints."[26] He argues, "Leadership mobilizes, naked power coerces. To be sure, leaders, unlike power holders, will have to adjust their purposes in advance to the motive bases of followers."[27]

Based on the above definition of leadership, Burns describes a transforming leader as one who looks "for potential motives in followers, seeks to satisfy higher needs, and engages the full person of the follower."[28] This leads Burns toward the interest of focusing on the nature of *moral leadership*, which "emerges from, and always returns to, the fundamental wants and needs, aspirations, and values of the followers."[29] Northouse also portrays transformational leaders as those who "set out to empower followers and nurture them in change. They attempt to raise the consciousness in individuals and to get them to transcend their own self-interests for the sake of the others."[30]

As Beli states,

> Organizations are modified continually by the relationships going on as work is done. It follows then that the purpose of leadership development is not to train a person to perform a specific task in a certain way (competency), but to create within the person capacity to find within the work itself shared with a relational community potential for learning and growth.[31]

The term "transformational leadership" was first coined by J. Downtown in 1973 and was later used by MacGregor Burns in his seminal work *Leadership* published in 1978.[32] In this book Burns laid down the foundation for transformational leadership, treating leadership as a process that occurs between the leader and the followers. In other words, he links the leadership role with that of the followers. With this approach he introduced transformational leadership theory, a theory that diverted leadership studies from approaches focused on great leaders and transactional management to the interaction of leaders and followers as workers toward "mutual stimulation and elevation."[33] Transformational leadership, as opposed to transactional leadership, focuses on the more personal aspect of organizational interactions. Burns describes transformational leadership this way:

> Such leadership occurs when one or more persons *engage* with others in such a way that leaders and followers raise one another to higher levels of motivation and morality. Their purposes . . . become fused. Power bases are linked not as counterweights but as mutual support for common purpose. . . . But transforming leadership ultimately becomes moral in that it raises the level of human conduct and ethical aspiration of both leader and led, and thus it has transforming effect on both.[34]

Some studies have used transformational leadership and charismatic leadership as synonymous terms.[35] The two are, however, two separate theories.[36] As J. Hunt and J. Conger emphasize in their research, "There needs to be more differentiation between than there has typically been in the use of the two terms."[37] Therefore, this article follows the line of those who focus on transformational leadership in its own right.

This theory provides a significant theoretical framework for understanding how Africa can intentionally work on equipping, raising, and empowering transformational leaders for the continent. As Burns indicates, the key to leadership is the discerning of key values and motives of both the leader and follower and, in accordance to them, elevating (forming and empowering) others to a higher sense of performance, fulfillment, autonomy, and purpose.[38]

For Burns, transformational leadership is experienced in organizational interactions. In other words, "such leadership occurs when one or more persons engage with others in such a way that leaders and followers raise one another to a higher level of motivation and morality. Their purpose becomes fused. Power bases are linked not as counterweights but as mutual support for common purpose."[39] This is similar to what Burns describes as the experience of those that emerged as transformational leaders such as Lenin, Mao, and Gandhi while engaging the needs of their public followers.[40] This is the reason why Burns refers to transformational leadership as "a socialized leadership"—a leadership "concerned with [meeting the demands or] collective good" of others (or the public).[41] Below I will show how this theory applies in the church context using the missional leadership conversation.

TRANSFORMATIONAL LEADERS AS MISSIONAL LEADERS

How is transformational leadership theory applied in the church context? This brings us to the missional church conversation in North America for the last few decades where the concept of leadership was discussed from a Trinitarian perspective. The missional church conversation started in North America as a response to Leslie Newbigin's critical analysis of the missionary encounter in the twentieth century. His identification and framing of crises and challenges in the way mission was understood and carried out in the Western world attracted American missiologists to engage in conversation—which resulted in the creation of the Gospel and Our Culture Network (GOCN). This conversation mainly addressed ecclesiology and mission, with a focus on the dynamic interrelations among gospel, church, and culture.

What the missional church conversation introduced was the Trinitarian reconceptualization of Christian mission. It resulted in a shift from understanding mission as a mere activity of the church to mission as rooted in God's purpose to restore the creation. The church is called to participate in this mission as part and parcel of the body of Christ.[42] The missional church is a church engaged in the ongoing creative work of the Triune God with a purpose of restoring the whole man. Missional leaders are formed and empowered when they are engaged in this mission and contribute their share to promote the well-being of the community.

According to Roxburgh and Romanuk, the missional church can be understood as the gathering of "the people of God, called to be *formed* into a unique social community whose life together is the sign, witness, and foretaste of what God is doing in and for all of creation."[43] This means there are three primary focuses or characteristics of missional churches: (1) *Life together* (community), (2) *Witness*: engaging the public by participating in the ongoing work of the Triune God, and (3) *Spiritual formation* and *empowerment* of each member, in which members are enabled for such ministry.

This is similar to what Gary Simpson identifies as the two roles of missional churches in their community: "the moral formation of their members" within the church and the church serving as "a meeting place of private and public life."[44] What Roxburgh and Romanuk identify under *spiritual formation* is what Simpson describes as "moral formation of members" because with the spiritual formation comes moral formation. The *witness* or public engagement of the church is described by Simpson as the public life of the church. *Life together* is the life of Christians as disciples of Christ, both forming their community and engaging the public.

Dimensions of Missional Church

The figure below demonstrates how I picture the three dimensions of a missional church described by Roxburgh and Romanuk. First is *life together*. The missional church as a community of believers is *life together*—together with each other as brothers and sisters in Christ and with the Triune God in their midst. It is this togetherness that defines their identity and shapes their ministry. What is mostly ignored in the missional church conversation is that togetherness also extends what Simpson describes as the church's

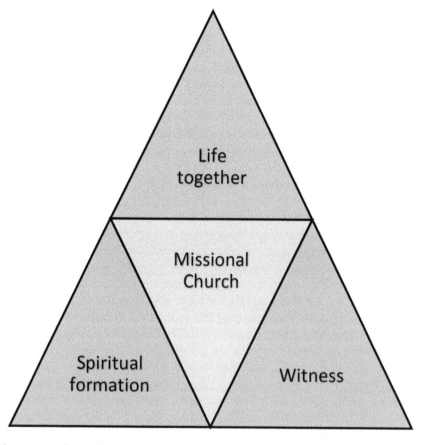

Figure 2.1. Three Dimensions of a Missional Church. *Image by Samuel Deressa.*

commitment as "public moral companions." In other words, the church as a community (*life together*) should "exist as a meeting place of private and public life."[45]

This leads us to the second dimension of the missional church, the church as a *witness*. The witness of the missional church is related to or founded on its *life together*. The church's *witness* is its public ministry. The missional churches become witnesses by engaging in the ongoing creative work of the Triune God through multiple kinds of ministries. The third dimension is *spiritual formation*. In *Missional Church* the concept of spiritual formation, or cultivating the Christian community, was emphasized as one of the main foci of missional church conversation.[46] The missional church forms and empowers people for God's mission in the world. The Triune God is the one that calls, forms (empowers), and sends God's people to engage the world.

Missional leadership is one of the topics in the missional church conversation. It is a theological concept that emerged from the understanding that leadership should be viewed from a Trinitarian perspective, a perspective that focuses on the ongoing involvement of the Triune God in human history. As Roxburgh rightly articulates, "Missional leadership is framed, understood, and articulated in relationship to the question of what God is doing in the world."[47] The starting point in framing missional leadership is a theological reading of God's ongoing creative work.

The Greek word *perichoresis*, the word used since the sixteenth century to describe the eternal co-relatedness of each person in the Trinity, is used as a framework within which we articulate missional leadership. Perichoresis is a useful theological framework to capture missional leadership because it connects the perichoretic understanding of the Trinity with the very reason for which the church exists (God's mission) and with the kind of leadership that the church has to exercise for this mission to manifest. The very reason why the concept of Trinity as perichoresis helps to frame our concept of missional leadership is that we as human beings are created in God's image, which would mean that our very existence can be perceived only in terms of our relationship to each other and God.[48]

If missional leadership is about formation of believers while engaging in the ongoing creating work of the Triune God, how can this be expressed in practical terms in such a way that it reflects the life and ministry of the church and those involved in ministry? Such leadership formation takes place in Eucharist fellowship. In the Eucharist the Triune God shares its entire perichoretic life with the Christian community and the whole creation, and the Christian community is formed and transformed as a result. As Luther explains, in the Eucharist "Christ has given his holy body for this purpose, that the things signified by the sacrament—the fellowship, the change wrought by love—may be put into practice."[49]

Eucharistic fellowship is a fellowship that requires willingness to share others' burdens and suffering. It is through the practice of such sharing that the Christian community is transformed and missional leaders emerge. We encounter God in and through each other's life. By carrying each other's burden with the love of Christ, we form a communal culture through which each member is formed into the likeness of Christ. As Luther emphasizes, "By the means of this sacrament, all self-seeking love is rooted out and gives place to that which seeks the common good of all; and through the change wrought by love there is one bread, one drink, one body, one community."[50]

For Luther, to experience such transformation, one must:

> Take to heart the infirmities and needs of others, as if they were [one's] own. Then offer to others [his/her] strength, as if it were their own, just as Christ does for [him/her] in the sacraments. This is what it means to be changed into one another through love. . . . To lose one's own form and take on that which is common to all.[51]

Burns's transformational leadership can be applied to missional leadership in different ways. To mention among many is that *transformational* leadership has a genuine concern for the needs, wants, motives, and values of followers. In other words, transformational leadership pays careful attention to those elements in the followers, looking for a point of contact where meanings and purposes can be realized. In fact, the main emphasis of transformational leadership is not necessarily on the mechanism of an organization. Rather, it focuses on the common good of society. Similar to Burns's transformational leadership, missional leadership pays careful attention to particular context and culture, where God is already at work. A missional church with a transformational leadership mind focuses on people with different spiritual gifts and always attempts to find a way to help them discern the values and purpose of their spiritual gifts. Below I will show how that applies in African context.

CREATING TRANSFORMATIONAL AND MISSIONAL LEADERS IN AFRICA

As discussed above, Africa is a rich continent. If properly managed, as Adeyemo rightly noted, "Africa is not only capable of feeding herself but also to feed the rest of the world." He adds, "Egypt in North Africa did that for years in biblical history. How did it happen? There was Josef in the land. Are there no 'Josefs' in modern day Africa?"[52] Below I will argue that many Josefs will arise in Africa if the Christian church is to focus on nurturing and equipping its members to be transformational and missional leaders in their communities.

One of the major problems in African leadership is leaders think of themselves as lords and masters rather than being servants of the people. It is common to observe an authoritarian or dictatorial style of leadership in most countries in Africa. For decades Africa has had bosses, not leaders. If some become successful in becoming better than others, their leadership style is more transactional—support and benefit only those who are on their side or provide service to them. However, as noted above, the central assumption in transformational leadership is the shift from a focus on great leaders (or a leader-centered approach) and a transactional approach to interactional or collaborative leadership which emphasizes relationships. For Burns, transactional leadership is a leadership praxis focused on an "exchange [of] one thing for another," while transformational leadership is mainly about looking for "potential motives in followers to satisfy [their] higher needs [by engaging] the full person of the followers."[53] At the core of transformational leadership theory is an emphasis on relationships. As Burns contends, "We must see power—and leadership—as nothing but as *relationship*."[54] As Burns argues, it is within the relationship of power that encompasses the needs and values of both the leader and followers that people are elevated to a higher level of moral development.[55]

Missional leadership is also opposed to a "big man" leadership approach as noticed in Africa.[56] Just as relationship is emphasized in transformational leadership, missional leadership helps us to consider the significance of considering a communal culture or shared leadership for leadership formation. The emphasis of missional leadership is equipping "saints for the work of ministry, for building up the body of Christ," and this is what we refer to as formation and empowerment of believers for ministry (Eph. 4:11–12). Saints are equipped in the missional church where the Word is preached and sacraments are administered. Equipping saints is the work of God, and that is why it is emphasized that "leadership formation must be asked only in terms of what God is doing in forming the social community known as ecclesia."[57] In the missional church, all of Christ's people are equipped so that they can function in a way that they all contribute to building the whole body by equipping each other as a community, and that they serve as transformational leaders in their larger communities.

Understanding missional leadership from the perspective of the Eucharistic fellowship also leads to the recognition of every believer as a leader, agent of formation, and empowerment. Eucharistic fellowship is an invitation to a shared leadership. It corresponds to the argument of Cladis that leadership in the missional church is exercised in a relationship (a team-based community).[58] When leadership is exercised in a relationship, everyone in the

Christian community becomes a *de facto* leader, which means that they all have a part to play by sharing each other's suffering and forming each other into the likeness of Christ.[59]

Missional leadership is not limited to the church context. It goes beyond that and includes the spheres in which the church, as participant in the Triune God's ongoing creative work, is engaged. This, according to Gary Simpson, includes the civil society in which the missional church

> exhibits a compassionate commitment to other institutions and their predicaments [which,] in turn, yields a critical and self-critical—and thus fully communicative—procedure and practice of public engagement; finally, the emerging missional church, as public companion, participates with civil society to create and strengthen the fabric that fashions a life-giving and a life-accountable world.[60]

Furthermore, the churches in Africa have been known for their major contributions in development and for continually advocating for holistic development. This holistic development that African churches have been advocating for, however, did not include leadership development for the most part. Therefore, for the church being the body of Christ, what it needs to do is to first play a role in challenging the African leaders to adopt the transformational leadership model. They need to intentionally and critically engage African leaders and seek for ways in which they can challenge, inform, and equip leaders with Christian values of leadership. Thirdly, the church needs to educate and equip its members to become transformational and missional leaders at every level, which would mean that they need to work on developing the human person physically, intellectually, socially, and morally. The African church has to shift its focus from achieving numerical growth and other secondary matters to nurturing its members with clear intention to raise young transformational and missional leaders that can make positive impacts within both the church and the larger governmental structure.

The church in Africa should play a major role in educating its members on how to be transformational leaders in their communities. Members of the church can be engaged in any type of duties of vocation, but if they are educated on what it means to be transformational and missional leaders, what they can each contribute can be a reason for the total transformation of Africa. This way they can challenge the minority that are privileged by the system. Transformational leadership is what promotes increased service to all and capacitates the less privileged for communal development and transformation.

As noted in the statement of the Association of Member Episcopal Conferences in Eastern Africa (AMECEA), the only way to bring impact in African communities is if the church or "the entire Christian community shares the life and mission of Christ" by embodying Christian values in all aspects of life. In other words, according to the AMECEA statement, "It is through the whole Christian people that the church is deeply presented in all aspects of life and activity of the world. We are convinced that it is only in our total involvement as living members of Christ that the church will be the salt, leaven, and light of mankind [sic] in our countries."[61]

CONCLUSION

Africa is in need of change. Africans are demanding a better and more developed life like people living on other continents have. Lack of transformational and missional leadership, however, left Africa in crisis. In this article I argued that the only way to bring change in the African context is if Christians that have adopted transformational and missional leadership styles are involved in leadership. The worst reaction to such a suggestion would be to convince oneself that nothing needs to change in Africa and to imagine that everything is "normal." African churches should react to such normalization and should be able to help those they are leading to discern the need for change and recast vision that can help their followers to move forward. What helps the leaders to succeed in today's context is to be "informed and empowered"—which has its own positive impact on decision-making. Leadership without information will probably result in failure.

Africa needs to adopt missional leadership because it pays careful attention to particular contexts and cultures where God is already at work. A missional church gives due consideration to transformational leadership in such a way that it nurtures the life and ministry of people with different spiritual gifts. The missional church always attempts to find a way to help people discern the values and purpose of their spiritual gifts. One major significance of transformational leadership is that it pays careful attention to talents and potentials in the followers, looking for a point of contact where meanings and purposes can be realized. In fact, the main emphasis of transformational leadership is not necessarily on the mechanism of an organization. Rather, it focuses on the common good of society.

NOTES

1. Tite Tienou, "Integrity of Mission in the Light of the Gospel in Africa: A Perspective from an African in Diaspora" (paper, 11th International Conference

of the International Association for Mission Studies, Port Dickson, Malaysia, July 31st–August 7, 2004), 3.

2. For example, some French journalists predicted that Africa would be wiped out in fifteen to twenty years. See *L'Express*, 27 (April 1990). See also American medias that take this issue out of proportion: *New York Times*, "Scramble for Africa," https://www.nytimes.com/1971/06/13/archives/scramble-for-africa-by-anthony-nutting-454-pp-dutton-10.html (accessed October 18, 2021). This problem is discussed in an article published by *Aljazeera* entitled "The Problem Is Not 'Negative' Western Media Coverage of Africa," https://www.aljazeera.com/opinions/2019/7/9/the-problem-is-not-negative-western-media-coverage-of-africa (accessed October 18, 2021).

3. Emeka Xris Obeizu, "The Church in Africa and the Search for Integral and Sustainable Development of Africa: Toward a Socio-Economic and Politically Responsive Church," in *The Church as Salt and Light: Path to an African Ecclesiology of Abundant Life*, eds. Stan Chu Ilo et al. (Eugene, Oregon: Pickwick Publications, 2011), 44.

4. See Chinua Achebe, *The Trouble with Nigeria* (Nairobi, Kenya: Heinemann, 1983).

5. Achebe, *The Trouble with Nigeria*, 3.

6. See Wes Granberg-Michaelson, "Think Christianity is Dying? No, Christianity is Shifting Dramatically," *The Washington Post*, May 20, 2015, https://www.washingtonpost.com/news/acts-of-faith/wp/2015/05/20/think-christianity-is-dying-no-christianity-is-shifting-dramatically/.

7. Joel Carpenter, "The Christian Scholar in an Age of Global Christianity," in *Christianity and the Soul of the University*, eds. Douglas Henry and Michael Beaty (Grand Rapids, MI: Baker Academic, 2006).

8. Quoted in Stan Chu Ilo et al., *The Church as Salt and Light: Path to an African Ecclesiology of Abundant Life* (Eugene, Origen: Pickwick Publications, 2011), 69.

9. Ilo, *The Church as Salt and Light*.

10. Tokunboh Adeyemo, *Is Africa Cursed? A Vision for the Radical Transformation of an Ailing Continent* (Nairobi, Kenya: WorldAlive Publishers, 2009), 22.

11. See Gary Simpson, "African Realities Today through Lutheran Lenses," https://crossings.org/african-realities-today-through-lutheran-lenses/?print=pdf.

12. See Saleem Ali et al., eds., *Africa's Mineral Fortune: The Science and Politics of Mining and Sustainable Development* (New York: Routledge, 2020). The book describes the challenges of natural resource governance, particularly related to leadership problems, suggesting ways in which mining can be more effectively managed in Africa.

13. Adeyemo, *Is Africa Cursed?*, 23.

14. Africa owns 40 percent of the world's hydroelectric power and yet was able to utilize only 11 percent of its capacity. It is a major exporter of coal. For details, see International Water Power & Dam Construction, "Tracking the Latest Hydropower Developments in Africa," *NS Energy*, May 3, 2021, https://www.nsenergybusiness.com/features/hydropower-africa/.

15. For details, see C. Bansikiza, "Poverty and Unemployment: A Challenge to the Church and Society in Africa," in *African Ecclesial Review* 46, no. 3 (2004): 279–80.

16. Tienou, "Integrity of Mission," 4.
17. Obeizu, "The Church in Africa," 44.
18. Yoweri Museveni, *What is Africa's Problem?* (Kampala, Uganda: NRM Publication, 1992).
19. Museveni, *What is Africa's Problem?*, 11.
20. Jacinta Ahiambo, "Education: An Effective Tool for Servant Leadership in Africa," *African Ecclesial Review* 54, nos. 3 & 4 (2012); Felix E. Enegho, "Integrity in Leadership and the Challenges Facing Africa: A Christian Response," *African Ecclesial Review* 53, nos. 3 & 4 (2011); George Kinoti, *Hope for Africa and What the Christians Can Do* (Nairobi, Kenya: AISRED, 1994).
21. Quoted in Gabriel Mmassi, "Palaver: Church Leadership in Africa," *African Ecclesial Review* vol. 52, nos. 2 & 3 (2010): 185–86.
22. See Philip Jenkins, *The Next Christendom: The Coming of Global Christianity* (Oxford: Oxford University Press); Dana L. Robert, "Shifting Southward: Global Christianity Since 1945," *International Bulletin of Missionary Research* 24, no. 2 (April 2000): 50–58; Lamin Sanneh, *Whose Religion Is Christianity? The Gospel Beyond the West* (Grand Rapids, Michigan: Eerdmans, 2003); Robert Wuthnow, *Boundless Faith: The Global Outreach of American Churches* (Oakland, California: University of California Press, 2009); and Mark A. Noll, *The New Shape of World Christianity: How American Experience Reflects Global Faith* (Downers Grove, Illinois: InterVarsity, 2009).
23. Peter Northouse, *Leadership: Theory and Practice*, vol. 4 (Thousand Oaks, CA Sage Publications, 2006), 176.
24. Peter Northouse, *Leadership: Theory and Practice*, vol. 5 (Thousand Oaks, CA Sage Pubns, 2010), 172.
25. James MacGregor Burns, *Leadership* (New York: Harper & Row, 1979), 11.
26. Burns, *Leadership*.
27. Burns, *Leadership*, 43.
28. Burns, *Leadership*, 4, 20.
29. Burns, *Leadership*.
30. Northouse, *Leadership: Theory and Practice*, 190.
31. See Skip Beli, "Learning, Changing, and Doing: A Model for Transformational Leadership Development in Religious and Non-Profit Organizations," *Journal of Religous Leadership* 9, no. 1 (2010): 95.
32. Burns, *Leadership*.
33. Burns, *Leadership*, 4. Burns's theory on transformational leadership has been the basis of more than four hundred doctoral dissertations.
34. Burns, *Leadership*, 20.
35. O. Behling and J. M. McFillen, "A Syncretical Model of Charismatic/Transformational Leadership," *Group & Organization Management* 21, no. 2 (1996): 163–92; J. Conger and R. Kanungo, "The Empowerment Process: Integrating Theory and Practice," *Academy of Management Review* 13, no. 3 (1988): 471–83.
36. To learn more about the difference between charismatic leadership and transformational leadership, refer to Mary Miller, "Transformational Leadership and

Mutuality," *Transformation* 24, no. 3 (July & October 2007): 180–92; Conger and Kanungo, "The Empowerment Process," 471–83.

37. J. Hunt and J. Conger, "From Where We Sit: An Assessment of Transformational and Charismatic Leadership Research," *Leadership Quarterly* 12, no. 1 (1999): 340.

38. Burns, *Leadership*, 4.

39. Burns, *Leadership*, 20.

40. Burns, *Leadership*, 129–30, 137, 252–54.

41. Burns, *Leadership*, 173.

42. Gary Simpson, "No Trinity, No Mission: The Apostolic Difference of Revisioning the Trinity," in *Word & World* 18, no. 3 (1998). See also Craig Van Gelder and Dwight J. Zscheile, *The Missional Church in Perspective: Mapping Trends and Shaping the Conversation* (Grand Rapids, MI: Baker Academic, 2011).

43. Alan J. Roxburgh and Fred Romanuk, *The Missional Leader: Equipping Your Church to Reach a Changing World* (San Francisco, CA: Jossey-Bass, 2006), 14. Emphasis mine.

44. Gary Simpson, "Civil Society and Congregations as Public Moral Companions," in *Word & World* XV, no. 4 (1995): 426.

45. Simpson, "Civil Society."

46. Darrell L. Guder, ed., *Missional Church: A Vision for the Sending of the Church in North America* (Grand Rapids, MI: Eerdmans, 1998). In this book formation of the missional church is described as the role of missional leaders. In fact, "Missional Leadership: Equipping God's People for Mission" was the title of chapter 7.

47. Alan J. Roxburgh, "Missional Leadership," in *Religious Leadership: A Reference Handbook*, ed. Sharon Henderson Callahan (Thousand Oaks, CA: Sage Publication, 2013), 130; Eddie Gibbs, *LeadershipNext: Changing Leaders in a Changing Culture* (Downers Grove, IL: InterVarsity Press, 2005), 38.

48. Gibbs, *LeadershipNext*, 117.

49. Martin Luther, *The Blessed Sacrament of the Holy and True Body and Blood of Christ, and the Brotherhoods*, eds. Theodore Bachmann and Helmut Lehmann, vol. 35 (Philadelphia, PA: Muhlenberg Press, 1960), 60.

50. Luther, *The Blessed Sacrament*, 67.

51. Luther, *The Blessed Sacrament*, 61–62.

52. Tokunboh Adeyemo, *Africa's Enigma and Leadership Solutions* (Nairobi, Kenya: WorldAlive Publishers, 2009), 5.

53. Burns, *Leadership*, 4.

54. Burns, *Leadership*. Emphasis in the original.

55. Burns, *Leadership*, 41–43.

56. For an in-depth analysis of the Big Man Syndrome, see Ibrahim S. Bitrus, *Community and Trinity in Africa* (New York: Routledge, 2017), 50–62.

57. Roxburgh and Romanuk, *The Missional Leader*, 118.

58. George Cladis, *Leading the Team-Based Church: How Pastors and Church Staffs Can Grow Together into a Powerful Fellowship of Leaders* (San Francisco: Jossey-Bass, 1999), 10.

59. Colin E. Gunton, *The Promise of Trinitarian Theology* (Edinburgh: T & T Clark, 1991), 26.

60. Gary Simpson, "A Reformation Is a Terrible Thing to Waste: A Promising Theology for an Emerging Missional Church," in *The Missional Church in Context: Helping Congregations Develop Contextual Ministry*, ed. Craig Van Gelder (Grand Rapids, MI: Eerdmans Pub. Comp., 2007), 93.

61. Quoted in Mmassi, "Palaver," 184.

Chapter 3

We Can't Breathe

The Role of Public Theology in the Midst of Social, Political, and Institutional Unrest

David L. Everett

"Public" is a word that resides at every turn in missional ecclesiology discourse. The word *ekklesia* itself emanates from the idea of a civic meeting, as does its Hebrew counterpart *qahal*, which refers to a deliberative assembly of the body politic. "Public" is associated with the New Testament word *kerygma* and its verbal vicissitudes. Usually translated "preaching," it is far removed from what we now label preaching. According to George Hunsberger,

> Its meaning field has to do with the function of the "herald," the news announcement by the official spokesvoice of one in power or authority. The public broadcast of the news, the "*public*ation" of it, is the form of witness the New Testament describes.[1]

Once clear that theology is in fact "public," we can move away from the passive portrayals of buildings on neighborhood corners, or ivory institutions on hills, and more toward the image of "*public*ans" pressed into the fabric of life, living it out in social contexts, and affected by the environmental dynamics shared by others.[2] Engagement then becomes the welcomed outcome of this public "sharing" because it is within such a space that theology can cultivate the essential virtues of citizenship. It is then and there that "public" theology can serve as a contemporary conscience,[3] weaving together opinion and power, highlighting Gary Simpson's point that "those who bear especially the impoverishing, dispossessing consequences of economic or democratic policy, or of any decision venue, must be full participants with effective voice in the decision-making bodies, processes, and procedures."[4] This represents a "democratic solidarity and publicity"[5] that addresses the crucial question of who discerns, deliberates, and decides by following what he terms "the participatory golden rule"—decision-makers must be consequence-takers, and consequence-takers must be decision-makers.[6]

In exploring a practical, inclusive way of thinking about "public" theology, an emphasis on the essential components related to equity—leadership, ownership, partnership—is key. The interpretation of "public" needs to be expanded to find ways to establish critical methods of engagement across social, economic, and political divides. Evidence suggests that institutions often reproduce rather than remedy social patterns. Thus, in seeking to understand these patterns, a "public" theology must acknowledge, interrogate, and reconcile the reality from whence they come—domination, colonization, and assimilation. This reality, however uncomfortable and upsetting, has created a tension of opportunity to discuss the historical, practical, and perpetual interpretation of "public" and the fundamental role institutions have, and continue to play, in its praxis. The need for an inclusive understanding of, and approach to, "public" is clear as the demands and realities of the social landscape become more contentious, divisive, and polarizing.

LEADERSHIP

"Do not be silent; there is no limit to the power that may be released through you."

Howard Thurman

Why is staying within the silos of "status quo" so natural and preferable? A sociological response could be that what is known breeds a certain level of security and comfort, but a reply from a "public" theology perspective would question whether security and comfort should, in fact, be goals at all. This has been the question at the core of missiology since Jesus dispatched the disciples:

> Behold, I send you out as sheep in the midst of wolves. Therefore be wise as serpents and harmless as doves.[7]

From either standpoint the underlying dual nature of context and content is significant—context being circumstances and conditions, content being realities that result. Hence, any "public" theology must be concerned with leadership dynamics—personal, interpersonal, and communal—if it is to be functional and effective during times of unrest.

According to Ronald Heifetz and Marty Linsky, leadership would be a safe undertaking if institutions faced problems for which they already have solutions. This is a critical lens through which to view "public" theology as it distinguishes *technical* challenges, those which people have the necessary expertise and procedures to tackle, from *adaptive* challenges, those that require experiments, new discoveries, and adjustments from numerous places within the institution.[8] As adaptive challenges present themselves, the tendency is for members of an institution to look to an expert to provide a technical solution: "Tell me/us what to do." This approach allows institutions (and individuals) to avoid the dangers, either consciously or subconsciously, of risk and vulnerability by treating adaptive challenges as technical. This is why routine management is more prevalent than actual leadership.[9]

To define leadership as an activity that addresses adaptive challenges considers not only the values that a goal represents "but also the goal's ability to mobilize people to face, rather than avoid, tough realities and conflicts."[10] The most difficult and valuable task of leadership relative to a "public" theology in times of unrest may be advancing goals and articulating strategies that promote adaptive solutions—undertaking the iterative process of examining where an entity is, how it arrived at that point, and what it needs to do to move forward. In other words, we need a direct engagement with context and content, fueled by the need for change and immersed in constant action. Thus, leadership requires disturbing people.[11]

The assertions of Heifetz and Linsky suggest that in addition to recognizing challenges, leaders must be careful to understand their historic, systemic, *and* structural nature while interpreting them in adaptive terms. As Barbara Crosby and John Bryson argue, in order to coordinate action and make headway on resolving complex problems, those involved need to be aware of the whole problem *system* and recognize that *it* has to undergo significant change.[12] Challenges require a process that addresses the various dimensions collectively, engaging the broad scope of systems and structures at both the macro and micro levels. A "public" theology would have to include careful attention to the historic nature of identity and community formation and allow that to inform an approach to, engagement with, and understanding of unrest. Yet throughout this process, a clear focus on leadership, perhaps even shared leadership, must be employed to avoid pitfalls of apathy, distrust, and silo pervasiveness. John P. Kotter explains that "needed change can still stall because of inwardly focused cultures, paralyzing bureaucracy, parochial politics, a low level of trust, lack of teamwork, arrogant attitudes . . . and the general human fear of the unknown."[13]

Given the climate of polarization, it would be prudent for leaders to imagine a different manner by which change can occur, particularly during unrest. Since attempting to create major change with simple, linear, analytical processes almost always fails, reactive participation must be replaced with proactive engagement. For a "public" theology, this might be very difficult, arguably impossible, given the aforementioned characterizations of the "church." But leadership that engages across silos embodies a transformational mindset that mobilizes rather than misconstrues—a traditional approach that will continue to be unsuccessful and non-relational because it inadequately engages the dynamics, factors, and variables beneath the unrest.

Unfortunately, a siloed mindset has been institutionalized, resulting in a culture that discourages leaders from learning *how* to lead. Ironically, this institutionalization is a direct result of past successes—the repetitive pattern of "doing what's always been done." The combination of institutions that resist change and leaders who have not been taught how to create change is lethal, particularly because sources of complacency, status quo, and business as usual are rarely adequately addressed. Urgency and change are not issues for "*public*ans" that are comfortable with, and simply seek to maintain, a current system of policies, processes, and practices. Leadership needs to take into account culture, as it "can smother those who want to respond to shifting conditions"[14] while promoting complacency. Therefore, a networked approach that includes a variety of cross-cultural, multi-representational stakeholder engagement and inclusivity is a better, more beneficial model to influence systems and structures:

> Change advocates have to engage in political, issue-oriented, and therefore messy planning and decision making, in which shared goals and mission are being developed as the process moves along. New networks must be created, old ones co-opted or neutralized. These networks range from the highly informal, in which the main activity is information sharing, to more organized shared-power arrangements.[15]

For leadership within a "public" theology to be effective, two premises must be accepted. First, a certain loss of autonomy will be experienced. Here an approach that Geoffrey Vickers calls "acts of appreciation" becomes a useful lens because appreciation merges judgment of what is *real* with judgment of what is *valuable*. Identifying problems involves new appreciation of how something works, what is wrong with it, and how it might become better—from multiple perspectives. This appreciation subsequently shapes the way a problem is defined, the solutions considered, and the experiences of those impacted.[16]

Second, an understanding of culture is pivotal. Edgar Schein distinguishes three levels of culture: artifacts, which are visible organizational structures and processes; espoused beliefs and values, which are strategies, goals, and philosophies; and underlying assumptions, which are unconscious, taken-for-granted beliefs, perceptions, thoughts, and feelings. Culture is inextricably linked to historical and perpetual realities. Not accepting this dynamic will undermine any engagement efforts, however genuine, authentic, and accommodating. As Schein points out:

> The most central issue for leaders, therefore, is how to get at the deeper levels of a culture, how to assess the functionality of the assumptions made at that level, and how to deal with the anxiety that is unleashed when those levels are challenged.[17]

I am not suggesting that this type of leadership is the only means by which "public" theology can be effective. However, I am asserting that anything other than an approach that consistently considers cultural dynamics and realities will always be subject to degradation as soon as the pressures associated with the unrest subside, i.e., protests, marches, etc. In this way, "public" theology has always played a prominent role in many of America's most important movements, from the pursuit of independence to civil rights. It was the personal stake and claim, or ownership, of "*public*ans" that connected moral obligation with social location to harmonize efforts of change.

OWNERSHIP

"In the end, we will remember not the words of our enemies, but the silence of our friends."

Martin Luther King, Jr.

To be effective, "public" theology needs to, once again, establish some level of obligation in terms of reaction and response. In most instances, if not all, systems and structures have a direct correlation to outcomes. A lack of obligation, or the practice of deflection, not only can manifest itself in "*public*ans" but can also be fostered in "*public*" by institutions that initiate, promulgate, and tolerate racism. Such habits left unchecked and uncorrected in a "public" theology can undermine trust and eventually take away from the collective understanding and addressing of key issues associated with unrest. To combat this, ownership should involve an embracing and unpacking of history, considering its effects at various levels, as well as its impact—leaving no structure, system, or institution unexplored.

Power and privilege dynamics are social institutional realities that can either help or hinder attempts at ownership. To make strides toward establishing accountability, "public" theology must begin with the frank acknowledgment that there are embedded causes of unrest—specifically, who has access and to what extent. This entails barriers and constraints that are more burdensome for the least of these with the least access, leading to "meaning-systems" that, "while originally only ideas, gain force as they are reproduced in the material conditions of society."[18] Power and privilege dynamics stem from the acceptance of social mindsets that result in conditions becoming a part of, and reinforcement for, contingent applications and meanings—directly resulting in distrust, limited (if any) inclusion, and lack of communication.

Given, as previously asserted, that culture is a critical component, it is essentially the construct of *"public"* theology that assigns value and validity in the practice of *"public*ans" as it comprises what people do, how they go about doing it, and why.[19] While the modern use of the term "culture" obscures the original, dynamic, and creative meaning of "tending, harvesting, or cultivating," retaining this active sense highlights the fact that culture is not some inert abstract reality but is always in process in that it is always affecting and always being actively produced. Specific historical context may inform culture, but different content influences it. Consequently, culture is not a monolithic stationary entity that should be rejected, accommodated, or even transformed but rather an existential reality that exists in a critical, discriminating, and constructive manner.[20]

So what is the implication for "public" theology? Mirroring a worldview predicated on lack of access directly places it among systemic and structural patterns of dominance, and possibly oppression. For these patterns to be purged, "public" theology must be viewed as a critical response to the need for change and understood as a moral mandate to challenge. Without clear intentionality and inclusiveness, "public" theology runs the risk of harboring the undertones and realities through which much unrest is viewed. And without inclusiveness, *"public"* theology is left to the "good intentions of well-meaning people," however culturally incompetent and insensitive.

Meaning can help "public" theology avoid the types of traps identified by Banaji and Greenwald as "mindbugs"—ingrained habits of thought and approach that lead to errors in perception, remembrance, reasoning, and decision-making.[21] Strategically used, *meaning* can prioritize perspectives, evaluate impact, and, most importantly, galvanize partnerships. This assignment of meaning can then serve as evidence of a *"public"* commitment that serves the shared purpose of fostering trust through cultural understanding. Meaning, therefore, must incorporate deep dives into the systemic and structural influences of unrest as a critical step in the acknowledgment of, and attempt to legitimately be, a *"public"* theology.

PARTNERSHIPS

"Not everything that is faced can be changed. But nothing can be changed until it is faced."

James Baldwin

"Public" theology is institutional as well as individual. Its very nature involves capacity *and* competency as both are required for full understanding and participation. The inerrant historical understanding and practice of equality implied that once equal rights were achieved, individual ills and conditions of underrepresented groups would be remedied. This ignored that a certain majority held the structural bloodlines "in society to infuse their racial prejudice into the laws, policies, practices, and norms of society."[22] It is ironic that such an understanding and practice would be so misapplied given that institutions have historically dealt with the problematic in ways that have recognized the underlying need for, and practice of, support, thereby making social transformation possible and standing as a structural principle in American democratic idealism through access.

Partnership is a powerful means to create access. It becomes a way of thinking that transforms silo mindsets into innovative pathways. Partnership, when done well, invites commitment, crosses boundaries, and encourages meaning. Internally, partnerships can help diagnose problems more comprehensively and clearly; externally, they may help identify sources that can help provide better solutions. The view that "public" theology is solely the responsibility of a particular group based on social location, power, and privilege is a fledgling concept. Simply put, partnerships work to define problems more broadly, expand strategic thinking, and explore collective solutions.

Whether referred to as "community engagement," "civic engagement," or "civil partnerships," collaborative constructs can gird "public" theology. Many of the partnerships necessary to create successful, equitable strategies and solutions can also protect against unrest as they involve building pathways of imagination and innovation, inside and outside the normal bounds of "*public*" and boundaries of "*public*ans." Approaching these as authentic relationship-building opportunities can be an integral step in building trust, removing misconceptions, and contributing to the realization that the need for relationships may not be just prudent but also transformational.[23]

Martin Luther King called the art of alliances complex and intricate. It can be argued that his assertion was accurate because building alliances is much more detailed than putting exciting combinations and ideas on paper. It involves an acknowledgment of self and common interests, validation of individual and group identity, and affirmation of isolated and shared resources.

If, as King argued, we employ the principle of selectivity along these lines, we will find millions of allies who, in serving themselves, also support the various institutions that house them, "and on such sound foundations unity and mutual trust and tangible accomplishment will flourish."[24]

Another aspect that is advantageous to explore is *who*, or *what*, has power.[25] This is to say, who or what is socially positioned to have access in order to exercise ability and authority. As they studied successful change efforts, Crosby and Bryson "realized that organizations had to find a way to tap each other's resources (broadly conceived) in order to work effectively on public problems. That is, they had to engage in sharing activities, which vary in level of commitment and loss of autonomy."[26] This brings to bear a critical point: systems and structures are either unwilling to forfeit or uncomfortable forfeiting autonomy and/or power. This is especially true where social hierarchy is the history. For *"public"* theology to advance, the philosophical approach must change to visualize what can be accomplished by a shared-power structure that, otherwise without, renders the "public" less informed, responsive, and resourceful. Shared-power arrangements may be most useful in creating a climate where those with little to less social *authority* feel a sense of *creative deviance* that enables them to step away from providing answers that soothe and readily raise questions that disturb.[27]

CONCLUSION

"I am invisible, understand, simply because people refuse to see me."

Ralph Ellison's *Invisible Man*

Ralph Ellison's stirring novel follows the coming-of-age journey of a young Black man in search of personal power, reflecting on his position in society and wandering through moments of deliberation and development as he drifts from encounter to encounter—some intense, others comical, and a few somewhat sad. Again and again, we find this young man questioning his very existence based solely on how he is perceived, received, and deceived by the individuals and institutions whom he encounters while traveling from the segregated American South to Harlem, New York. *Invisible Man* took aim at the complex social, psychological, and political assumptions, beliefs, and practices of those in power to relegate America's Black population to an inferior category of citizenry through forces seen and unseen.

Fast forward to now. Amid the nationwide protests in the US spurred by the recent killings of Ahmaud Arbery in Georgia, Breonna Taylor in Kentucky, and George Floyd in Minnesota, Ellison's portrayal resonates with me as a

Black man: in Minnesota, in institutions, in society . . . I am invisible. Some may criticize the riots that are occurring, and rightfully so, as I do not condone the actions and behaviors that have taken place during the evening hours across America. But I also get the fact that suddenly, Black people's fight and plight have become plainly and *pain-ly* visible.

Tell me, how should I feel when greeted upon entering a store while wearing a suit and tie, but followed when my fraternal brands and familial tattoos are visible? How should I feel when treated as a knowledgeable professional when my titles and credentials are known and yet microassaulted/aggressed when they are not? How should Black people feel when we've tried in every way—nonviolence, marches, sit-ins, protests, petitions, workshops, trainings, courageous conversations, safe spaces, brave spaces, healing circles, restorative practices—to bring attention to the oppressive, stifling, and traumatic experiences we're constantly subjected to and NOTHING changes?

John Wesley once made the declaration, "I went to America to convert the Indians, but oh, who shall convert me?" I believe anger can be a moral and ethical response to injustice; however, it cannot and should not lead to further harm and injury. Instead of focusing on who or what we may deem to be *right*, I suggest a shift to recognizing what may in fact be *righteous*. Righteous indignation goes beyond racial lines and posits itself in the womb of humanity. For me as a human being, did not four little girls dying from a church bomb cause righteous indignation? Similarly, as a nation, under God, indivisible, with liberty and justice for all, should not racism, in any form, cause righteous indignation?

Black America is angry, and we are exhausted. For those who harbor racist ideology, those who are complicit with silence, and those who choose to be blind and/or indifferent to the struggles, experiences, and hurt caused by individuals, institutions, systems, and structures in this country, I leave you with this:

> . . . *for he who does not love his brother whom he has seen, how can he love God whom he has not seen?* (1 John 4:20, NKJV)

Please, "public" theology . . . start to SEE.

NOTES

1. George R. Hunsberger, "The Missional Voice and Posture of Public Theologizing," in *Missiology: An International Review* 34, no. 1 (2006), 17.
2. Hunsberger, "The Missional Voice," 18.

3. Philosopher Joseph Butler believed that the most fundamental aspect of human nature is the conscience which he defines as the reflective or rational faculty which discerns the moral characteristics of actions. For Butler, conscience is a type of moral reason which distinguishes right from wrong.

4. Gary M. Simpson, "God in Global Society: Vocational Imagination, Spiritual Presence, and Ecclesial Discernment" (keynote address, The Missional Church and Global Civil Society Consultation, Luther Seminary, St. Paul, MN, November 2008).

5. Solidarity is a key condition for developing moral wisdom, thereby playing a constitutive role in a publicly effective moral epistemology allowing critical issues to be identified, distilled, and framed—manifesting itself through proposals, programs, and practices for moral and cultural formation, or critical reformation. Publicity takes what has been critically identified, morally framed and formed, and programmatically proposed and makes that fully public, meaning that in a transparent and accessible manner, publicity connects what it discovers concerning the social condition to the systems of power that can cause and effect change.

6. Simpson, "God in Global Society."

7. Matthew 10:16, NKJV.

8. Ronald A. Heifetz and Marty Linsky, *Leadership on the Line: Staying Alive through the Dangers of Leading* (Boston: Harvard Business School Press, 2002), 13.

9. Heifetz and Linsky, *Leadership on the Line*, 14.

10. Ronald A. Heifetz, *Leadership without Easy Answers* (Cambridge: The Belknap Press of Harvard University Press, 1994), 23.

11. Heifetz and Linsky, *Leadership on the Line*, 20.

12. Barbara C. Crosby and John M. Bryson, *Leadership for the Common Good: Tackling Public Problems in a Shared-Power World* (San Francisco: Jossey-Bass, 2005), 9.

13. John P. Kotter, *Leading Change* (Boston: Harvard Business School, 1996), 20.

14. Kotter, *Leading Change*, 27.

15. Crosby and Bryson, *Leadership for the Common Good*, 9.

16. Crosby and Bryson, *Leadership for the Common Good*, 9.

17. Edgar A. Schein, *Organizational Culture and Leadership* (San Francisco: Jossey-Bass, 2004), 37.

18. Ian Haney López, *White by Law: The Legal Construction of Race* (New York: New York University Press, 2006), 10.

19. Kathryn Tanner, *Theories of Culture: A New Agenda for Theology*, Guides to Theological Inquiry (Minneapolis: Fortress, 1997), 27.

20. Darrell L. Guder, *Missional Church: A Vision for the Sending of the Church in North America* (Grand Rapids: William B. Eerdmans, 1998), 151.

21. See Mahzarin R. Banaji and Anthony G. Greenwald, *Blind Spots: Hidden Biases of Good People* (New York: Bantam Books, 2016).

22. Robin DiAngelo, *White Fragility: Why It's So Hard for White People to Talk About Racism* (Boston: Beacon Press, 2018), 22.

23. See Lee G. Bolman and Terrance E. Deal, *Reframing Organizations: Artistry, Choice, and Leadership* (San Francisco, Jossey-Bass, 2008).

24. James A. Washington, ed., *A Testament of Hope: The Essential Writings and Speeches of Dr. Martin Luther King, Jr.* (New York: HarperCollins Publishers, 1986), 310.
25. Defined as the ability to construct, control, coerce, and/or change.
26. Crosby and Bryson, *Leadership for the Common Good*, 17.
27. See Heifetz, *Leadership without Easy Answers*.

Chapter 4

Native Christian Mission in Burma

Pum Za Mang

In popular culture, history, literature, art, and public memory, Western missionaries have become revered not just as religious proselytizers but also as an eternal symbol of modernization, with native Christians extolling that missionaries sacrificed everything, including their lives, when they came, lived, and worked with and for them. Underscoring the full extent of suffering they endured, native Christians tell and retell how their missionaries such as Adoniram Judson underwent misery after misery. During the first Anglo-Burmese war, the Burmese falsely accused Judson of being a British spy and imprisoned him, shattering his entire family.[1] He died in 1850 after almost four decades of missionary service, and many missionaries—who came after him—also lost their lives and the lives of their children while working among and with the Karen, Kachin, Chin, and more, demonstrating their selfless commitment and costly sacrifice. In recognition of their work of love, which led to the notable modernization of illiterate and backward people, native Christians have endlessly cherished their missionaries.

To be more specific, Duwa Zau Lawn, the former Minister for the Kachin, affectionately told Gustaf A. Sword, who replaced the legendary American missionary Ola Hanson, "We [the Kachin] shall never forget that you gave us the Kachin script, the school books and schools, and above all you gave us the Bible in our own language and you brought us our Christian faith. We are fully aware that what we are today we owe to the missionaries who came here and gave their lives for us."[2] Delighting in the amazing progress his people made with the help of missionaries, San C. Po, the father of the Karen, similarly recorded in his 1928 book, "Every Karen must be ever grateful to the missionaries and the people that send them, of whatever nationality, for the sacrifice of time, talent, money, and men on their behalf."[3]

My knowledge of church history in Burma allows me to say that the missionaries deserve such profound gratitude, respect, love, and affection, but the story of native missionaries also deserves to be recognized, told, and written, historically because it has been no less dynamic and noteworthy. Whereas scholars and students keenly interested in Burmese studies have written a host of journal articles, books, and dissertations about the illustrious history of foreign missionaries, they mostly neglected the fascinating stories of native missionaries actively involved in proselytizing and converting their own people with enduring consequences. I, therefore, explore this overlooked subject, present the notable role of native missionaries in the making of Christianity, and look at how the new religion they adopted has served and helped ethnic minorities to protect their ethnic identity and keep their distance from their far more powerful neighbors.

THE KAREN CHURCH

American Baptist missionaries started mission and evangelization enterprises among the Karen in the early nineteenth century, and many Karen, especially the Sgaw, accepted the teachings of missionaries without much difficulty, thanks to their old folklores of the "lost book," "white brother," "Ywa," and, indeed, British colonialization, along with troubled race relations between the Burman and Karen.[4] The constructive impact of that religious conversion elevated their social status, stirred their national awakening, and influenced their future destiny so much so that one cannot fully comprehend Karen society and history without understanding the church. It must be noted that when they adopted Christianity, many Karen Christians also became abused, persecuted, imprisoned, enslaved, and martyred, demonstrating the high price of embracing missionaries and practicing Christianity. Karen churches, however, firmly withstood religious repression and ethnic persecution, which agonizingly tested and seemingly reinforced their new faith, as more Karen increasingly accepted Christianity in the years and decades that followed. They not only survived such challenges but also adopted the vital idea of self-support.[5]

What is more, early Karen converts cherished the underlying notion of the Karen proselyting the Karen and other highlanders, implying that the history of Karen Christianity would remain incomplete without making mention of determined Karen missionaries and schoolteachers proselytizing the Karen, Kachin, Chin, and more during and after the nineteenth century. This striking church history started with the unpromising encounter between Judson and Ko Thabyu, who reportedly killed some thirty persons. Known as an infamous murderer, Ko Thabyu played a crucial role in changing the course of Karen religion and history by proselytizing his people with notable success. Judson purchased him, and the Rev. George D. Boardman baptized him in Tavoy on May 16, 1828, marking the birth of Karen Christianity. Seeking to spread the gospel to his people, he went to the deep valleys and steep hills in much of lower Burma, which resulted in thousands of the Sgaw adopting Christianity.[6] He inspired Saw Quala, who contributed to preaching the gospel and converting many Karen afterward.

Driven by the deep desire and tenacity to reach all Karen communities with the gospel, the Sgaw Karen Baptists formed the Bassein Karen Home Mission Society (BKHMS), the first native Karen missionary organization, in 1850, which would forever change the course of religious landscape in Burma. Whereas Western missionaries faced uphill challenges of linguistic, cultural, social, and geographic barriers, the early Karen Christians went through the remote jungles, hills, and valleys, visiting Karen villages, living among Karen villagers as missionaries, and Christianizing them.[7] That means that the Christian Karen played an indispensable role in the process of their conversation to Christianity and the formation of the Karen Baptist church. Whenever we think of the history of the Karen church, we must also recall that the emotional, ethnic, and social impact of the Karen mission for the Karen must not be underestimated. In seeking to spread the gospel to other hill people, the BKHMS sent Karen missionaries and teachers to live and work among the Chin, Kachin, and other races after the 1870s.[8]

That the overwhelming majority of the Chin and Kachin now practice Christianity historically links to the salient contribution of the Karen Christians investing so much of their resources in evangelizing Chin and Kachin societies. It is important to note that Western missionaries extensively proselytized and educated the Karen from the start for the sake of mission efforts, given that between 1828 and 1929, some 150 Western missionaries, along with two thousand Karen native missionaries, worked among the Karen.[9] It must be added that in geographical terms, lower Burma populated by the Karen was easily accessible to missionaries, so it made every sense when American missionaries used their assets for the Karen mission and lifted their collective situation. Mission education positively impacted and transformed the course of Karen history beyond all recognition, and it is hard to exaggerate their holistic advancement.

When missionaries founded various renowned mission schools for Karen children and vigorously advanced education for the once illiterate Karen, they consistently focused on Christianizing them.[10] In other words, they educated the Christian Karen, primarily because they held that those Karen would best evangelize their own people in the future, and church history absolutely proved them right. There were, for instance, 231,818 Christians from all ethnic groups in Burma, according to the 1921 census, and the Karen Christians alone represented 178,225, underscoring the widespread mission work of Western missionaries among the Karen and the growing vitality of Karen Christianity. It must be further reiterated that Karen missionaries toured Karen villages across lower Burma and proselytized their people with remarkable success, demonstrating the historical fact that the Karen were crucial agents and players in the course of their conversion to Christianity.[11]

The story of this native mission has not stopped here, as many Karen Christians, trained and educated at mission schools and seminaries, likewise went to the Chin, Kachin, and other hill people across the land as missionaries and schoolteachers. With unbreakable resolve, spirit, and passion for bringing the gospel to the non-Karen races, they lived with Chin and Kachin villagers, learned their languages, earned their confidence, and evangelized them. What is, therefore, fondly cherished and immortalized in Burmese church chronicles is that the early Christian Karen made a vital contribution to the treasured history of converting the Chin and Kachin with permanent ramifications. Remember that the first converts among the Chin and Kachin were the product of the labor of patience, sacrifice, and, indeed, love by Karen missionaries. Had the Christian Karen not sacrificed their lives and used their immeasurable resources for mission work among the Chin and Kachin, things may have gone very differently.

What must not be overlooked meanwhile is that Karen missionaries lived and worked with the ethnic Lahu and played a significant role in the formation of the Lahu Baptist church. While underlining what they did for the Lahu, James H. Telford, a missionary in Kengtung, for instance, penned in 1927:

> A historical sketch of the Kengtung Mission would not be complete if we failed to make mention of the great part the Karen Christian workers have had in the development of the Lahu church. . . . Much of the success . . . has been largely due to their splendid consecration and complete abandonment to the work. For years the Karen churches of Bassein . . . have sent evangelists and pastors to the Lahus, for whose financial support the Karen churches have assumed entire responsibility. The services over a period of years by such men as Po Tun, Ba Te, Chit Swe, and numerous others, live as a fragrant memory in the hearts of the Lahus.[12]

Like the Karen who evangelized them, the Christian Lahu continued the tradition of evangelization by proselytizing their own people, with David and Maya Bradley recounting, "This movement has continued and become indigenized, with Lahu Christians continuing to proselytize and convert other Lahu."[13] Karen missionaries, meanwhile, continued preaching and evangelizing the Lahu and Wa. Saw Aung Din, a graduate of renowned Judson College and Myanmar Institute of Theology (MIT), worked among the Lahu and Wa between 1941 and 1957. Later he became Director of the Wa-Lahu mission field for MBC (then known as the Burma Baptist Convention). As a testament to the growing importance of the Lahu Baptist church, Angela Pun, a Lahu scholar, served as a professor at MIT, and her nephew, Robert Pun, now serves as associate general secretary of Myanmar Baptist Convention (MBC). Karen missionaries also worked among the ethnic Akha, and the first Akha Baptist church was founded in April of 1936 as a result of the labor of love by Thra Tun Gyaw and his wife for a decade.[14] Ardently involved in the labor of reaching the non-Karen races with the gospel and Christianizing them, Karen missionaries proselytized the Naga in western Burma and the Chinese in the borderland between Burma and China.[15]

It must be added that the Christian Karen have typically placed great emphasis on education since the 1830s, when many of them started adopting Christianity and establishing vernacular schools where future pastors, preachers, and evangelists were educated.[16] By 1931 there were 888 Baptist mission schools in the country, and 611 schools were for the Karen.[17] The once-illiterate Karen highly valued education, as they thought education was the fundamental source of holistic modernization for them. In this particular connection, Ardeth Maung Thawnghmung, a Karen scholar, writes, "The introduction of a written script and the availability of material in the Karen language were central to the growth of literacy, spread of knowledge and education, and strengthening of ties among the traditionally weakly linked Karen communities."[18] In all, the Christian Karen have always enthroned education, and Karen missionaries, evangelists, pastors, and schoolteachers brought this splendid tradition with them when they lived and worked among and with other illiterate races.

THE CHIN CHURCH

Living in much of modern-day western Burma, the Chin once practiced the tribal religion of their ancestors, but most of them are now Christians, thanks to American and Karen missionaries bringing Christianity to the Chin country. The Karen Christians in lower Burma played an important part in the formation of Chin churches in the early twentieth century, given Karen and American missionaries evangelized the Chin together, a key breakthrough in Chin history that changed the collective destiny of the Chin as a people forever. In March of 1899, Arthur E. Carson, an American missionary; Laura Carson, his wife; and San Win, a Karen missionary, arrived in Hakha, the principal village in the Chin country. In the years that followed, more Karen missionaries, namely Pu Kut, Shwe Zan, Maung Gone, Maung Kya, and

Kyi Ghine, followed them and worked among the Chin. The new religion they brought gradually penetrated Chin society, and a group of eleven Chin Christians at the village of Khuasak, where Shwe Zan lived and worked, converted to Christianity and founded Khuasak Baptist Church, the first Chin church in history, on February 17, 1906. Shwe Zan became the pastor of that church, and the first Lord's Supper in Chin history was held the next day, February 18, marking the beginning of Chin Christianity, which has permanently transformed the course of Chin history.[19]

What is more, historically education has always been vital to missionaries evangelizing the illiterate races, and American missionaries proselytizing the Chin also founded multiple schools to educate Chin children. Karen missionaries and teachers taught at such schools on weekdays and preached at churches on Sundays, boosting relations between the two races socially, religiously, and ethnically. Karen churches, as stated before, enthroned education, which notably elevated the shared status of the Karen, and Karen teachers and missionaries endeavoring to help the Chin in terms of education, thus, taught Chin children. Thra San Win was, for instance, a preacher, the headmaster of the Hakha mission school and subinspector of government schools in the Chin country.[20] Intending to prepare Chin men for church leadership, Chester U. Strait, an American missionary, opened the Bible school in Hakha in May of 1928 with thirteen students but discontinued that school after 1931, when his students completed their studies and graduated. He used the same school building as a teacher's training school, where men and women were trained to become preachers and teachers, which would impact the larger Chin society. After they lived with and for the Chin for thirty-five years, Karen missionaries and teachers returned home in 1934, for enough Chin students studied and graduated from the teachers' training school.[21] While underscoring how indispensable their role was to the Chin mission, Robert G. Johnson, the last missionary to the Chin, quoted Joseph H. Cope, a missionary before him, as recording:

> We owe everything to the Karens. We do not know what we would do without them. When Mr. Carson first came up he brought three or four Karen with him and from that time on, with a few exceptions, they have proven splendid men on whom one could place no end of responsibility. For a long time, they were the only evangelists here. They went out to strange villages where no preparations had been made for them and where they were threatened direly. The first Chin Christians came seven days' journey from Haka where a Henzada Karen, Thra Shwe Zan, worked alone, seeing the missionaries only once a year. The Chin preachers were put under these Karens and some of our finest workers were trained by them. They learned the language, learned the ways of the people, and won their confidence. In the first literary work I did, it was the Karens who

helped me. In the school work as well we have Karen headmasters, and they proved as valuable there as in the evangelistic work.[22]

Native Chin missionaries made a significant contribution to proselytizing and converting their own people, given Christians in the north went to the south to evangelize their brethren, who still practiced Chin tribal religion. After their conversion to Christianity, Sakhong from the Zophei area and Lian Kar from the Senthang area, for instance, became missionaries and teachers and opened a school in Matupi, the main village in the south, in 1933. In 1944 Rev. That Dun and Rev. Pa Hrek from the Zophei area, likewise, went to Matupi and served there as native missionaries, acquiring deep affection and reverence from Christians in the Matupi area.[23] What made this native mission remarkable and different from the foreign mission was that different tribes of the Chin, who once fought and killed each other, accepted one another as one race.[24] In epitomizing the social and religious bonds such Chin missionaries made in the south, the Chin in the Matupi area founded That Dun Baptist Church in Matupi and have been able to speak the Lai dialect.

It must be noted here that all foreign missionaries left the Chin country in April of 1942 due to the war and returned only in February of 1946, which means Chin Christians ardently supported themselves when native Chin missionaries went to the south in 1944, amplifying the growing confidence and vitality of Chin churches at that time. In his book Robert G. Johnson wrote that native Chin churches staunchly faced their tough reality, overcame the uphill challenges, and even flourished during the four years of their absence.[25] More people converted to Christianity, and church growth continued despite constant interruptions and destructions caused by the war. In this respect Robert G. Johnson pertinently wrote, "The war years revealed the solid foundation laid by the American Baptist Mission in developing national leadership and self-support, and thus during the war years the Christians continued and even much increased their zeal. In fact, deprived of foreign money and leadership, and thrown in full reliance on the Spirit, they entered into a time of revival."[26]

The Chin, meanwhile, joined the state of modern Burma when it became independent from the British in 1948, and peace was, more or less, restored in what has become known as Chin State. The period of political stability was short, however, as democracy evaporated in 1962, when the military arrested all top elected political leaders and seized power, marking the start of military dictatorship. The junta then expelled missionaries from the country and nationalized all mission schools in the 1960s, which resulted in depriving native Christians of positive social impact on mainstream Burmese society, especially education. The departure of Western missionaries has, meanwhile, allowed the Chin Christians to demonstrate the resolution, vitality, and resilience of their faith, as Chin church leaders at that time vowed to remain committed and faithful to their new religion. In his 2006 book, Robert G. Johnson recounted, "What pleased me most as I left the Chin Hills was the determination of the Christians to stand true to the gospel of Christ, no matter what happened in their country, no matter what lay before them."[27] It must be stressed that the exodus of foreign missionaries actually corroborated the claim of the Chin that Christianity has been their own religion.

Thanks to the strong zeal and resolve of Chin native missionaries restless in preaching the gospel and converting their people, more Chin became identified with Christianity and church growth consistently continued despite political violence and religious persecution. In 1972 the Methodists in the Kalay area, for example, sent missionaries to the Dai tribe of the Chin living in much of southern Chin State.[28] Compelled to spread the gospel among their own people in the south, the Presbyterians in the Kalay area also started proselytizing the Dai in 1975. The Baptists came earlier in 1952. I taught at Myanmar Theological College (MTC), Mandalay, the most consequential Methodist seminary in Burma, for years and visited the hilltop town of Mindat, southern Chin State, twice, which allowed me to understand the lasting impact and vitality of Christianity among the Dai. It has been observed that virtually all the Dai are now Christians and that there are many highly educated Dai church leaders and theological educators.

What is more, the Baptists held a consultation in the picturesque town of Falam from May 13 to 17 of 1981 and decided to undertake mission enterprise among the Chin, who still practiced Chin tribal religion.[29] Driven to make the entire Chin population Christian by 1999, a century after the arrival of the first missionaries in 1899, they started what has become known in Chin church history as the Chins for Christ in One Century (CCOC) mission in 1983. The single most historically important and consequential mission work started by the Chin, 906 young men and women evangelized their people, mostly in the south, and revived existing churches elsewhere, which led to the conversion and baptism of 20,051 people by 1999, when they held the Chin Evangelical Centenary. Between 1983 and 1999, they spent 74,424,116.15 kyat (the national currency) and six of those missionaries gave their own lives.[30] That mission epitomized the unprecedented ties among the subtribes of the Chin and protected their distance from the Burman.

The cost of being different from the Burman religiously and racially is not cheap, however, considering the successive juntas dominated by the Burman have deliberately and systematically targeted the Chin for ethnic persecution, religious restriction, and political suppression. In underscoring how they have painfully endured the banality of military assaults, Benedict Rogers notes, "Famine, the burning of villages and the destruction of rice barns were to become regular features of Chin life a century later, under the rule of the

Tatmadaw."[31] Our military rulers have stripped our people of their homes, their properties, their churches, and often their own lives. I lived most of my childhood life in our mountainous but romantic state and witnessed the plight of our people. The situation was so difficult and precarious that hundreds of thousands of our people left our native land and permanently resettled in many Western countries.[32]

THE KACHIN CHURCH

The Kachin country never saw missionaries before 1837, when Eugenio Kincaid entered territories north of Mandalay and Ava in the heartland of Burma and arrived in Mogaung, where he met what he fondly called the friendly, progressive, and open-minded Kachin. That contact was so moving for him that he pleaded with mission leaders in the United States to send missionaries to the Kachin, but without success. Dr. Rose, another missionary among the Karen, visited Bhamo in 1868 and 1875 for potential mission work among them, as he held the view that the Karen and Kachin were ethnically related. In his 1954 book, Gustaf A. Sword quoted him as remarking, "If I were young again I would make the Kachins my people and their beautiful mountains my home. There may be as many beautiful jewels among the Kachins as among the Karens."[33] Karen missionaries, together with American missionaries, eventually arrived in the Kachin country in 1877 and played key roles in the course of proselytizing and converting many Kachin to Christianity, accordingly bolstering religious, ethnic, and social ties between the two races with long-term consequences before and after Burma became independent. In his book Herman G. Tegenfeldt wrote, "It is worthy of note that the first Baptist missionary to set forth in a Kachin village was not an American, but a Karen."[34]

Karen missionaries visited rural Kachin villages, lived with them, spoke their languages, entered their real world, earned their hallowed trust, and evangelized them with much success. Thra S' Peh, who arrived with Josiah N. Cushing in 1877, for example, lived in Bunwa village near Bhamo for years, and a group of seven Kachin villagers subsequently adopted Christianity as a result of his labor, but he waited until after William H. Roberts returned from his furlough in the United States. Four Karen missionaries and Alice Buell, the wife of Roberts, sang hymns, and Roberts baptized the first seven Kachin Christians on Sunday, March 19, 1882, marking the birth of Kachin Christianity. The first-ever Kachin communion followed that evening, and a Karen missionary read the text of 1 Corinthians 11 from the Karen Bible and explained the theological meaning of the rite in Kachin (Jingphaw). Roberts and L.W. Cronkhite, another American missionary, broke the bread and poured the wine respectively, as they led that solemn communion.[35] In displaying his zeal, determination, and commitment, Thra S' Peh wrote in his letter (January 11, 1878):

> I pity this people very much. They want very much to learn; but at present I am all alone on the mountains among them. Owing to fighting among the Kachins and Burmans, I cannot travel about as freely as I wish. The Burmans have given out that they would massacre all the Kachins from fifteen years old and upward, and I was a little afraid. Teacher Cushing told me not to fear; if the Burmans attached one mountain, to flee to the next, and if they take all the mountains, to flee into China. I did as he said, and stayed on the mountains. I am all ready to cast in my lot with these poor Kachins, to suffer with them, and to lead them with my whole heart to Christ, as Moses cast in his lot with the children of Israel.[36]

The history of Kachin Christianity and the remarkable contribution of Karen missionaries to the Kachin mission were historically intertwined, given that Karen missionaries lived among the Kachin for eighty-five years. Bogalay (1876–1877), S' Peh (1877–1887), Koteh (1878–1892), Naythah (1878–1879), Shwe Gyaw (1879–1919), Maukeh (1879–1898), Kan Gyi (1895–1925), Po Nyo (1895–1911), John Thwe (1898–1900), Shwe So (1892–1937), Tha Dwe (1899–1929), Kyaw Dwe (1906–1936), Ba Thaw (1911–1952), Po Zan (1918–1927), Tha Htoo (1919–1962), and Sein Nyo (1924–1938) lived among and with the Kachin as missionaries. At least six of them died in Kachin country and were buried in Kachin graves. Apart from Karen missionaries sent and supported directly by Bassein Karen churches, there were Karen pastors and schoolteachers employed by American missionaries to work among the Kachin.[37] The fact that virtually all the Kachin have now practiced Christianity is historically connected to the ultimate sacrifice, perseverance, patience, and commitment of Karen missionaries.

Factors influencing the amazing success of mission work among the Kachin encompassed elements of Kachin tribal religion, including the idea of a supreme being, flood story, and lost book tradition. The mutual distrust existing between the Burman and Kachin also played an important role.[38] The Kachin seemingly thought they needed to adopt Christianity, for Buddhism would eventually absorb those who still practiced animism, which would lead to what has become known as Burmanization.[39] Remember that practicing Christianity has served them well to preserve their ethnic identity and their distance from the Burman. And the emotional and social influence of Karen missionaries learning and speaking the Kachin language while preaching the gospel to them must not be underrated. To be more specific, the first Karen missionary, Bogalay, studied the Kachin vernacular [Jinghpaw] and preached to the Kachin in Jinghpaw. In highlighting the profound influence Karen missionaries wielded upon the Kachin while evangelizing them at the time, Bertil Lintner precisely writes, "It was easy for the Kachins to relate [to] them [the Karen]—they shared a similar hill tribe culture and also a deep-rooted mistrust of the Burmans. Christianity gave them new strength to face the superior power that for centuries had tried to subjugate them."[40]

Karen nurses and medics, moreover, actively assisted American medical missionaries serving the Kachin community in upper Burma. In his 1943 book, the famed American medical missionary, Dr. Gordon S. Seagrave (1897–1965), who spoke Karen as his first language and worked in the town of Namkham, recounted how Karen medical professionals, including Dr. Ba Saw, the son of Karen missionaries to the Chin, lived and worked in Kachin community.[41] Known as Burma Surgeon and spending some twenty years of his life in Burma, Seagrave built a well-known hospital, treated countless patients with various diseases, and trained local women to be veteran nurses.[42] Karen nurses working with him at Harper Memorial Hospital in Namkham even volunteered to provide much-needed medical services to the wounded in 1944, when the British and American forces surrounded and finally seized Myikyina.[43] Embodying the undying spirit of American and Karen medical missionaries dedicated to the need of all races in northern Shan State, the stone two-story building from that missionary era has been still there as the one-hundred-bedded public hospital serving all Namkham residents from diverse races and faiths.[44]

The often unnoticed but important impact of Karen missionaries on racial and religious ties between the Karen and Kachin was that Naw Seng, the ablest commander in the Burma Army and the war hero known for his storied battles against the Japanese during WWII, played no small part in saving the young nation when he led the successful combats against the communists in central Burma, symbolizing the legendary military prowess of the Kachin. When he was ordered to attack the Karen rebels, Naw Seng, a Kachin Christian, refused and instead joined the Karen uprising.[45] Lintner writes, "Naw Seng had no desire to fight his fellow Christian Karens on behalf of the Burmans, whom he had in any case never fully trusted. On 21 February at the front in Toungoo in central Burma, he took his entire battalion and went over to the Karens."[46] It must be further recalled that when Gen. Smith Dun, the first commander-in-chief of the Burma Army, was fired in early 1949, he also sought refuge in Myitkyina, the state capital of Kachin State.[47] A Baptist Karen, who never fully trusted Burman nationalist leaders, Smith Dun most likely thought his life would be safe only in Kachin State.

The new religion they adopted has, moreover, lifted their political and social situation, partly because the missionaries founded mission schools for Kachin children, and by 1911 the Bhamo mission school had 221 students and the Myikyina mission school had seventy-five Kachin students. Mission education also produced for the first time in history educated Kachin elites, who would shape the fate and future destiny of the Kachin, given famed Kachin leaders, including Duwa Zau Lawn and Maran Brang Seng, were educated at mission schools. When many Kachin youth graduated, they took over much of the work previously undertaken by Karen missionaries.[48] While emphasizing the historically close interplay between mission education and Kachin ethnic awakening before independence, Mandy Sadan contends, "Although the numbers of Kachin people professing Christianity remained relatively small during the colonial period, many of them through their contact with missionary education systems . . . undoubtedly increased their abilities to occupy socially, economically and politically niche spaces."[49]

With the zeal and determination to make all the Kachin Christian, the Kachin Christians undertook mission and evangelization work among other Kachin in upper Burma and western China. It is notable that they sent missionaries to the Kachin in China and converted hundreds of them to Christianity by the 1930s.[50] They also sent missionaries to the ethnic Naga, Palaung, and Shan, who have extensive social interactions with the Kachin.[51] In 1977, which marked a century of the advent of American missionaries in the Kachin country, Kachin Baptists held an anniversary event and proclaimed that they would send three hundred young missionaries (known as the 3/300 mission) to evangelize all the Kachin who still practiced animism. They started that mission in 1978, and Kachin church leaders stated Christians represent 99 percent of the entire Kachin population following this native mission.[52] Through this native mission enterprise, they make it clear to everyone that the religion they have practiced has been their own religion, not Western religion, which contradicts the narrative of Buddhist nationalists against minority Christians in contemporary Burma.

All in all, exploring and stressing the remarkable, but often overlooked, accounts of native missionaries proselytizing and Christianizing their people, this essay clearly demonstrates that the Chin, Kachin, and Karen Christians have in historical and practical terms played a key role when they accepted the Christian faith. That means that they are active agents in the making of Christianity and that they display to everyone, especially the Burmese authorities, that Christianity is their own religion. Finally, practicing Christianity has served them well to protect their ethnic identity and keep their distance from their powerful lowland neighbors.

NOTES

1. Helen G. Trager, *Burma through Alien Eyes: Missionary Views of the Burmese of the Nineteenth Century* (New York: Asia Publishing House, 1966), 57–62.
2. Gustaf A. Sword, *Light in the Jungle: Life Story of Dr. Ola Hanson of Burma* (Chicago: Baptist Conference Press, 1954), 112–13.
3. San C. Po, *Burma and the Karens* (Bangkok: White Lotus, 2001), 58. This book was originally published in 1928.
4. Harry I. Marshall, *The Karen People of Burma: A Study in Anthropology and Ethnology* (Columbus: The Ohio State University Press, 1922), 297.
5. Randolph L. Howard, *Baptists in Burma* (Philadelphia: The Judson Press, 1931), 43, 65, and 68.
6. Ardeth Maung Thawnghmung, *The Other Karen in Myanmar: Ethnic Minorities and the Struggle without Arms* (New York: Lexington Books, 2012), 24; Harry Marshall, "The Karens: An Element in the Melting Pot of Burma," *Southern Workman* 56, no. 28 (1972): 30; and Howard, *Baptists in Burma*, 59.
7. Linus P. Brockett, *The Story of the Karen Mission in Bassein, 1838–1890: Or, the Progress and Education of a People from a Degraded Heathenism to a Refined Christian Civilization* (Philadelphia: American Baptist Publication Society, 1891), 29–42; and Yoko Yahami, "Karen Culture of Evangelism and Early Baptist Mission in Nineteenth Century Burma," *Social Sciences and Missions* 31 (2018): 261.
8. Herman G. Tegenfeldt, *A Century of Growth: The Kachin Baptist Church of Burma* (South Pasadena: William Carey Library, 1974), 84; and Marshall, *The Karen People of Burma*, 301.
9. Alexander McLeish, *Christian Progress in Burma* (New York: World Dominion Press, 1929), 60.
10. Yahami, "Karen Culture of Evangelism and Early Baptist Mission in Nineteenth Century Burma," 264.
11. McLeish, *Christian Progress in Burma*, 18, 19, and 22.
12. Cited in Genevieve Sowards and Erville Sowards, *Burma Baptist Chronicle* (Rangoon: The University Press, 1963), 318.
13. David Bradley and Maya Bradley, "Standardisation of Transnational Languages in Asia: Lisu and Lahu," *Bulletin VALS-ASLA* 69, no. 1 (1999): 87.
14. Genevieve Sowards and Erville Sowards, *Burma Baptist Chronicle*, 404 and 419.
15. Tegenfeldt, *A Century of Growth*, 94; and Marshall, *The Karen People of Burma*, 301.
16. Helen James, *Governance and Civil Society in Myanmar: Education, Health, and Environment* (New York: Routledge, 2005), 95.
17. Howard, *Baptists in Burma*, 115.
18. Thawnghmung, *The Other Karen in Myanmar*, 26.
19. Robert G. Johnson, *History of the American Baptist Chin Mission*, vol. 1 (Valley Forge: Robert G. Johnson, 1988), 57, 64, 65; and Jones Mang Hup, *Laimi Khrihfa Thawhkehnak* (Hakha: Chin Association for Christian Communication, 2014), 50.
20. Howard, *Baptists in Burma*, 117.

21. Lian H. Sakhong, *In Search of Chin Identity: A Study in Religion, Politics, and Ethnic Identity in Burma* (Copenhagen: NIAS, 2003), 172.

22. Genevieve Sowards and Erville Sowards, *Burma Baptist Chronicle*, 388.

23. Johnson, *On the Back Road to Mandalay*, 186; and Sakhong, *In Search of Chin Identity*, 174.

24. It must be noted that due to language differences and geographical difficulties, Chin society remains divided, but, overall, what unites them is by far greater than what divides them.

25. Johnson, *History of the American Baptist Chin Mission*, 656.

26. Genevieve Sowards and Erville Sowards, *Burma Baptist Chronicles*, 391.

27. Johnson, *On the Back Road to Mandalay*, 328.

28. Van Hong, *A History of the Upper Myanmar Methodist Mission in Mindat Area* (Master of Theology Thesis, Myanmar Institute of Theology, 2022), 6.

29. Thlaawr Bawihrin, *The Impact of Missionary Christianity on the Chins* (Indianapolis: Thlaawr Bawihrin, 2002), 155.

30. Hup, *Laimi Khrihfa Thawhkehnak*, 157–59.

31. Benedict Rogers, *Burma: A Nation at the Crossroads—Revised Edition* (London: Random House, 2015), 106.

32. The vast majority of them have lived in the United States and founded hundreds of Chin diaspora Baptist churches there. See Bawi Bik Thawng, "Contextual Leadership within Chin Immigrant Churches in the United States" (2021).

33. Sword, *Light in the Jungle*, 48.

34. Herman G. Tegenfeldt, *A Century of Growth*, 95.

35. Bertil Lintner, *The Kachin: Lords of Burma's Northern Frontier* (Chiang Mai: Teak House, 1997), 63–64.

36. Howard, *Baptists in Burma*, 81.

37. Tegenfeldt, *A Century of Growth*, 366.

38. Lintner, *The Kachin*, 73–74; and Tegenfeldt, *A Century of Growth*, 82.

39. Mandy Sadan, *Being and Becoming Kachin: Histories beyond the State in the Borderworlds of Burma* (Oxford: Oxford University Press, 2013), 391 and 397.

40. Lintner, *The Kachin*, 61.

41. Gordon S. Seagrave, *Burma Surgeon* (New York: W. W. Norton, 1943), 33, 103, and 104.

42. Rennie B. Schoepflin, "Making Doctors and Nurses for Jesus: Medical Missionary Stories and American Children," *Church History* 74, no. 3 (2005): 589.

43. Lintner, *The Kachin*, 95.

44. Gen. Ne Win nationalized all mission schools and hospitals after his military coup in 1962.

45. Though Naw Seng and his men joined the Karen uprising, most Kachin soldiers remained in the Burma Army.

46. Lintner, *The Kachin*, 114–15.

47. Gen. Smith Dun, *Memoirs of the Four-Foot Colonel* (New York: Cornell University Press, 1980), 24–25.

48. Bertil Lintner, *The Kachin*, 74.

49. Sadan, *Being and Becoming Kachin*, 374.

50. Lintner, *The Kachin*, 78.
51. Tegenfeldt, *A Century of Growth*, 226–29.
52. Sadan, *Being and Becoming Kachin*, 382.

Chapter 5

Diakonia and Justice in an African Context

Highlights from the Kenya Evangelical Lutheran Church

Margaret Kemunto Obaga

Historically, the church's diaconal ministry has followed closely on the classic six works of mercy announced by Jesus to feed the hungry, quench the thirsty, welcome the stranger, clothe the naked, heal the sick, and accompany the imprisoned (Mt 25). The church must now capitalize on our deep knowledge and expertise by bringing this knowledge and expertise to the public policy-making table for actualizing ever more just ways of life. Diaconal ministry now inextricably links together works of mercy with prophetic works of justice. In this way, the church's essential diaconal ministry continues to grow in new contexts and times across the prophetic (critical solidarity), the sapiential (wisdom for everyday living), and the pacific (just peace building) dimensions of diakonia.[1]

These words were said by Gary Simpson on the "New Opportunities on Lutheran Diaconal Work in Africa" during the Consultation on Poverty and the Mission of the Church in Africa held in Arusha, Tanzania, on September 2, 2006.

In this quote Simpson captures the meaning of diakonia in the changing times and contexts. This essay will explore, in part, these topics, including diakonia as love and faith in action, church governance and diakonia, pursuit for justice and diakonia, the challenge of a dominating patriarchy, and diakonia as the space for compassion and of assurance and hope in Christ.

The essay draws insights from the Kenya Evangelical Lutheran Church (KELC) in exploring a contextual diakonia. The term "contextual diakonia" refers to making a response to the needs experienced by individuals and communities in their particular situation and the changing social milieu.[2] This calls for systematic efforts to meet people where they are in church and society, supporting them to determine their own futures, understanding how their particular social-economic environment affects them, and taking relevant mitigation measures in partnership with them to help them meet their specific needs. Thus, diakonia responds to the context of individuals, communities, and all of creation. One, therefore, becomes open to the new and creative ways in which diakonia is understood, adapted, and practiced. In the context of the KELC, diakonia work is structured as a department within the larger church structure. Diakonia, as a KELC department, has few employed staff with a large population of volunteers at the grassroots. Experience on the ground has shown that the needs of these targeted groups differ from one region or parish to another. Thus, we recognize that the solutions initiated by the department of diakonia in its partnership with the people on the ground are not universal; they are contextual.

METHOD AND DESIGN

Written interviews were used to explore the nature and understanding of diakonia work in the Kenya Evangelical Lutheran Church (KELC). Nine leaders in the KELC were interviewed. Among them were five women and four men out of whom were two laypersons, two deacons, two evangelists, and three pastors. Finding them was easy since they already work in the field of diakonia within the church structures. The interview comprised four open-ended questions and a fifth one which was optional to allow the respondent to give added views on diakonia. The questions were as follows:

1. How is diakonia understood in the KELC? Give examples.
2. How is diakonia organized in the Church District (*Majimbo)*, parish, congregation (*Mtaa)*?
3. In what ways do the African culture and the KELC's gender policy guide and shape diakonia work?
4. What is the impact of diakonia work on the church's culture and practice?
5. Any other comment?

The interviewees responded in writing to all the questions. This essayist collected the data, merged them into common themes, and analyzed and interpreted them for the main theme. Interviewing was an explorative and flexible method for the questions to the thematic areas of diakonia. This form of interviewing was chosen because it offered easy access to the respondents through email and telephone follow-up. Nine out of the twelve participants contacted took part in the interview and sent their written responses.

The interviews elicited various answers through written texts. Four broad, open-ended questions were emailed to twelve people in the church.[3] The interviewer, with the vision of seeing it grow into a national KELC image for Christian service and witness, introduced the topic of diakonia to the twelve people contacted earlier. The participants are well known to the interviewer as knowledgeable members of the Lutheran church, and each one of them plays a leadership role. The interviewer assured them of confidentiality for the purpose of this essay. Open-ended questions were aimed at encouraging more information to be given on diakonia in the community and all levels of church organization.

In the final essay, only a few responses were highlighted for the purpose of focus on the theme under discussion. These responses rely on prior writing skills and practices of the participants. The downside is that not all participants seemed to possess the skill, comfort, and confidence to write full accounts.[4] It is for this reason that some terms were retained in the Kiswahili language. For example, question 2 combines English and Kiswahili, which is the common language of communication in the KELC. The words *Mtaa* (congregation) and *Majimbo* (districts) refer to the smallest church unit and the one larger than a parish, respectively. Using the Kiswahili language was beneficial to the interviewees as experienced and knowledgeable persons in the area of interview.[5] The *Mtaa* and *Majimbo* form part of the KELC's organizational and governance structure. "Governance is the decision-making process in which the leadership of the organization exercises power to mobilize resources and direct those resources in a transparent and accountable manner."[6] This is the overall goal for diakonia, especially in its resource mobilization, use, and sustainability.

Findings from the Interviews

The overall goal of the interview was to find out how people understood and practiced diakonia in the various church units of the Kenya Evangelical Lutheran Church. The interviewer received the responses each by email, read each one of them, and assigned codes[7] in order to create content. Patterns of the content were identified and highlighted. Common themes were identified in all the responses from the nine participants that gave feedback. The themes were reviewed, tabulated, and named for the final essay as follows:

1. Diakonia as Love and Faith in Action

2. Church Governance and Diakonia
3. Diakonia and the Pursuit for Justice in Africa
4. The Ever-Dominating African Patriarchy and Diakonia
5. Diakonia: Space of Assurance and Hope in Christ

DIAKONIA AS LOVE AND FAITH IN ACTION

The theme of diakonia as love and faith in action is interesting because it defines diakonia. Diakonia is an integral part of God's mission, encompassing proclamation, service (diakonia), and advocacy.[8] Discussions on whether mission is about proclamation *per se* or if it involves both proclamation and service are ongoing, but from the responses there is an understanding that there is no separation between proclamation and service (diakonia). For the communities and people in need, these two themes offer service to the needy, holistic care, compassionate ministry, and humanitarian aid in addition to the much-needed care for the environment.

Diakonia as love is biblically based. Acts 6 points to the importance of diakonia in the congregation. It is an expression of both what the church is by its very nature and what is manifested in its daily life, plans, and projects.[9] In the Gospel of Matthew, chapter 25, the eschatological message of Christ highlights the meaning of Christian love and the practice of faith. "Whatsoever you do to the least of these . . . that, you do unto me,"[10] says Jesus Christ to his followers then and now. To love is a mandate given to all who bear the name of Christian. The test of faith is the practice of love among Christians to themselves and to others, as well.

Faith in action is reflected in the interview responses. For example, "support was sent by the head office to the various stations";[11] "giving food, school fees and other basic needs";[12] and "acts of compassion to the needy: widows, orphans, persons living with disabilities and those affected with chronic diseases."[13] This understanding of diakonia reflects the generally held notion that diakonia means support from the church's main head office; the people on the ground seem to be mere recipients of the support of funds or material provided. So most "people look like they are waiting for *manna* to drop from above"[14] instead of being directly involved in full diaconal ownership. "It is only through many seminars and lessons that this tendency is slowly changing."[15]

The mentality of receiving help from the head office, which seems common and longstanding, has serious implications for mission and justice in church and society. The implications include what one respondent refers to as "Mother church provides help for the underprivileged."[16] The term "Mother church" connotes overseas "donor dependency syndrome"[17] with "a basket of 'goodies' [for relief]."[18] This description of the people's understanding of diakonia leaves one with a sour taste in the mouth. It suggests that the local church sees diakonia as an external 'giver' of whatever it asks for. This type of understanding and practice of diakonia cultivates a church's attitude of dependency on outside help and support. The basis of this, perhaps, does not require much effort to understand. Most certainly, outside support is not a problem; dependency on outside help is the problem. By "outside help" I refer to congregations depending on the head office or the head office depending on support from overseas. Dependency lowers human dignity and the basic human rights of the other. If this is the case, how or why is it, then, that such dependency has continued to exist?

Donor dependency syndrome seems to be a perennial problem in the majority of African faith-based organizations. It raises the question, are North-South church partnerships a problem? The quick answer is, "No." North-South church partnerships are not a problem in themselves; it is actually a good thing to maintain these partnerships as expressions of Christian witness, mutuality, and unity in a changing world. The problem lies in understanding the practice of partnership itself. Obaga and Obaga argue that mutuality and sharing ensure that "true reciprocity excludes one-sided dependency."[19] They add that partners recognize each other in a two-way perspective, that is, "both as needy receivers and rich givers" of whatever they possess. Furthermore, as needs and riches are not measured only financially, partners need to work out joint priorities based on each other's needs and to raise questions that challenge one another in an authentic spirit of mutual reciprocity to enrich the experience of bilateral participation in the *missio Dei*.[20] This view can be applied in the African context in line with what one respondent says, that is, "It is only through many seminars and lessons that this tendency is slowly changing."[21] When the partnership relations with the West will be viewed as mutually global and mutually local will this dependency syndrome get solved.

This mutual aspect of partnership will be realized when donations and funding for social welfare programs are seen purely as expressions of friendship. Dependency syndrome is an injustice which is a threat to justice.[22] Therefore, diakonia is a service that becomes a transformative tool[23] for justice in church and society, where it becomes "'faith in action' to touch and improve people's lives."[24]

CHURCH GOVERNANCE AND DIAKONIA

Church governance is important for keeping the church in check in its Christian witness and sustainability. In the KELC this is done "by having committee members representing the grassroots to the national level."[25] The KELC Secretary General, Luke Mwololo, further observes that the KELC's devolved or decentralized services are aimed at strengthening church governance. He states, "Devolution is to prepare for [the] expansion of the church, the center [sic] has no capacity and, importantly, that the principle of devolution in decentralizing services and programs, points the church to grow from the base or grassroot outward."[26] Also, devolution is for the church aligning itself to the changing environment so that the lower units can raise leadership at the district levels and, in so doing, strengthen those districts. The district leaders on the ground know the needs of their units and can work on meeting them. It is important that the lower units of the church develop the necessary structures, own the church, and see to it that it can be sustained. Through the "making and sustaining of the clergy" or KELC's "*Kujitegemea*"[27] programs, the church districts are made to understand that "head office" is not the KELC; rather, KELC is a system of governance that begins from the congregation (*Mtaa*) through the national office. The head office only facilitates plans made at the district level. The church districts should be able to raise the leadership capacity of the church unit, that is, the congregation, to a point of taking proper care of their staff members. KELC's "Operation *Kujitegemea*" was initiated for this purpose.

The devolved system of governance aims at strengthening leadership and implementing programs and governance at the grassroots.[28] KELC's church governance, therefore, is the decision-making process in which the leadership of the organization exercises the power to mobilize resources and direct those resources in a transparent and accountable manner. Governance involves the stewardship of resources[29] to ensure justice, fairness, and honesty in the church organization such that efficiency and quality services are to be promoted and maintained. This involves "doing the right things" compared with "doing things right."[30]

The challenge in church governance lies in the implementation and monitoring of programs and general operations. Serious challenges exist in some, if not most, of the churches in Africa. Given the dwindling donations from Western churches, it is important for the African church to urgently strategize for resource mobilization for training, planning, monitoring, and reporting. These strategies will help the church to be self-sustaining and to utilize existing resources effectively in order to avoid over-dependency on external donors. Sustainability is about the church's capacity to work through its own efforts. With limited support from different stakeholders, both locally and globally, the African church should develop the capacity to achieve sustainability with a reduction of its dependency on donors,[31] bearing in mind that dependency is an injustice against human dignity.

DIAKONIA AND THE PURSUIT FOR JUSTICE IN AFRICA

Martin Luther King Jr. has stated that "injustice anywhere is a threat to justice everywhere."[32] This famous quote was first introduced to me by Simpson during my studies at Luther Seminary in the class "The Vocation of a Theologian" in 2009. At that time this quote reminded me of the work I had done in the KELC's women's desk in Kenya before joining Luther Seminary for my theological studies. I remembered how at one time during an official church visit to a community in a remote part of Kenya nearly twenty years ago, I saw a level of poverty I had never before imagined possible. I stared poverty right in the face; it was a ferociously intimidating experience. I saw human beings just sitting on bare, hot sand, literally waiting for death. I was revulsed and thought to myself, *How could this be? Is this really part of my country? This is unfair!* I felt angry, very angry, and wanted to get answers from the government of that time.

After I completed my visit, one woman handed me a small plastic paper bag with 250 grams of dry beans. I hesitated at first as I did not find it morally right to take it, but a colleague nudged me to accept it. He said, "Take it, don't refuse. It is the right thing to do," according to African tradition. This little amount of beans in a tattered plastic paper bag from the generous heart of this very poor woman who was staring at death from famine and starvation convicted my conscience and to me became a "moral means to awaken the conscience of an oppressive adversary and of a wider passive public."[33]

Years later I have returned to work in the diakonia department of my church, and in this position I have once again seen prevalent poverty as an injustice against the affected communities. Injustices were visible in the lack of basic human rights, such as the right to water, education, housing, and food. My office was inundated with requests for help and support in some rural areas. The school fees program became overwhelmed with hundreds of students in need of tuition fees for primary and secondary schools and post-secondary education and training institutions. During the Covid-19 pandemic, requests for sanitary items such as soap and masks were in high demand by the church's districts. Understandably, during the pandemic help was needed to relieve people from the effects of this pandemic. Besides this, the devastating effects of climate change were also felt, and communities needed food relief. In both situations the poor were the most affected. The church, through the diakonia department, has been involved in these relief efforts.

My diaconal journey seems to have started at the time I took Simpson's class on Martin Luther King Jr. I have since utilized every opportunity available to be in solidarity with the poor, suffering, vulnerable, and marginalized.

My work at the diakonia department has offered me the space through which to be in solidarity with the poor. The respondents of my questionnaire lifted up phrases that describe the perception held about current diaconal work in the KELC, including "care and concern to humanity," "I am because we are," and "humanity towards others."[34] These responses describe this type of solidarity and the generosity extended by the church as service to humanity through its diakonia space. The small gift of dry beans by the pathetically poor woman symbolized a manifestation of human generosity at its highest form; it was a gift of sacrificial selflessness, an *ubuntu* expression at its best. The interview responses point to the *ubuntu* spirit that indwells the people in their lived culture, an African philosophy on life. It is a deeply held African ideal of one's personhood rooted in one's interconnectedness with others.[35]

Ubuntu philosophy is relevant for diaconal work at the KELC. It is "care and concern to humanity." One experiences it through being in solidarity with those who suffer injustices. Just as Christ suffered on the cross for the sake of the world, a congregation as a public moral companion "becomes an encumbered community,"[36] encumbered with the moral and economic predicaments of its neighbors. KELC has created a Diakonia Day which is celebrated on the last Sunday of February, which is usually in the Lenten season. The celebrations include almsgiving in support of those in need. In the most recent event, food and clothes were also collected and distributed. Congregations have since discovered the joy of giving, and some have decided to organize such an event every three months. The idea has further evolved to include supporting Christians in neighboring parishes and faraway districts. They now see it as their vocation and a moral obligation, in the spirit of *ubuntu*, to share what God has given them.

The *ubuntu* spirit inherent in the people moves them to find validity and completeness in the other person's humanness and personhood. As archbishop Desmond Tutu says, "I am a person through other people. My humanity is tied to yours."[37] Since *ubuntu* is expressed in community, respect, co-responsibility, dignity, social justice, compassion, solidarity, and such, these values form an important aspect for education and training on the nature and practice of justice. These values should form part of the moral formation of the congregation as a community of faith. Simpson rightly states, "When our everyday lifeworlds overlap in regular and patterned ways, they take on more ritual, organizational, or institutional dimensions and thereby grow more resilient and determinative. When these dimensions materialize, the public space called civil society emerges."[38] In this case the principle of "do unto others what you would them do unto you" is applicable.

Tools and systems are created to address issues of justice. At KELC the constitution, human resources, and financial and gender policies are some of the tools developed and adopted to address the need for justice for all. The gender dimension and diakonia and justice is also significant. "Stating that the protection and promotion of human rights of women are fundamental to the sustainability of development, that sustainable development requires gender equality and the full leadership of women in all the development process, and that all assessment, planning, monitoring and evaluation in development work requires a gender perspective and analysis which values the work and experience of women."[39] The responses from the interview showed that the much-needed diakonia work among women and girls is challenged by the impact of an overbearing patriarchy in some communities. The congregation needs to do more to address this situation in its context.

THE EVER-DOMINATING AFRICAN PATRIARCHY AND DIAKONIA

Patriarchy is a contextual reality and a challenge to diakonia work which the church must address. Mercy Oduyoye, a prominent African scholar on African women's theology, poignantly observes, "Mama carried more responsibility in the church without getting any more authority, because westernization was teaching Africa the advantage of keeping women invisible."[40] On Westernization, missionary Christianity, and African women, Mwaniki writes, "It is notable that as agents of the church of England, where women did not play any significant roles in church leadership, and also the fact that missionaries were colonial agents of civilization, more emphasis was put on civilizing Africans than liberating women from patriarchy."[41] This Western patriarchal stance resonated with African patriarchy. It coerced African women "to fit into the church in the way white Western and African men deemed fit."[42]

Serene Jones observes that women feel excluded and silenced by men's ways of speaking and knowing.[43] This exclusion or marginalization leaves women to find gendered alternative spaces in such areas as taking care of children, cleaning the church, doing hospitality, and singing in church choirs. These areas are in no way less important. Rather, such areas of women's responsibility are used to perpetuate male dominance. Oduyoye notes that "women's experience of being persons primarily in relation to others—as mother or wife—predominates in Africa. A woman's social status depends on these relationships and not on qualities or achievements of her own."[44] Dorcas Dah echoes this view when she states, "Women tend to be limited to certain roles in Africa which become prescribed. Although women are the ones responsible for providing for the needs and welfare of their families and the society, they are treated with little importance by those they serve."[45] In reality, these tasks are basic to human life and existence, without which community and church will not function.

Patriarchy hampers justice for women which requires intentional mitigation measures. On this issue the respondents in the study observed that gender policy in KELC will ensure privileges are shared by involving women in various participations.[46] Furthermore, KELC's gender policy has reorganized them and also empowered them on the issues of their rights as well as demanding and standing up for their rights. KELC's gender policy has also shown that men and women can work hand in hand to reach out to the less fortunate in society.[47] The gender justice policy of the church advocates for equal opportunities by utilizing available resources and opportunities and promoting equality in terms of participation in all decision-making platforms. This includes advocating for justice of equal rights for all and empowerment of the vulnerable in the public space. It should be noted that KELC's gender policy does not discriminate; it advocates for fairness for all people in society.

These responses show an awareness that the church ought to be committed to addressing the issues of patriarchy in the church and in society. Women's active participation and representation in the various levels of leadership validate the church's commitment to addressing the gender dimension. KELC's strategic plan for 2020–2024 clearly outlines women's empowerment through scholarships and economic activities, for leadership and representation, and for participation in the various levels of church structure. KELC's gender policy is one such tool which speaks into the question of injustice against women in patriarchal contexts.

DIAKONIA: SPACE OF ASSURANCE AND HOPE IN CHRIST

The theme of hopelessness and despair is all too common in the African continent. The faces of hopelessness include the Covid-19 pandemic; effects of climate change such as drought and hunger; illiteracy; unemployment; vulnerability of girls, children, women, people with disability, and immigrants; and poverty. In addition, hopelessness is manifested in drug and alcohol abuse, gender-based violence, poverty associated with aging, and rising mental illness. Churches are challenged to act boldly through their diaconal ministry to accompany communities experiencing these issues in a commitment to lift up justice, peace, and the integrity of creation.[48] In other words, diakonia should be challenged in its action to seek to intervene in the spiral of hope and to take initiatives of accompaniment to move people from one step to another by means of "envisioning transformation, reconciliation and empowerment."[49]

Diakonia in an African context reflects the ability of its vocation not only to accompany the people for the sake of justice but also to care for the environment with all its dimensions: social, political, religious, economic, and cultural. Women, for instance, have fewer economic opportunities, hence greater vulnerability to injustice and impoverishment. Poverty traps women in multiple layers of discrimination and hinders their ability to claim their rights.[50] It is worth noting the importance of diakonia work among the suffering people in Africa. Some responses to the interview question "Any other comment?" elicited comments identifying diakonia as "a space of hope" and "visible and touchable faith in action." These responses were based on experience and affirmed the relevance of diakonia's utilization of the space of hope to strengthen its actions and to creatively explore new ways of accompanying the people as a church.

Women as a specific part of the church are also identified as an indispensable partner of the church's diakonia work among the poor, the sick, children, and youth. There was, therefore, an appeal that the diakonia department partner network with the women's department in the spirit of interdependence as enshrined in the "ubuntu" philosophy and way of life. It also lifts out the aspect of networking among people and the church organization. This is important for the strengthening of work and the results that it offers in the areas of justice and reconciliation. Diakonia is a space of assurance and hope in Christ, and through it "the church must . . . capitalize on our deep knowledge and expertise by bringing this knowledge and expertise to the public policy-making table for actualizing ever more just ways of life."[51] Diakonia must be an open and free space for all to participate in response to the Great Commission and the hope we have in Christ Jesus.

CONCLUSION

The work of diakonia is integral to the being of the African church and important to its life. It is part and parcel of the church's mandate of holistic proclamation. The gospel is a message of hope and salvation which is made complete as faith active in love. Diakonia is the service ministry of the church which is a culmination of proclamation and communion.[52] During his earthly ministry, Christ proclaimed good news which incorporated service to the poor and the sick. Christ said, "For I was hungry and you gave me something to eat, I was thirsty and you gave me something to drink, I was a stranger and you invited me in, I needed clothes and you clothed me, I was sick and you looked after me, I was in prison and you came to visit me."[53] Christ not only cared for the souls but was also compassionate for the physical needs of the people.

While diakonia is an indispensable part of the church's mission, it experiences certain challenges in African contexts where patriarchy is prevalent and its effects include the marginalization of women and children. The church needs a reform of policies that promote holistic human dignity. Diakonia's work on justice issues such as accompanying the poor and needy highlights the prophetic role of the church and its critical solidarity with the people. Issues of justice are experienced widely in Africa. The church is challenged to address itself on this situation through its diaconal ministry. Diakonia is a space for promoting hope in the lifeworld of the people and, ultimately, hope in Christ Jesus.

Although doing good works is an integral part of new life in Christ, Lutherans are suspicious when good works are lifted up as a prerequisite rather than the outcome of faith in Christ. One is justified by faith through grace alone, but the response is gratitude through the good works of love extended to neighbor, that is, fellow human beings. This means that the gift of faith from God is completed in the response embodied in the acts of love. This understanding informs diaconal work as promoted and practiced by the congregations of the Kenya Evangelical Lutheran Church. To serve humanity with the intention of obtaining merits before God and fellow human beings undermines the principle of justification by faith alone. But good works are "visible expressions of the new life in Christ given by faith."[54] The Bible describes "diakonia as a ministry of distribution of resources, so that everyone may have a fair share in this world of poverty in the midst of affluence."[55]

We need the good works of diakonia through caring for the needy as a ministry that is central to mission and praxis in the church. Diakonia, therefore, is the visible way in which the church demonstrates its solidarity with the poor through the congregations. In this case it is right to say that diakonia activities are responses to issues of injustice, and where there is injustice, there is no reconciliation. Congregations in KELC, through the creative interventions of diakonia, are indeed prophetic and public moral companions of the community. We can only agree with Simpson's echoing message from Martin Luther King Jr. that the time is NOW for action to transform societies. For Martin Luther King Jr., time is a myth, so instead of taking a laissez-faire attitude to time, we must act with great urgency now, not later.

We must also reject the attitude of fatalism common among African societies that do not notice the wheels of progress or justice. Christians must come together and through diakonia become co-workers with God, and in this way "we must help time and realize that the time is always ripe to do right."[56] Churches should strive to utilize available resources to develop and promote the ministries of diakonia at all church levels and ground them at the congregational level. The spirit of compassion should thus be realized through to support the mission of the church, "that all may have life in abundance."[57]

NOTES

1. Gary M. Simpson, "Africa Is the Lord's and the Fullness Thereof," in *So the Poor Have Hope, and Injustice Shuts Its Mouth: Poverty and the Mission of the Church in Africa*, eds. Karen L. Bloomquist and Musa Panti Filibus (Geneva: Lutheran World Federation, 2007), 162.
2. Peter Ignatius Gichure, *Contextual Theology: Its Meaning, Scope and Urgency* (Nairobi, Kenya: Publications Department, the Catholic University of Eastern Africa, 2008), 71.
3. Kathy Charmaz, *Constructing Grounded Theory: A Practical Guide through Qualitative Analysis* (CA: Thousand Oaks: Sage Publications, 2006), 26.
4. Charmaz, *Constructing Grounded Theory*, 36.
5. Herbert J. Rubin and Irene Rubin, *Qualitative Interviewing: The Art of Hearing Data*, 2nd ed. (Thousand Oaks, CA: Sage Publications, 2005), 64.
6. Martin Oluoch, "Governance and Leadership," (presentation, KELC's Diakonia, Building Capacity and Institutional Strengthening Training, Malindi, Kenya, 13–14 July 2021).
7. Coding is part of the interviewing process of a research project.
8. Kjell Nordstokke, ed., *Transformation, Reconciliation, Empowerment: The LWF Contribution to the Understanding and Practice of Diakonia* (Geneva: Lutheran World Federation, 2009), 9 & 27.
9. Nordstokke, *Transformation, Reconciliation, Empowerment*, 28.
10. Matt. 25:40.
11. Question 1, respondent 5.
12. Question 1, respondent 8.
13. Question 1, respondent 1.
14. Question 1, respondent 3.
15. Question 1, respondent 3.
16. Question 1, respondent 4.
17. Question 1, respondent 3.
18. Question 1, respondent 3.
19. William Obaga and Margaret Obaga, "North-South Partnerships: A Bird's View from a German Context," in *Reformation in the Context of World Christianity*, eds. Frieder Ludwig et al. (Wiesbaden: Harrassowitz Verlag, 2019), 220.
20. Obaga and Obaga, "North-South Partnerships."
21. Question 1, respondent 3.
22. Gary Simpson, "Changing the Face of the Enemy: Martin King Jr., and the Beloved Community," *Word & World* 28, no. 1 (Winter 2008): 57.
23. Question 1, respondent 4.
24. Question 1, respondent 4.
25. Question 2, respondent 1.
26. Luke Mwololo, Secretary General for KELC, interview by author, Nairobi, Kenya, October 28, 2021.
27. *Kujitegemea*, or "The Making and Sustaining of Clergy," is a KELC program for pastors' care.

28. Luke Mwololo, phone conversation with author, October 28, 2021.
29. Oluoch, "Training on Capacity Building."
30. Oluoch, "Governance and Leadership."
31. Joseph Nzioki and Sr. Margaret S. Shinga, "Towards Sustainable Resource Management: The Case of Catholic Religious Organizations in Kenya," in *From Embers to Flames: SPU 2nd Integral Missions Conference* (Nairobi, 2018).
32. Simpson, "Changing the Face of the Enemy," 57.
33. Simpson, "Changing the Face of the Enemy," 62.
34. Question 3, respondent 6.
35. Michael Battle, *Ubuntu: I in You and You in Me* (New York: Seabury Books, 2009), 32.
36. Gary M. Simpson, "Civil Society and Congregations as Public Moral Companions," *Word & World* 15, no. 4 (1995): 426.
37. Battle, *Ubuntu*, 32.
38. Gary M. Simpson, "Missional Congregations as Public Companions with God in Global Civil Society: Vocational Imagination and Spiritual Presence," *Dialog* 54, no. 2 (2015): 139.
39. Nordstokke, *Diakonia in Context*, 78.
40. Mercy Amba Oduyoye, "Be a Woman and Africa Will Be Strong," in *Inheriting Our Mothers' Gardens: Feminist Theology in Third World Perspective*, eds. Letty M. Russel et al. (Philadelphia, PA: John Knox Press, 1988), 46.
41. L. Mwaniki, *Gender and Imago Dei: A Postcolonial African Reading of 1 Corinthians 11:1–16* (Phoenixville, PA: Borderless Press, 2018), 19.
42. Oduyoye, "Be a Woman," 46.
43. Serene Jones, *Feminist Theory and Christian Theology* (Minneapolis: Fortress, 2000), 24.
44. Mercy Amba Oduyoye, *Hearing and Knowing: Theological Reflections on Christianity in Africa* (Accra, Ghana: Sam-Woode Ltd, 2000), 122.
45. Ini Dorcas Dah, *Women Do More Work Than Men: Birifor Women as Change Agents in the Mission and Expansion of the Church in West Africa: Urkina Faso, Cote D'Ivore and Ghana* (Accra, Ghana: Regnum Africa, 2017), 2.
46. Kenya Evangelical Lutheran Church, *Gender Justice Policy 2020: Gender Justice Advocacy to Transform Church and Society* (working document of the Kenya Evangelical Lutheran Church).
47. Question 3, respondent 1.
48. Question 3.
49. Nordstokke, *Diakonia in Context*, 19.
50. Nordstokke, 14.
51. Simpson, "Africa is the Lord's," 162.
52. Nordstokke, *Diakonia in Context*, 20.
53. Mt. 25:35–36.
54. Nordstokke, *Diakonia in Context*, 34.
55. Musawenkosi Biyela, "Called and Empowered by God to Act," in *So the Poor Have Hope, and Injustice Shuts Its Mouth: Poverty and the Mission of the Church in*

Africa, eds. Karen L. Bloomquist and Musa Panti Filibus (Geneva: Lutheran World Federation, 2007), 133.
  56. Simpson, "Changing the Face of the Enemy," 59.
  57. John 10:10.

Chapter 6

Global Public Theologians in Rural Contexts

Malawi and Wisconsin: Equipping Prophetic Public Companions for God's Mission in Rural Communities

Laurie Skow-Anderson

This chapter will explore three pathways the Northwest Synod of Wisconsin (NWSWI) follows as it engages as a public church:[1] 1) *Global Pathway*-learning alongside the Evangelical Lutheran Church of Malawi (ELCM) to be a public church, 2) *Rural Pathway*-discovering ways to be a public church in a rural synod, and 3) *Leadership Pathway*-raising up leaders for a public church in a rural context through the Lay School of Ministry of the NWSWI. These three pathways run parallel and at other times intersect for rich learning about being a public church in a global and rural context.

A GLOBAL PATHWAY: MALAWI AND NORTHWEST WISCONSIN

The office of the ELCM is located in Lilongwe, Malawi. Lilongwe is a *long way* from Chetek, Wisconsin, the synod office of the NWSWI. Eight thousand six hundred miles separate these rural outposts for Christian ministry. Both provide fertile soil, holy ground for growing global public church leaders. Like Moses, standing before the burning bush on holy ground,[2] called to address the injustice, suffering, and oppression of God's people in Egypt, Lutherans in Malawi and Wisconsin stand on God's holy ground, called to work for justice and peace in all the earth.[3]

The NWSWI and ELCM have been companion synods[4] since 2001 and continue to discover what it means to accompany each other in ministry. We read the same Bible, walk on the same planet, worship the same triune God, and study the same catechism. Guided by the same Holy Spirit, we are co-journers,[5] followers in the way of Jesus. Since it began, the ELCM has had one bishop, Bishop Joseph Bvumbwe, and the NWSWI has had four. In my interviews with the former bishops Robert Berg, Duane Pederson, and Richard Hoyme, I learned each bishop struggled to understand the accompaniment model of companion synod relationships. "Accompaniment is defined as walking together in a solidarity that practices interdependence and mutuality. The ELCA lives out accompaniment in relationships with global companions, striving to share God's love and participate in God's mission together."[6] It has often felt one-sided with the wealthy Americans sending money to the poor Malawians. Bishop Pederson mentioned that the challenge was to "move from a position of rich Americans of privilege and wealth . . . to a relationship . . . [in which] accompaniment needs to be constantly worked. It is easy to lapse into old models of rich Americans helping the poor."[7] Bishop Hoyme remarked that the instinct is to come to Malawi and fix things. Both former bishops recognize that the key to accompaniment is relationships. Bishop Berg indicated that accompaniment is not natural. It took time for them to grow into an understanding of accompaniment and learn to walk together.

Over the years the NWSWI has provided humanitarian aid, and individual congregations are partnered with congregations in Malawi to encourage more personal connections and relationships. A highlight of this accompaniment relationship has been learning together at the Pastor's Academy in Malawi.[8] Together we also support efforts to improve community infrastructure; dig wells; invest in agriculture; build churches, infirmaries, and feeding stations; and provide for transportation and seminary education. Most importantly, we have invested in relationships. We have hosted the bishop and many friends from Malawi, and we have been the guests of the ELCM. Now during COVID we communicate through WhatsApp and Zoom. We are continuously learning from each other and nurturing this relationship.

Former Bishop Robert Berg initiated the companion synod relationship with Malawi. Berg explained that prayer is the most important way we accompany the church in Malawi. They pray for us, and we pray for them. It is more important than the money. The companion congregations program matched congregations from NWSWI with individual congregations in ELCM so that they could pray specifically for each other. We are able to pray for a church, pastor, and people by name. Bishop Pederson notes that we benefit the most from the deep spirituality of the Malawi church. Deacon Diane Kaufmann, the first companion synod coordinator for the NWSWI, reflected on how the ELCM's Women of Prayer serve as the spiritual leaders that grew the church in Malawi. The Women of Prayer were both the pray-ers and the do-ers in the church. Prayer was their foundation, and from it they moved out into the world doing ministry for Jesus's sake. They staffed the feeding centers and did many other service projects. Bishop Bvumbwe describes the work of the Women of Prayer as the backbone of the church.

> The (Women of Prayer) group is a powerful force of spirituality in each congregation. Their activities include prayer, singing, Bible studies, service, and leading worship services, including preaching. . . . The group believes that every challenge we face has its roots in what God wants us to do. Like Jesus, we are called upon to see, hear, and respond to the needs of our neighbour. Doing this will sometimes involve work and service to others, as Jesus did. The group therefore strongly believes that it must provide for healing services to those who suffer. The spirituality of the Women's Group of Prayer can therefore be understood more in their services to others in need rather than as an end to itself.[9]

We learned about the power of prayer and were inspired by the deep spirituality of the Women of Prayer and the leaders of ELCM. We learned that through prayer we are called out to serve our neighbor. Berg shared, "We learned about joy and thanksgiving for life from the people who often didn't know from week to week which of their friends would die from HIV/AIDs or malaria."

By accompanying the ELCM, we grew in our understanding of what it means to be a public church. Berg shared that Bishop Joseph Bvumbwe was a major leader among the churches in sub-Saharan Africa. Everyone knows and respects Bishop Bvumbwe. At one point there was a great political upheaval and division between political parties in Malawi over the president's desire to change the constitution and be elected to a third term. Bishop Joseph Bvumbwe was invited to mediate the dispute. During the early years of the HIV/AIDs crisis, the Malawian government was slow and at times unwilling to engage in educating the public about the dangers of being infected. Under Bvumbwe's public leadership, the ELCM stepped in to convene educational gatherings that gave clear, frank information about how AIDs is sexually transmitted. Over the years the ELCM established schools, training centers, hospitals, clinics, and feeding stations. From the start these institutions were not just for the Lutherans or Christians. All were welcomed. The Bergs were in attendance at a dedication for an educational training center. At the dedication the local imam was present and spoke. He thanked the ELCM.

He said, "What you are doing is not just for the Lutheran Christians. You are helping all of us." Berg mentioned that at other times when the Lutherans gathered, they would invite the tribal chief and honor him, even if he wasn't a Christian. The community recognized that the Lutheran feeding centers and medical centers were there for the community, for everyone, not exclusively for Lutherans.

The lessons we learned from our accompaniment with the ELCM in their work to overcome the HIV/AIDs epidemic inspire us in our efforts to overcome COVID and the other issues facing the Northwest Synod of Wisconsin. As the leader of the Lutheran church in Malawi, Bvumbwe made it clear that for a public church to be faithful in proclaiming the gospel of Jesus Christ, it needed to do the following:

1. *Partner with other groups to work for peace and justice.* Bishop Bvumbwe notes,

> Right from its inception, the ELCM took social involvement as one of its prime concerns. Deliberate efforts have been made for the church to be holistic in its approach. Parallel with preaching and teaching the gospel, the ELCM has been deeply involved in the social [well-being] of its members and the citizens of Malawi, in general. A small, rapidly growing church, the ELCM is an active member of various ecumenical organizations, both locally and internationally, to the point that its impact has been felt as a partner in the gospel and in the effort to bring about peace with justice in the suffering world today.[10]

Like the church in Malawi, the rostered leaders and lay leaders of the NWSWI are learning to tend to more than just the spiritual needs of their churches and are connecting deeply with the needs of their communities. Like their counterparts in Malawi, most congregations in NWSWI participate in some food distribution or community meal program. During the Coronavirus pandemic, we intentionally reached out beyond denominational lines in an effort to keep the public safe and get the vaccine to more people with our work with the Wisconsin Council of Churches.

2. *Be an advocate and agent for change for the poor.* Like the ELCM, the NWSWI is primarily a rural synod. Poverty, food insecurity, housing, transportation, and access to health care in the rural areas in Wisconsin are significant issues. COVID-19 has made rural poverty in Wisconsin more visible. Bvumbwe describes the rural poverty in Malawi:

Most of its members live in rural areas and are generally poor. The situation has been worsened by the presence of killer diseases, such as HIV/AIDS. In addition to the primary responsibility of preaching the Word of God, the ELCM can also be described as the voice of the voiceless and an advocate, as well as an agent, of change for the betterment of those marginalized in society—the poor (usually widows and orphans). In this regard, and for the sake of these young children, the church feels compelled to operate hope projects such as feeding centers for orphans and small-scale income generating projects for widows, as well as skill training opportunities for the young people. The ELCM has also engaged in adult literacy programs, dug wells, HIV/AIDS care and prevention education, job skills training, primary and secondary schools, mobile clinics, gender violence, and scholarships.[11]

As leaders in a public church, the pastors, deacons, and Synodically Authorized Ministers (SAMs)[12] of the NWSWI are learning to identify the needs and the gaps that exist for services to the rural poor. We are paying attention to the movement of the Holy Spirit, discerning the needs, and using our assets to meet those needs.

3. *Be prophetic.* Some leaders in the NWSWI struggle with what it means to be prophetic. We live in such a politically polarized area that even preaching on the Beatitudes will get a pastor in trouble for sounding too political. Many preachers, pastors, and teachers are challenged to find their prophetic voices and create safe spaces to have conversations about the issues dividing our churches and our country today. Bishop Bvumbwe calls us to strive to be prophetic.

The prophetic role of the church needs to be revived and even emphasized, naming sin by its name, and pointing to the will of God for all God's people in all countries of the world. The ELCM, like other African churches, will need to provide leadership in this effort. . . . God's promises remain the source of hope for those who live in poverty and injustice. The church must remain strong in its ministry, based on the knowledge that God has promised to be present with it up to the end. . . . The ELCM believes that such a time has come, and churches have the opportunity for such a witness to the world. Such effort will need the church to take a leading role to seek justice for and on behalf of the millions who suffer in the world today. I personally believe that as a church we will need to be more vigilant in seeking justice more than sympathy.[13]

The leaders of the NWSWI are inspired by Bishop Bvumbwe's call to be prophetic in our particular time and place in history. At a synod-wide event, we discussed the book *Preaching in Hitler's Shadow: Sermons of Resistance in the Third Reich.*[14] For some of our pastors, prophetic preaching feels as dangerous today as it was for the pastors in Germany. The temptation is to protect our jobs, be safe, and say nothing. History has condemned the German pastors who said nothing during the Holocaust. We wrestle to find ways to have conversations around topics such as racism, immigration, climate change, gun violence, and COVID protocols in the NWSWI without alienating members. Only one pastor in this synod has been threatened with violence for prophetic proclamation, so the comparison to Nazi Germany isn't accurate, but it is thought-provoking.

4. *Address uncomfortable subjects.* Bishop Bvumbwe was a leader in HIV/AIDs education and worked to help de-stigmatize those who were infected. "HIV/AIDS has left no family untouched. In the wider community, there is no household that has not been affected one way or the other by the pandemic."[15]

He continues to call for honest, frank conversation about sex in a country where it is a taboo subject. Victims of AIDS are shunned, and women are shamed and silent about being attacked/raped. He speaks out against violence toward women, specifically rape. The most recent youth gathering in Malawi in 2021 focused on violence against women and girls. The NWSWI has also needed to respond to issues impacting the care of women and children impacted by violence. In October of 2020, partial county funding was stripped from Embrace, the only domestic abuse shelter serving four counties in the northwest corner of Wisconsin. This was done to oppose a Black Lives Matters sign Embrace displayed in its offices. I wrote a letter in support of Embrace.[16] Since George Floyd's murder in May 2020, conversations around race, racism, white privilege, and white supremacy have made many feel uncomfortable in our synod. An entire church council resigned in part for a comment I made in a recorded sermon about white privilege. A backlash against gun regulations has led to a second amendment sanctuary movement in some communities in NWSWI. As bishop I joined many of the area pastors across denominations in signing a letter opposing this movement. Several ELCA pastors had very uncomfortable conversations with angry church members, and one was threatened. Engaging in these conversations is important. These issues impact the health and well-being of Wisconsin communities. We are learning to be comfortable with uncomfortable conversations for the well-being of the community.

5. *Engage in the public and political arena.* Joseph Bvumbwe reports that just as the church in South Africa had a significant role in the struggle against apartheid and the church in Malawi helped to remove a dictator from office and bring about a multi-party rule, so should the church today

be engaged in the public arena. In his case it was a call to be engaged in the HIV-AIDS crisis.

> From the onset, the African churches have played a key role in national and local community efforts to deal with difficult issues or challenges. This has always been the case, that African churches have led the way in the struggle communities face.[17] It is our understanding that the church cannot isolate itself in time of crisis; it must be part of the peoples' suffering. . . . In many African countries, churches and church based organizations are called upon to take a leading role in influencing people's behavior and social change. All over Africa, churches are taking an active part in the fight against the HIV pandemic. They form part of the lobby and advocacy groups for people living with AIDS. They are part of the local commission, e.g., the country coordinating mechanisms (CCMs), and other committees at the local level or community level; it is often the churches which take the lead in mobilizing resources for home-based care, counseling, social support and education for the young. In Malawi, like elsewhere in Africa, government is lacking in medical services . . . it is the churches and other faith-based NGO's and Christian organizations that moved in to fill the gap.[18]

The churches in the NWSWI can learn from Bvumbwe's faithful witness to be a more public church. In light of the current issues we face, such as the COVID-19 pandemic, racial justice struggles, climate change, and political divisiveness, the public churches in the NWSWI have found inspiration from Bvumbwe to engage the crisis of the moment with faithful voices and calls to action. When one suffers, we all suffer together. Public faith leaders need to be visible in the community, lean into the biblical narrative to frame responses to the issues of the day, and be the hands, feet, and voice of God in their communities. Be the church in the community, for the sake of the community, for God's sake.

6. *Read the Bible.* In John 9 we read that Jesus heals a man born blind.

The disciples asked, "Who sinned, this man or his parents that he was born blind?" Bvumbwe explains that when we read Scripture, we learn that judging people isn't the point. When we read Scripture, we move past judging those infected with HIV/AIDs. We remove the shame, guilt, and stigmatizing shadow that has been cast over their lives and work to comfort them in their suffering. Jesus violated the Sabbath law and healed the man born blind. He was teaching his disciples and

> . . . is inviting us to join him in providing for the healing of the world. There is too much darkness and hopelessness out there, and we are invited to join Jesus

in providing hope and healing for those who suffer. Jesus stopped at nothing. He had to break rules and traditions of every kind in order to provide sight to the man born blind so that he could see. Yes, the lepers in both the Old and New Testament were isolated for fear of infecting others and some diseases were seen and understood to be punishment or curses for sins, yet Jesus, without any hesitation or condemning the old practices, preached the love of God for sinners and the cursed, regardless of their sins. Like Jesus, we must be the light of the world. The light shines out of darkness, providing hope for those who live in darkness. There are many who are living in hopelessness. Jesus is inviting us to shine with him now, so that together we can provide hope to many who are hopeless.[19]

Dwelling in the Word and Dwelling in the World are two of the foundational faith practices used in our synod. Dwelling in the Word is a spiritual practice "in which people listen to Scripture together, sharing words of phrases that capture their imagination or questions the text provoked in them."[20] Dwelling in the World is a practice of reflecting back on the week and a relational encounter and "asking what might God be up to in that encounter and what God might want them to do if they reentered that encounter."[21] At many of our gatherings, we read God's Word and let it soak in. We let the Word work on us and in us so that we might with the help of the Holy Spirit discern God's will in our rural context for ministry. We also are learning to Dwell in the World and reflect back on our one-to-one meetings and larger gatherings and wonder what God might be up to in those connections. These are the faith practices that will move us forward as a church beyond judgment to compassion. These are the faith practices that will lead us to love our neighbor and be public leaders engaged in civil society.

This global pathway illustrates accompaniment at work. As rural faith leaders in Wisconsin, we are growing in our understanding of what it means to be a public church, and we are grateful for the lessons we've learned from Bishop Bvumbwe and our companions in Malawi. We have learned lessons about partnering with civic groups to work for peace and justice in our respective countries, advocating for the poor and vulnerable, taking risks and being prophetic, addressing uncomfortable subjects, engaging in the political arena, and listening deeply to Scripture and paying attention to the movement of God's Spirit in our daily work.

A RURAL PATHWAY

Both the Evangelical Lutheran Church of Malawi and the Northwest Synod of Wisconsin, ELCA, are rural church bodies where approximately 90 percent of the congregations are located in rural areas, small towns, or villages.[22]

Wisconsin's land mass is 97 percent rural, but only 30 percent of the population lives in the rural areas.[23] In Malawi 82 percent of Malawi's population lives in rural areas. These rural places are holy ground for growing a public church.

In Malawi 11.4 percent of the population have electricity, 50 percent live in poverty, and of those 20 percent live in extreme poverty. It is one of the poorest countries in the world. 80 percent of the population is employed in agriculture.[24] The literacy rate is 70 percent. The ELCM has over 101,000 members, with seventy-two Parishes and Mission Areas. Just over 4 percent of the population has received COVID-19 vaccinations as of October 2021.[25] In the twenty counties that make up the NWSWI, the highest poverty rates are in Sawyer County (17.7 percent), Rusk County (15 percent), and Eau Claire County (14.5 percent). The literacy rate in Wisconsin averages 93 percent. The NWSWI has 90,000 members and 198 congregations. Some of the lowest COVID-19 vaccination rates in the state are in the NWSWI. As of October 2021, Taylor and Price counties had a vaccination rate of less than 30 percent.

On the one hand, it is impossible to compare Malawi to Northwest Wisconsin. The economic differences alone make some comparisons unhelpful. On the other hand, both of our church bodies are relatively small and decidedly rural, and a conversation about being a public church in a rural context is helpful.

Rural Wisconsin has changed over the years. There are fewer red barns with silos and small herds of content black-and-white dairy cows grazing in a green pasture and fewer blue-eyed farm families. Today the iconic red barns are decaying and have been replaced by metal pole buildings with automated feeding and milking machine systems. Tall silos have been replaced by enormous white plastic bags filled with silage. Family farms are replaced by factory farms and immigrant laborers from Mexico working around the clock to milk 5,000 head of cows three times a day. Wisconsin produces 15 percent of the nation's dairy products, more than any state in the US.

Rural life in Africa has changed too. There are still many smallholder subsistent farms, but rural Malawi also includes large farms with cash crops of tea and tobacco. Malawi is ranked thirteenth in world producers of tea.[26] Workers on these large farms receive low wages. Smallholder farms and individual family plots grow vegetables, especially corn to make the national dish called Nsima. Nsima is a thick corn porridge—the basic corn porridge eaten every day by many Malawians. Subsistence farmers are victims of frequent floods, and droughts still result in famine.

This is our context for ministry. Being a public church in rural Wisconsin and rural Malawi presents unique challenges and opportunities.

Challenges Facing Rural Public Churches

If you ask me where I live, I'll tell you that I'm about an hour east of Minneapolis/St. Paul, Minnesota. I won't tell you the name of the small town I live near because you've never heard of it. I'll tell you where I live in relationship to a major urban area. The U.S. Census Bureau defines rural as what is not urban—that is, after defining individual urban areas, rural is what is left over.[27]

Rural life is more than a negative. It is more than what is not urban. In rural areas it is more likely that people and places can be known. In an urban community, one is less likely to be known. Urban areas are marked by "more anonymity in day-to-day life," rural areas by familiarity.[28] In a Pew Research Center Report about urban and rural polarization, "folks who value open space, like-minded neighbors and conservative political views tend to favor living in rural communities."[29] They put a high value on trust, community, and knowledge of who one's neighbor is.

"Rural" does not necessarily mean farming. Folks who live in rural areas are less likely today to be connected to agriculture in direct ways than they were years ago. In 1930 21 percent of the population engaged in farming; in 1980 it was 3.4 percent. Today about 20 percent of the US population lives in rural areas, and less than 2 percent of the US population is actively engaged in farming.[30]

Rural people and rural communities are complex. In a survey given to a group of ministers of the NWSWI, 50 respondents helped identify five themes in rural ministry that will guide a more publicly engaged church.

1. *Pay careful attention to personal relationships.* Public church leaders in rural areas need to develop one-to-one relationships in the congregation, in other congregations, and with unchurched neighbors before introducing any programmatic venture.
2. *Assume everyone is related.* Small and rural congregations often feel like extended family. One survey response noted that in rural congregations the "grief runs deep and collective memory is long." Like families, some congregations may be dysfunctional. Dysfunctional congregations lack healthy decision-making practices, triangulate, and hold on to conflict for years. Know the history and the family trees in the rural church.
3. *Develop the ability to navigate community connections.* To be a public church, leaders need relationships with the community leaders. They need to know elected and unelected community leaders and the influencers. Borrow a page from Faith Based Community Organizing and do intentional one-to-ones[31] and initiate meetings with groups of

community leaders. Time is well spent attending community functions. Sit on the hospital ethics committee. Attend school board, township board, and city council meetings. Volunteer to coach. Frequent the local restaurants and businesses. Be present.
4. *Practice agile adaptive leadership.* COVID-19 has proven that some small membership congregations are nimble and flexible, able to pivot quickly when needed. They can be resourceful and creative and have willing workers. On the flip side, change and new ideas can be a hard sell. Pastors and the few lay leaders in some small rural congregations sometimes over-function and burn out. Burnt-out leaders are in survival mode and are less willing to be publicly engaged.
5. *Accept the demographics.* Being small and getting smaller can have a negative impact on a congregation and community's self-image. Rural communities in America have experienced so much loss: declining population, talented young people moving to the city, hospitals and businesses on main street closing, and schools consolidating. Church leaders are "called to abide: to stay put long enough to be made from the dust of a place . . . caring for a place, practicing the ministry of presence, living into an appropriate smallness."[32]

The summary above from a brief survey of ministers serving rural and small-town churches lifts up insights into rural public ministry: nurture relationships, be adaptable, commit to remain faithful, accept the demographics, and stay long enough to learn to love a place and a people. It is recognizing that doing rural ministry in these challenging days is standing on God's holy ground. We are committed to learning more about rural public ministry accompanying our companion synod in Malawi in the years to come.

There are many challenges to being a public church in Rural Wisconsin. Authentic rural ministry is about abiding and loving the people and the place and acknowledging the current reality of both the ministry and rural community. It is also acknowledging that all is not as God intended. Church leaders are required to "speak into being that which could be, to infuse God's dreams into the congregations and communities."[33] Leaders are called to befriend rural congregations and communities. "At its heart, befriending rural communities is all about coming to the basic realization that the destiny of the rural church is tied to the destiny of the rural community. Wherever we are going in the rural places, we're going there together. In the church, this means we begin to act as a friend of the community, not just as an actor with the community. As the community goes, so goes the church. The thriving of one is the thriving of the other."[34] This is a call for those serving in rural congregations to take seriously the work of being engaged public theologians in the rural arena.

The rural areas of the United States have as many social problems as urban areas do. Per capita poverty in rural areas is higher than in urban areas. "According to the most recent estimates from the 2019 American Community Survey (ACS), the non-metro poverty rate was 15.4 percent in 2019, compared with 11.9 percent for metro areas."[35] There are significant food insecurity[36] in rural areas, food deserts, and hidden homelessness.[37] But the rural problems tend to fall through the cracks. The population is less dense and spread out over a larger geographic area, and so poverty is less visible. As church leaders and public theologians in rural congregations and communities, we are to mind the gap between what is and what God wills. Public faith leaders and public churches fill in the gap in rural areas.

In rural areas there is a gap between the needs of the rural poor and the resources and agencies to provide assistance.[38] As a public church, ministers in a rural context call attention to this injustice and raise awareness about the injustices in rural areas. In addition to the poverty and hunger of rural areas, transportation is often a major issue. Urban dwellers often are able to use mass transit, bus, or train. In rural areas the gaps between the needs and resources are often hundreds of miles wide. Many lack affordable ways to cover the miles to the nearest hospital or clinic. Seeing a specialist of any kind often requires hours on the road. Transportation to educational opportunities and even to a store with fresh produce is challenging for the rural poor. According to Rev. Dr. Mark Yackel-Juleen, Director of Rural and Small Town Ministry at Wartburg Seminary, public theologians in rural areas mind the gap by working with a team from the congregation and the community to make a difference in Jesus's name. This is his model for rural public ministry:[39]

1. *Community Needs Assessment.* This could be as simple as informal conversation or as intentional as a meeting of community leaders and survey of residents.
2. *Identify the Gap.* From the data gathered from the needs assessment, identify the needs and create a prioritized list.
3. *Raise Awareness of the Gaps.* Communicate the process, the needs, and the list using whatever method makes sense in your setting.
4. *Network.* This is a problem-solving step. Involve as many people as possible to discover tools, available resources, and people who can begin to address the needs.
5. *Collaboratively Design and Implement a Plan to Address the Needs.*
6. *Evaluate and Repeat the Process.*

Public theologians in rural communities have prophetic voices using the language of our faith traditions to speak to the justice issues, the gap between what is and what God wills. Some find their way by writing using various social media platforms. Some of the leaders in NWSWI write columns in the local small-town newspaper. Others are serving on school boards, the food shelf board, the local ministerial group, or other community development organizations. Minding the gap and finding a path to access necessary agencies and resources is what a public leader in a rural context is about.

COVID-19 vaccination rates in some of our rural counties were significantly lower than the state average. Local congregations did what they could to host vaccination sites and address the false information that circulated about the vaccine. In August 2021 Taylor County had only a 26-percent vaccination rate compared to 50 percent statewide. A pastor of the NWSWI in Taylor County hosted Wisconsin Governor Evers at a press conference to announce a vaccination incentive program. This was a model of prophetic public witness in a small rural community.[40] However, members of the community protested at the press conference, and a member left the church because of the church council's decision to host the press conference. There is risk in being a public witness and public church in rural Wisconsin, and it may cost relationships.

A LEADERSHIP PATHWAY: THE LAY SCHOOL OF MINISTRY

The Northwest Synod of Wisconsin's Lay School of Ministry is holy ground for training lay leaders for a public church.[41] The purpose of the Northwest Synod of Wisconsin's Lay School is to equip lay leaders to live out their baptism in their daily lives and specifically in the public arena. The lay school is designed to help lay people become public theologians engaged in civil society. When asked to talk about what it means to be a leader in a public church or a pastor to be a public theologian, former director of the Lay School Greg Kaufmann said, "It is the ability of the person lay or rostered to connect their faith with the actual world in which they live and have their being. Public theologians are lay leaders that are confident enough in their faith skin to make a difference in the place where God has planted them."[42]

Kaufmann, reflecting on what it means to be a leader in a public church, said, "I changed how I taught the Bible. I moved away from just studying the historical details of the text to asking about how a text connects and relates to real life here in rural Wisconsin. This gave students permission to participate in God's ongoing work in civil society. Living out our faith in the biblical conversation moves it out of the past to inform how we live with our neighbor down the street today."

The Lay School has set a high bar for the students. It is a two-year course of study. It meets nine times a year, one weekend a month for six hours of intensive coursework with the expectations of readings, homework, and faith-formation group meetings between the sessions. The two-year curriculum[43] includes Old and New Testament, church history-systematics, worship, faith formation, and missional leadership. The church history and systematics course is taught by Dr. Gary Simpson, who has taught at the Lay School since 1994.

Over the years the Lay School has continued to evolve. "By the time the 5th group of students started in 1998, graduates of the previous classes demanded that the Lay School add a continuing education class for them."[44] These continuing education classes have had fifty to seventy-five participants a year for the last twenty years. During the COVID-19 pandemic, the Lay School continued and moved to a Zoom platform. Even during the pandemic, there were fifty students on Zoom for the continued education sessions. The continuing education courses continue to shape students to be public theologians in a public church. The Zoom platform removes geographic barriers, and students can now join from across the country.

Current director of the Lay School, Rev. Dr. Phil Ruge-Jones, structures the continuing education courses on a two-year cycle; one year focuses on the Bible, and the second year focuses on public witness. According to Ruge-Jones, the purpose of the Lay School is to provide tools for lay people to live lives faithfully. Recently, the Lay School has had series of in-depth courses on the Repudiation of the Doctrine of Discovery, racism, immigration, interfaith relationships, eco-theology, and how to read Scripture through a variety of lenses. As director, Ruge-Jones is intentional in seeking out younger, more diverse instructors for each of these series. He believes that this course of intentional study is forming these lay leaders into strong public witnesses to their faith. They live out this witness in all the communities of the NWSWI. The continuing education program of the Lay School is forming public theologians.

The Lay School unintentionally became a seminary prep program. At least twenty Lay School students have gone on to seminary to become ordained pastors. Two became deacons. Others have discerned that living out their baptismal covenant means they will serve in their local congregations as Synodically Authorized Lay Ministers. (SAMs). Currently, we have twenty-one Synodically Authorized Lay Ministers serving congregations in our synod.[45]

The original purpose of the Lay School was *not* to produce seminary students or SAMs. It is now an expectation that all SAMs will have finished Lay School and, in addition, take preaching and pastoral care courses and participate in a colleague group led by an experienced pastor.

The Lay School has been effective in achieving its purpose of building bridges among congregations, the synod, and the greater church. It has also been effective in raising up public theologians for our public churches. Evidence of that claim can be found in this case study of one of the LSM graduates, Mary Meierotto.

A CASE STUDY

Mary Meierotto[46] is a long-time member of Bethesda Lutheran Church in Bayfield, Wisconsin. In 2010 Meierotto graduated from the LSM two-year program, and she has since completed ten years of the LSM's continuing education program. In 2016 she began serving as a Synodically Authorized Minister (SAM). The coursework of the Lay School inspired her to live out her baptismal covenant in new ways. The continuing education program gave her new insight into the Doctrine of Discovery and immigration issues, both major topics in the Lay School's continuing education curriculum.[47]

Bethesda and Immanuel form a small two-point parish in the northernmost part of the synod on Lake Superior. Average worship attendance is thirty winter / fifty summer at Bethesda and twenty-five winter / forty summer at Immanuel. They are both congregations committed to public ministry and are currently doing justice and loving their neighbor in two significant ways. Meierotto, walking alongside this parish, has developed new relationships with the Red Cliff Band of Lake Superior Chippewa and in July 2020 started a Native/Lutheran worship service that gathers once a month on Sunday mornings. A member of the Red Cliff tribal council, Jim Pete, tells me that Meierotto has been a member of the community for such a long time that she is accepted. He shared with the tribal council that Meierotto's two churches were learning about the Red Cliff culture.[48] This testimony at a tribal council meeting is no small thing. This relationship grew as Meierotto studied the Repudiation of the Doctrine of Discovery during the 2017–18 Lay School continuing education program year.

Meierotto also walked with Bethesda and Immanuel in their work to start the Lake Superior Bridge Builders. This is a group of church and community members who are working with an immigrant family seeking asylum. They remodeled the basement of their church building in Bayfield into a three-bedroom apartment in order to be better equipped in the future to host and support families seeking asylum. This ministry is an outgrowth of the study that Meierotto did while part of the Lay School of Ministry.

This SAM and parish are providing leadership for the whole community to be a family: a family that cares and watches out for its neighbors. It is a family that cares and is now able to stretch that caring out to Red Cliff Band of Lake Superior Chippewa and to those who have crossed the border and entered the US without documentation. A church member remarked that by connecting with Red Cliff neighbors and asylum seekers, the parish is doing what big churches do. Little churches like theirs usually just take care of their own.

Through the LSM Meierotto has participated in a Border Immersion Trip to Arizona and Texas and traveled to Pine Ridge Indian Reservation. Meierotto said that these experiential learning opportunities helped her to care for those who weren't members or even Christians in the community. In addition, Mary has visited Malawi, our companion synod, and her parish is providing tuition for a female seminary student in Malawi. Mary Meierotto is a baptized child of God, a SAM, a Lay School graduate, and a public theologian.

In conclusion, the Northwest Synod of Wisconsin has discovered three pathways that have guided its ministry as a public church: 1) It has learned about being a public church, responding to a health crisis from its companion synod, the Evangelical Lutheran Church in Malawi, and Bishop Joseph Bvumbwe; 2) it has embraced its rural context and the relational nature of ministry as avenues to mind the gap in addressing social justice issues; and 3) the Northwest Synod of Wisconsin gives thanks to God for the ways the Lay School has formed public theologians and leaders in our rural public churches. In this chapter we've "held theology and praxis close together."[49] This revealed a practical public theology lived out on holy ground of the fields and pastures surrounding rural faith communities in both Malawi and Wisconsin. This rural public church is grounded in the biblical and historic Lutheran teachings and lived out through missional congregations and the baptismal vocation of believers. This lived theology and praxis is relational, risky, and potentially revolutionary. This lived theology and praxis is certainly a public endeavor. As Luther Seminary Professor Emeritus Gary Simpson notes:

> The church is always public. Its public character is rooted in its most basic identity constituted through public worship's proclamation of the gospel, distribution of the sacraments, and outcries of prayer as it anticipatorily groans and rejoices in communion with the Holy Spirit and with all creation. Public theology begins and ends its critical reflection on this publicness. Vocation is the outworking of ceaseless prayer. Public theology therefore reflects also on the vocation of congregations as public companions with God in global civil society.... The church is an eschatological communion that anticipates already now in its life together with the world the coming reconciliation of all things when the triune God will be all in all.[50]

NOTES

1. The Northwest Synod of Wisconsin (NWSWI) is one of the sixty-five synods of the Evangelical Lutheran Church in America.

2. Ex. 3:1–5 (NRSV).

3. *Evangelical Lutheran Worship* (Minneapolis, Augsburg Publishing, 2007, 2019), 243.

4. Each of the sixty-five synods of the ELCA has at least one international companion. "These relationships are rooted in 'accompaniment,' which promotes the values of mutuality, inclusivity, vulnerability, empowerment and sustainability. The purpose is to strengthen one another for life and ministry through prayer, study, communication, exchange of visitors and sharing of resources." https://www.elca.org/Our-Work/Global-Mission/How-We-Work/Companion-Synod-Relationships?_ga=2.233576026.519101991.1638030020-256581953.1608055964 (accessed November 26, 2021).

5. Co-journer is a term used by the Franciscans in Rochester, MN, for their lay associates.

6. Evangelical Lutheran Church in America, https://www.elca.org/Our-Work/Global-Mission (accessed November 26, 2021).

7. Former Bishops Robert Berg, Duane Pederson, and Rick Hoyme and former Companion Synod Coordinator Deacon Diane Kaufmann, interviewed by author, August 2021.

8. The Pastor's Academy is a weeklong continuing education event for ELCM pastors held in Lilongwe, Malawi, and sponsored by the NWSWI.

9. Joseph Bvumbwe, "Can the Pulpit Also Be Used? A Handbook for Pastors and Lay Leaders: On Breaking the Silence on HIV/AIDS," (D.Min Thesis, Luther Seminary, 2004), 106, 108.

10. Bvumbwe, "Can the Pulpit Also Be Used?," 17.

11. Bvumbwe, "Can the Pulpit Also Be Used?," 18.

12. Pastors and deacons are ordained ministers in the ELCA. Synodically Authorized Ministers (SAMs) are lay leaders, and they participate in an ongoing training and mentoring program. SAMs are authorized to do ministry including the sacraments by the synod bishop and synod council.

13. Bvumbwe, "Can the Pulpit Also Be Used?," 19–20.

14. Dean Stroud, *Preaching in Hitler's Shadow: Sermons of Resistance in the Third Reich* (Grand Rapids: Eerdmans Publishing, 2013).

15. Stroud, *Preaching in Hitler's Shadow*, 48.

16. Laurie Skow-Anderson, "Message from Bishop Laurie Skow-Anderson," Constantcontact.com, October 22, 2020, https://myemail.constantcontact.com/A-message-from-Bishop-Laurie---10-22-20.html?soid=1101126434512&aid=V-MKm3oYejY.

17. Bvumbwe, "Can the Pulpit Also Be Used," 96.

18. Bvumbwe, "Can the Pulpit Also Be Used?," 106, 108.

19. Bvumbwe, "Can the Pulpit Also Be Used?," 106, 108.

20. Dwight Zschiele, *The Agile Church: Spirit-Led Innovation in an Uncertain Age* (New York: Morehouse Publishing, 2014), Kindle edition, loc. 1479.

21. Zscheile, *The Agile Church*, 1496.

22. Evangelical Lutheran Church in Malawi, "About Us—Evangelical Lutheran Church in Malawi," https://elcm.weebly.com/about-us.html (accessed October 5, 2021).

23. Malia Jones and Mitchell Ewald, "Putting Rural Wisconsin on the Map: Understanding Rural-Urban Divide Requires Complex Spectrum of Definitions," *Wiscontext*, May 17, 2017, https://www.wiscontext.org/putting-rural-wisconsin-map.

24. World Bank of Malawi, "Overview," March 2021, https://www.worldbank.org/en/country/malawi/overview.

25. Joseph Mwale, "Malawi Misses September Covid-19 Vaccine Target," *The Nation Online*, https://mwnation.com/malawi-misses-september-covid-19-vaccine-target/ (accessed October 4, 2021).

26. Alice Chen, "The World's Top Tea-Producing Countries," *World Atlas*, September 17, 2020, https://www.worldatlas.com/articles/the-worlds-top-10-tea-producing-nations.html.

27. Michael Ratcliffe et al., "Defining Rural at the U.S. Census Bureau," U.S. Department of Commerce, Economics and Statistics Administration, December 8, 2016, https://www.census.gov/library/publications/2016/acs/acsgeo-1.html.

28. Brad Roth, *God's Country: Faith, Hope and the Future of the Rural Church* (Harrisonburg: Herald Press, 2017), 29.

29. Roth, God's Country, 30.

30. Mary Bellis, "History of American Agriculture," *ThoughtCo.*, https://www.thoughtco.com/history-of-american-agriculture-farm-machinery-4074385 (accessed October 5, 2021).

31. See descriptions of community organizing and one-to-ones at the Gamaliel Network: https://gamaliel.org/.

32. Roth, God's Country, 60.

33. Roth, God's Country, 88.

34. Roth, God's Country, 194.

35. Tracey Farrigan, "Rural Poverty and Well-Being," *U.S. Department of Agriculture, Economic Research Service*, September 17, 2021, https://www.researchgate.net/publication/317932288_The_Spatial_Concentration_of_America's_Rural_Poor_Population_A_Postrecession_Update.

36. Alisha Coleman-Jensen et al., "Household Food Security in the United States in 2019," *U.S. Department of Agriculture, Economic Research Service*, September 2020, https://www.ers.usda.gov/webdocs/publications/99282/err-275.pdf?v=9813.1.

37. Farrigan, "Rural Poverty and Well-Being."

38. Mark Yackel-Juleen, Director of Rural and Small Town Ministry, Wartburg Seminary, Zoom conversation with author, January 20, 2021.

39. Yackel-Juleen.

40. Pastor Elizabeth Bier, Nazareth Lutheran Church, Withee, WI, email to author, August 2021.

41. Greg Kaufmann, interview by author, August 2021. Pastor Greg Kaufmann, synod minister and former director of the Lay School of Ministry (LSM), served with four bishops and taught the Bible course for the LSM for over twenty-five years. After the formation of the ELCA in 1988, the congregations in this synod were inwardly

focused and barely aware of the other Lutheran congregation across the street or across the township road. The synod staff wondered what they could do that would shift the culture and learn to be church together for the sake of the world. From this conversation the Lay School of Ministry was born. The hope was that students from the lay school would help the whole synod to understand what it meant to be church together. These trusted lay people could advocate for the synod and wider church, and they would be bridges to connect the whole synod. The first class started in 1993.

42. Kaufmann.

43. Northwest Synod of Wisconsin, "Lay School of Ministry," http://www.layschoolofministry.org/LSMCurriculum.html (accessed October 4, 2021).

44. Kaufmann, email to author, October 13, 2021.

45. Northwest Synod of Wisconsin, "Synodically Authorized Ministers," http://nwswi.org/leadership/sams (accessed October 4, 2021).

46. Mary Meierotto, Synodically Authorized Minister, interview by author, July 2021. Permission to use her story in email to author received November 2021.

47. Northwest Synod of Wisconsin, "Lay School of Ministry History," http://www.layschoolofministry.org/LSMhistory.html (accessed October 4, 2021).

48. Jim Pete tells the story of the Red Cliff Band of Lake Superior Chippewa history as part of the NWSWI Land Acknowledgement, https://vimeo.com/536144242.

49. Clive Pearson, "Editorial: Stretching Definitions," *International Journal of Public Theology* no. 13 (2019): 383, https://brill.com/view/journals/ijpt/13/4/article-p383_1.xml?language=en.

50. Gary Simpson, "Missional Congregations as Public Companions with God in Global Civil Society: Vocational Imagination and Spiritual Presence," *Dialog: A Journal of Theology* 54, no. 2 (June 2015): 142.

PART II

Implications for Ethics and Social Responsibility

Robert Kolb demonstrates that Luther and his followers, though often criticized for political passivity, present countless historical examples of civic leadership and intervention in the public arena, with both positive contributions and negative critiques. Although Luther lived in a vastly different environment than today, Kolb argues that Luther's insights into the nature of the God-designed shape of human life, with its callings to be responsible for the individual and welfare of others, lay a foundation for godly embodiment of God's life-restoring action in Jesus Christ. Kolb asserts that Luther's perspectives remain valid for twenty-first-century cultures and deserve attention today.

George R. Hunsberger leads the reader on a curious journey into Lesslie Newbigin's idea of a "Christian society." Surprised that Newbigin would assert such a possibility, Hunsberger searches out antecedent hints and clues to the idea as it was brewing for Newbigin; then he examines three major essays in which Newbigin commends the idea of a Christian society as an orienting vision—and even an agenda—for Christian public witness in Western secular society. Hunsberger provides a clear response to Newbigin's proposal and suggests that, despite controversies and shortcomings, it frames important territory for public missiology and public theology to engage.

John R. Stumme argues that Christian ethics, when it turns to Luther, should go beyond Luther's understanding of love in thesis 28 of the *Heidelberg Disputation*. His argument challenges the century-long hold on Christian ethics exerted by Andres Nygren's *Agape and Eros*, which interprets thesis 28 as defining what Luther means by love. Stumme critically appraises thesis 28 as missing a doctrine of creation; he argues that other Luther writings, which incorporate creation, provide other ways into love in Luther and therefore offer more promise for Christian ethics today.

Putting the social Trinity (Jürgen Moltmann) in conversation with Philip Hefner's idea of human beings as "created co-creators," Marie-Louise Ström lays the foundation for a civic ecclesiology of *cooperatio*, in which citizens are co-creators of a good society through co-creative relationship with God. In light of current crises in democracy and civic life, she proposes that the church has profound theological resources to take leadership in overcoming polarization and promoting a paradigm shift toward understanding democracy as everyone's work. Using its profound theological resources, the church becomes a site for civic learning and democratic empowerment, giving new meaning to Christian service and Christian civic agency.

Robert O. Smith draws upon political theory and religious sociology to offer a response to the epochal developments experienced through the Covid-19 pandemic. He became convinced through his ELCA synodical leadership that church leaders needed tools to comprehend and address the society-wide challenges of the pandemic moment. He advocates for religious communities to develop "societal chaplaincy," which is a vocational stance that broadens comprehension of their call beyond their primary congregations/communities to include community-wide and societal well-being. He envisions that comprehension of life's broad systems would critically restructure community relationships and provide holistic care and concern within society.

Chapter 7

The Polis in Luther's Theology

Robert Kolb

"Through civil rulers, as through our own parents, God gives us food, house and home, protection and security, and he preserves us through them.... [It] is also our duty to honor and respect them as the most precious treasure and most priceless jewel on earth. Those who are obedient, willing and eager to be of service, and cheerfully do everything that honor demands, know that they please God and receive joy and happiness as their reward. On the other hand, if they will not do so in love, but despise authority, rebel, or cause unrest, let them know that they will have no favor or blessing."[1] With such an orientation toward life in civil society, is it any wonder that followers of Martin Luther are often thought of as politically submissive, without much sense of individual responsibility for the larger society? But why indeed, in that case, have "Lutherans," beginning with Luther himself, throughout their five centuries of participation in societies around the world often provided significant civic leadership, both with positive contributions and negative critiques of injustice and tyranny?

FOR THE HISTORICAL RECORD

Lutherans have lived in four different settings. The lands in central and northern Europe in which they were a cornerstone of the establishment differed from their environment in the persecuted churches in Europe's East (first as victims of the Counter-Reformation and later of National Socialism and/ or Soviet imperialism). Beyond Europe Lutherans were first in establishing a mission church in the Global South, in India. In the nations of Africa and Asia, these Lutherans have always been a minority. Though never "establishments" in their societies, Lutheran immigrant churches in the Americas,

Australia, and South Africa have largely enjoyed until recently living within Christian establishments that did not disadvantage them. In all these situations, the Lutheran form of the Christian faith has at times succumbed to the inevitable negative elements in enculturation that come to God's people as he propels his gospel into each individual culture. (However, it must be also noted that God's message in Scripture is designed to be integrated into the thinking of every people and tongue.)[2] But they have also functioned as cultural pioneers and cultural critics in all four settings. Does that have anything to do with their being "Lutherans," who to one degree or another take seriously the person and often the teaching of Martin Luther?

Lutheran political theology has its roots in the Wittenberg experience of leading the introduction of significant reform to the Western church. Luther's call for reform had broad cultural significance, and not only in its initiating a revolution in public communication through effective use of the printing press.[3] It also had societal implications, beginning with Luther's 1520 deconstruction of piety in his *Open Letter of the German Nobility*, with its call for changes in ecclesiastical life and public life in general.[4] The targets of his critique included "extravagant and costly dress," spices from foreign lands, and the abuses of eating and drinking to excess, all protests against overindulgence and luxury (although Luther advocated modest enjoyment of God's temporal blessings and contentment with what he gives). Added to that list were usury, since the pursuit of Mammon was among the most powerful idols he condemned,[5] and brothels, since Luther regarded sexuality and the family as keystones to society's functioning.[6]

Lutheran political comment blossomed in the generation of Luther's and Melanchthon's students, whom the attempts of Emperor Charles V to eradicate Lutheran teaching in the 1540s drove into the political arena. The so-called "Gnesio-Lutherans" advocated and practiced resistance against what they perceived as imperial-governmental tyranny. Their Magdeburg *Confession* of 1550, issued in the midst of the imperial siege of Magdeburg, defined its faith in seven articles summarizing the teaching of the Augsburg Confession and outlined the calling of Christians in their specific spheres of social responsibility to oppose governmental abuse and oppression.[7] The *Confession* influenced the formulation of the resistance theory for French Huguenots and other persecuted Reformed groups by Theodore Beza. Through him it impacted theories of resistance to unjust government in England and thus in North America.[8]

Such thinking brought the Lutheran leadership of the county of Lippe, clergy and lay, to resist the imposition of advancing Calvinist absolutism in their principality in the late sixteenth century and early seventeenth.[9] Paul Gerhardt exemplifies a larger picture of quiet and not-so-quiet defiance of rulers by Lutheran clergy in the later seventeenth century.[10] James Stayer points out that it was not the classical liberal theologians in the train of Albrecht Ritschl and Adolf von Harnack but those whose theology was grounded in the Lutheran Confessions who discarded initial enthusiasm for Adolf Hitler to undercut and oppose National Socialist ideology.[11] Though Paul Althaus and Werner Elert did not share the open, active critique of National Socialism voiced already before Hitler became chancellor of Germany in 1933 by their colleague Hermann Sasse,[12] they worked to frustrate "German Christian" forces as professors in Erlangen.[13] Dietrich Bonhoeffer not only taught underground when German theological faculties had largely succumbed to National Socialist influences and provided pastoral care for supporters of the resistance. He also participated in formulating the post-war plan of the Christian Democrats for a "social market economy."[14] Others, including leading laity in politics and the military, consciously used Luther's distinction of two realms to formulate their own ideas regarding active resistance to the Hitler regime.[15]

Lutherans in other lands also played a variety of roles in public life. As in Germany, Lutherans in Nordic lands made many positive contributions to the public life and culture of their peoples. In nineteenth-century Denmark Nikolaus Grundtvig (1783–1872), with his institution of popular education and other social measures, represents Wittenberg concerns for the broader society.[16] Nathan Söderblom (1866–1931) pursued Luther studies even though he cast what he gained from the reformer into a framework shaped by nineteenth-century liberalism. Söderblom is best known for his social concerns, exhibited in his organizing the movement "Life and Work."[17] In very different circumstances in twentieth-century Norway, Bishop Einar Berggrav (1884–1957) echoed the critique of tyranny voiced by Luther and by the Gnesio-Lutherans of Magdeburg.[18] The German-Russian pastor Heinrich Wilhelm Dieckhoff (1833–1911) pioneered Russian education for the blind and the deaf, enlisting the aid of the tsarist court for his schools.[19] The rise of a Slovak literary culture and national consciousness stemmed not from the majority of the population that had been returned to Roman obedience by the Counter-Reformation persecutions but instead from the Lutheran pastor Josef Miloslav Hurban (1817–1888), the Lutheran layman L'udovit Štur (1815–1856), and other products of the Lutheran secondary schools. Twentieth-century Slovak political leaders, such as Milan Rastislav Štefánic (1880–1919), a founder of the Czecho-Slovak republic in 1919, and Alexander Dubcek (1921–1992), deposed leader of the first attempt to loosen Soviet domination of the Czechs and Slovaks, were baptized by their Lutheran families even if little of Luther's doctrine remained in their consciousness.[20] Likewise, the association of Louis Kossuth (1802–1894) with the Lutheran church of Hungary, in which he was baptized, remained strong throughout his life, a life spent partially in exile because of his leadership of the rebellion of the Hungarians against Habsburg domination in 1848–1850. Many of his fellow Lutherans supported the cause of Hungarian autonomy.[21] The strong voice of Bishop Lajos Ordass (1901–1978) protested publicly against the Hungarian Marxist regime's suppression of the freedom of the church and was jailed for his critique.[22]

In the twentieth century, mission churches produced Lutheran theological and ecclesiastical leaders whose voices have echoed across their society. In India Lutheran thinkers have promoted the welfare of the Dalits, the outcastes of Hindu society, and some have contributed significantly to the development of "Dalit theology."[23] Ethiopian Lutheran leaders such as Gudina Tumsa (1929–1979) paid the ultimate price for their speaking the gospel in the face of the hostility of the Marxist regime of Mengistu Heile Mariam; many others, including his wife, Tsehay Tolessa, suffered torture and imprisonment as they opposed the injustice and cruelty of the Communists.[24]

LUTHER AND THE POLIS

Is there any reason, however, to link such efforts with Martin Luther other than the fact that these individuals or groups bear his name? Luther's own political theology has often been ignored and, recently, more often misrepresented. But his view of the world's operation under God's often mysterious governance has trickled down through the ages and reasserted itself against both amnesia and distorting caricatures in various ways. It deserves attention today.

Luther's hermeneutic for reading God's design for human life in his created world centers on four distinctions that provided the equipment for dealing with reality, a reality that he found resting on the personal relationship of the Creator to his entire creation, human and non-human. His teachers had trained him to think in terms of Aristotle's substances as the fundamental units of reality. He learned that eternal rules and regulations held them together—rules that were clear to human reason. Reason serves as every individual's means of dealing with the substances of what exists. Without a personal god, Aristotle posited an unmoved mover, but movement, once generated, operated within this substantial framework of reality, managed by human reason according to eternal law. Early in his study of Scripture, Luther had recognized that the biblical writers perceived reality as fundamentally relational rather than substantial, a totally different way of beginning to think about creation and life. At the core of human existence stands trust in the Creator and the service to him and other human creatures that proceeds from that faithfulness.

The first of the four distinctions that framed his reading of Scripture and life—he found in the stories of Scripture "a mirror of life" as experienced in his day-to-day activities[25]—set forth God's two ways of addressing the human situation, with a presentation of what he is doing for sinners in the promise of the gospel of Christ and with a description of his design for good human living in the law that sinners encounter as the crushing and accusing account of the Creator.

Alongside this categorization of God's actions in his Word, Luther worked with three anthropological axioms that distinguished passive and active righteousness, human bondage and human freedom, and the vertical and horizontal realms in which human life takes place according to God's design. The first distinguishes two kinds of righteousness, or the twofold identity of human creatures. In regard to the origin of their ultimate identity as creatures and as children of God, they are passive, just as babies receive without any merit or worthiness in them the DNA of their parents. Luther first called this a righteousness from outside ourselves (*iustitia aliena*), later "passive righteousness" since it involved God's unconditional gift. Secondary identities flow from the human nature reborn through his creative or re-creative Word. In these identities we perform an active righteousness, "proper" righteousness. These identities belong to individuals (*iustitia propria*) and demonstrate themselves in their being the creatures, God's newborn children, that he has created anew according to eternal law, without any merit or worthiness in us.

Luther's anthropology contrasted freedom and bondage in two ways. He experienced that the choices his own will made when trusting in an object of ultimate reliability were always bound to rest on something God created rather than on the Creator as his Lord and Maker. Freedom of the will was worse—or less—than an illusion.[26] But Luther also used the term "freedom" for the deliverance from sin, death, and Satan that Christ has won for his people through his death and resurrection. This freedom bonds believers to those around them as the freedom to be truly human and not turned in upon oneself by sin.[27]

Passive righteousness or identity and the activities of loving service that flow from trusting God's new-life-bestowing promise are experienced in the true freedom which bonds human creatures to each other. This re-created way of life takes place within a framework constituted by the two distinct dimensions or "realms" that God has built into humanity. Confusion has resulted from the reformer's using the same word, "reich," for both the "kingdoms" of God and Satan and the "realms" of our relationship with him and our relationships with other creatures. Luther did not equate the church as institution with the relationship of believers with God, or their passive righteousness with God's rule. He did not equate earthly institutions with our relationships within the created order, or human activity with Satan's rule. Since the fall

God's exercise of his sovereignty has been in constant conflict with Satan's attempt at exercising sovereignty in both dimensions of human life. In the vertical dimension, the gospel has re-created sinners into God's children, and the law tells them how to respond in praise and prayer, while in the horizontal dimension, the law confronts sinful ideas of proper conduct of active righteousness with God's design as the gospel moves his people to trusting obedience. Bondage in the vertical realm gives way to Christ's liberating victory over sin, death, and Satan, which produces the freedom to live out God's gift of new life in both realms. Marius Timann Mjaaland argues that Luther's description of the identity God bestows in his gift of passive righteousness has profound implications for societal-political participation of the faithful, responsible child of God in promoting justice and the common welfare.[28]

H. Richard Niebuhr's characterization of Luther's understanding of the relationship of these two realms as "Christ and culture in paradox," helpful as his analysis is in many ways, mislabels Luther's distinction.[29] It is not a paradox to distinguish relationship with parents from relationship with siblings. A person is dependent upon and then grateful for parents; siblings command respect, love, care, and concern—at least ideally. Bernd Wannenwitsch provides a clear perspective on how Luther's distinction of the two dimensions of human life actually functions.[30] He cogently argues that this metaphor should be understood not in spatial terms but rather in temporal. In this world, throughout the horizontal dimension of life, believers remain "citizens" of the vertical dimension of life established by God's promise that here and now they possess and act out their new identity as no-longer-sinner but instead God's child. Believers acknowledge and use the tools provided by God's creative ordering of life for horizontal relationships with other creatures, but as people governed by their Lord at the same time. Believers do not cease being God's children when they exercise the assignments God gives them to preserve his gifts as best they can be preserved in the midst of evil. This means that they act in the horizontal realm with the same outwardly turned concern for other creatures that overcomes the sinful desire to protect oneself by turning inward. They pursue justice for others with instruments used to restrain wickedness and selfishness that recognize the sinfulness that turns people into less than fully human paths of action because they recognize how deeply sin has permeated the fallen human condition. As Luther maintained from the 1520s on, the person who turns the other cheek for his or her own person uses the sword against those who perpetrate injustice and wrong against the neighbor.[31] Brett Muhlhan contrasts Luther's approach to these situations as "personal-social" and "official-social."[32]

This enables believers to be sharply critical of their own cultures and neighbors in the face of the practice of ungodly actions and beliefs, while they are highly appreciative of what God is giving with his cultural gifts and his active participation as Giver in daily life. This enables believers to consciously maintain their identity as God's children while using the tools of God's law to preserve peace and order in his world to the greatest extent possible. According to Luther, they do this in the context of God's structure for human life. The Wittenberg reformer altered the definition of the proper human roles in the horizontal realm within the context of the medieval social theory. Its structure had molded the world in which he grew up and functioned his entire life. It presumed that societal life took place in three "*status*," or "*Stände*"—situations or walks of life: the *ecclesia*, or "*Lehrstand*"; the *politia*, or "*Wehrstand*"; and the *oeconomia*, "the *Nährstand*," which embraced both family life and economic activities. In each of these situations, individuals exercised their "*officia*," or "*Ämter*," their responsibilities, which encompassed both role or position in society and the functions that these positions demanded be exercised for the neighbor. Medieval theory placed each individual in one of these situations and held that those in the "*ecclesia*" were by virtue of their office as priest, monk, or nun holier than those engaged in the mundane activities of this worldly existence. They had a "calling"—"*Beruf*" or "*vocatio*"—from God which gave them a steeper but shorter way to heaven.[33]

Luther overturned this theory in certain critical details even if he retained its structure. All people are called by God, he taught, and are equally worthy in his sight by virtue of their trust in the work of Christ. Works in none of these walks of life merited salvation; works in all of them were equally treasured if they proceeded from faith (Rom. 14:23). Luther also perceived that each individual has responsibilities in all three situations while treating the third in its two distinct aspects: family and economic life, along with their callings in the church and in society. In this way his application of the "three" walks of life foreshadowed societies shaped by the Industrial Revolution. In his Table of Christian Callings, which completes the Small Catechism, he labeled every one of these situations a "holy order and walk of life."[34]

It might be thought that Luther's "political" thought falls neatly into the medieval category of "*politia*," which his contemporaries defined chiefly in terms of governing officials. Luther, like many of his time, saw society in broader terms, with the institutional responsibilities of the church as well as the activities of family and economics playing significant roles in life together in the commonwealth, in the community that enveloped all of daily life for believers and those outside the Christian faith together.

Nonetheless, the realm of the secular governing authorities played a significant role in his thinking of that public life. Luther emphasized obedience to those authorities because of God's commands in Scripture, frequently citing Romans 13:1–4, Matthew 22:21, 1 Peter 3:13–14, and other passages. His reading of these passages took place in the context of widespread revolts of the peasantry in 1524–1526 and against the background of the nearly one hundred and fifty earlier regional revolts by peasants since 1500. These revolts had caused suffering for many, fellow-peasants of the rebels suffering most. Fear of disorder determined public thinking across the social spectrum.[35]

Nonetheless, Luther recognized the faults of rulers, especially courtiers, and he never shied away from public criticism of them and their masters. His public altercations with Duke George of Saxony and King Henry VIII of England are only the most famous of his open calls for repentance in the highest ranks of society.[36] His admonitions to princes touched on not only ecclesiastical matters, as was the case with these two. Commenting on the Joseph narratives in his Genesis lectures in the 1540s, he outlined how Joseph had modeled God-fearing, prudent, and just rule. Joseph's example provided Luther a framework for sharply criticizing princely tyranny and negligence in office. The ambition and arrogance of rulers enflame them against God and their people.[37] They do not listen to the proclamation of God's Word, and they fail to exercise their rule properly. They ignore crime.[38] They fail to support the church and its pastors.[39] They raise taxes unreasonably.[40] Worse than the princes are their counselors. Those who are efficient in the exercise of their duties too often administer their responsibilities to their own benefit rather than the benefit of their princes' subjects, for whose benefit they are supposed to be ruling. They resemble wolves, foxes, vultures, and other birds of prey in their striving for their own advantage.[41] Luther directly criticized Johann Friedrich's court for its wastefulness to his students in his exposition of the story of Joseph.[42]

Luther viewed the pastor's admonishing civic leaders to repent of unjust actions toward subjects as part of their calling as shepherds of their congregations. Commenting on Psalm 82 in 1530, Luther emphasized that preachers of God's Word are obligated to call governing officials to repentance. "It would lead to much more rebellion if preachers would not condemn the vices of their rulers," he wrote. Failing to hold rulers accountable makes the mob angry and discontented, and it also strengthens the tyrants' wickedness. The preachers become accomplices of such evil and bring guilt upon themselves when they avoid such a preaching of repentance to government officials. For "the office of the Word is not the office of a courtier or a hired hand. He is God's servant and agent."[43]

Not because they had read Luther carefully enough to encounter such passages, but because they imagined him as the defiant friar facing the might of pope and emperor, some eighteenth-century Enlightened figures and their successors heralded Luther as a forerunner of modern Western conceptions of individual freedom and democracy. They did not pay close enough attention to texts to note the texts that tell what formed his perception of the necessity and value of civil order and obedience to secular authority. Luther did not believe that a minimally educated peasantry had the ability to construct a government that could ensure the welfare of the entire population. Therefore, in commenting on four forms of government, monarchy, aristocracy, democracy, and oligarchy, he found aristocracy—leadership by those prepared and trained to act for the good of society—was best because it took care of the needs of the population with understanding, respect, and virtue.[44]

Nonetheless, Luther's insistence that every individual bears responsibility as a human creature of the God who assigns or calls everyone to positions that require exercising concern for others did influence some who retained something of the Germanic common law notions of community decision-making, especially in the Anglo-Saxon world. Building on structures that remained in that world after Roman law had diminished them on the continent, Luther's concept of the Christian's calling, as conveyed also through the thinking of John Calvin,[45] indirectly fostered attitudes necessary for functioning democratic societies.

Where does Luther's view of the public arena fit into twenty-first-century cultures, Western-style or the several alternatives in other parts of the world than Western Europe, North America, and Australia? Human beings experience life in the four walks of life or situations he describes. This perspective on life remains valid for human existence in our time. For all the alterations and transformations that have changed forms for organizing public life through the Cartesian, industrial, scientific, and political revolutions of the past four centuries, daily life takes place in these four "locations." Christ remains lord of all four and of the realm of our core identities as well. Human defiance of his lordship has not changed either, even if technologies have intensified the misery and disruption that one person or one societal force can visit upon others. Although Luther lived in a vastly different environment than any Lutherans do today, his insights into the nature of the God-designed shape of human life, with its callings to be responsible for the individual and common welfare of others, lay a foundation for godly embodiment of God's life-restoring action in Jesus Christ.

NOTES

1. Irene Dingel, ed., *Die Bekenntnisschriften der Evangelisch-Lutherischen Kirche* (Göttingen: Vandenhoeck & Ruprecht, 2014 [henceforth *BSELK*]), 984/985, 6–18; Robert Kolb and Timothy J. Wengert, eds., *The Book of Concord* (Minneapolis: Fortress, 2000 [henceforth *BC*]), 407, §150–151.

2. Lamin Sanneh, *Translating the Message: The Missionary Impact on Culture* (Maryknoll, NY: Orbis, 2009).

3. Andrew Pettegree, *Brand Luther: 1517, Printing, and the Making of the Reformation* (New York: Penguin, 2015).

4. Martin Luther, *D. Martin Luthers Werke* (Weimar: Böhlau, 1883–1993 [henceforth *WA*]), 6:465,25–467,26; Martin Luther, *Luther's Works* (Saint Louis/Philadelphia: Concordia/Fortress, 1958–1986 [henceforth *LW*]), 44:212–15; Timothy Wengert, ed., *The Annotated Luther, Volume 1: The Root of Reform* (Minneapolis: Fortress, 2015), 460–63.

5. Martin Luther, *BSELK* 932/933; *BC* 387; cf. his critiques of an array of sins in the economic realm, *BSELK* 1006–18; *BC* 416–20.

6. Martin Luther, *Large Catechism*, Sixth Commandment, *BSELK* 1000–07; *BC* 413–16.

7. Nathan Rein, *The Chancery of God: Protestant Print, Polemic and Propaganda against the Empire, Magdeburg 1546–1551* (Aldershot: Ashgate, 2008); David Whitford, *Tyranny and Resistance: The Magdeburg Confession and the Lutheran Tradition* (Saint Louis: Concordia, 2001); cf. its text in *Controversia et Confessio: Theologische Kontroversen 1548–1577/80; Kritische Auswahledition*, ed. Irene Dingel (Göttingen: Vandenhoeck & Ruprecht, 2008–2021), 2:2–69.

8. Robert M. Kingdon, "The First Expression of Theodore Beza's Political Ideas," *Archiv für Reformationsgeschichte* 46 (1955): 88–101; David M. Whitford, "John Adams, John Ponet and a Lutheran Influence on the American Revolution," *Lutheran Quarterly* 15 (2001): 143–58.

9. Heinz Schilling, *Konfessionskonflikt und Staatsbildung: Eine Fallstudie über das Verhältnis von religiösem und sozialem Wandel in der Frühneuzeit am Beispiel der Grafschaft Lippe* (Gütersloh: Mohn, 1981).

10. Johannes Ruschke, *Paul Gerhardt und der Berliner Kirchenstreit: Eine Untersuchung der konfessionellen Auseinandersetzungen über die kurfürstlich verordnete „mutua tolerantia"* (Tübingen: Mohr/Siebeck, 2012).

11. James Stayer, *Martin Luther, German Saviour: German Evangelical Theological Factions and the Interpretation of Luther, 1917–1933* (Montreal/Kingston: MicGill-Queen's University Press, 2000), 79–95.

12. Hermann Sasse, "Die 'Krisis der Religion' und die Verkündigung der Kirche," and "Die Kirche und die politischen Mächte der Zeit," in *Kirchliches Jahrbuch für die evangelischen Landeskirchen Deutschlands 1932* (Gütersloh: Bertelsmann, 1932), 129, 30–113. See Arthur Cochrane, *The Church's Confession under Hitler*, 2nd ed. (Pittsburgh: Pickwick, 1976), passim. Noteworthy is the statement by Cochrane, a devoted Barthian, "It is to the lasting credit of Prof. Hermann Sasse, of the University of Erlangen, that he was the first to declare that because of this one plank in the Party's program [the embrace of positive and negative racism] the Church could in no way approve of Nazism. It had to be categorically repudiated. The fact that Sasse eventually broke with the Confessing Church in the interest of a narrow Lutheran confessionalism, and thereby greatly weakened the church's opposition to National Socialism, must not obscure the prophetic role he played at the outset" (36). Cf. Lowell C. Green, *The Erlangen School of Theology: Its History, Teaching, and Practice* (Fort Wayne: Lutheran Legacy, 2010), 289–98.

13. Lowell C. Green, *Lutherans Against Hitler: The Untold Story* (Saint Louis: Concordia, 2007), 325–57; Green, *Erlangen School*, 231–309.

14. Sasse recalled Bonhoeffer's trajectory from liberalism to a commitment to making Luther speak to his own time, a trajectory somewhat similar to his own, in a seminar in which the author of this essay participated, Concordia Seminary, Saint Louis, winter quarter 1964–1965. Cf. Michael de Jonge, *Bonhoeffer on Resistance: The Word against the Wheel* (Oxford: Oxford University Press, 2018), Michael de Jonge, *Bonhoeffer's Theological Formation: Berlin, Barth, and Protestant Theology* (Oxford: Oxford University Press, 2012), 83–128; Michael de Jonge, *Bonhoeffer's Reception of Luther* (Oxford: Oxford University Press, 2017); and Harald Jung, "The 'Simul-Dimension' and Its Possible Contribution toward a View of Social Theory: The 'Freiburg Ordo-School' and Its Concept of Ethics and Political Economy in Christian Resistance during the NS-Regime," in *Simul: Inquiries into Luther's Experience of the Christian Life*, eds. Daniel Johansson, Torbjörn Johansson, and Robert Kolb (Göttingen: Vandenhoeck & Ruprecht, 2021), 165–76.

15. Uwe Siemon Netto, *The Fabricated Luther: Refuting Nazi Connections and Other Modern Myths*, 2nd ed. (Saint Louis: Concordia, 2007).

16. A. M. Allchin, *N.F.S. Grundtvig: An Introduction to His Life and Work* (Aarhus: Aarhus University Press, 1997).

17. Carl Alex Aurelius, "Luther in Sweden," *Word & World* 18 (1998): 299–306; Carl Alex Aurelius, *Luther I Sverige, Svenska Lutherbilde runder fyra sekler* (Skellefteå: Artos & Norma, 2015).

18. Arnd Heling, *Die Theologie Eivind Berggravs im norwegischen Kirchenkampf* (Neukirchen-Vluyn: Neukirchener Verlag, 1992).

19. Matthew Heise, "Heinrich Wilhelm Dieckhoff," in *Dictionary of Luther and the Lutheran Traditions*, ed. Timothy J. Wengert (Grand Rapids: Baker Academic, 2017), 193–94.

20. Ján Juríček, *Milan Rastislav Štefánik* (Elmhurst, NY: Našy Snahy, 1980).

21. Tibor Fabiny, *Bewährte Hoffnung: Die Evangelisch-Lutherische Kirche Ungarns in vier Jahrhunderten* (Erlangen: Martin-Luther-Verlag, 1984), 42–48.

22. László G. Terray, *He Could Not Do Otherwise: Bishop Lajos Ordass, 1901–1978*, trans. Eric W. Gritsch (Grand Rapids: Eerdmans, 1997); H. David Baer, *The Struggle of Hungarian Lutherans under Communism* (College Station: Texas A&M University Press, 2006).

23. Gurukul Lutheran Theological College in Chennai has actively engaged Christian theological address of the injustices visited on the disadvantaged in Indian society; cf. Samuel Meshack, ed., *Mission with the Marginalized: Life and Witness of Rev. Dr. Prasanna K. Samuel* (Tiruvalla: Christava Sahitya Samthi, 2007).

24. Samuel Yonas Deressa and Sarah Hinlickey Wilson, eds., *The Life, Works, and Witness of Tsehay Tolessa and Gudina Tumsa, the Ethiopian Bonhoeffer* (Minneapolis: Fortress, 2017).

25. Heinrich Bornkamm, *Luther and the Old Testament*, trans. Eric W. and Ruth C. Gritsch (Philadelphia: Fortress, 1969), 11–44.

26. Robert Kolb, *Bound Choice, Election, and Wittenberg Theological Method: From Martin Luther to the Formula of Concord* (Grand Rapids: Eerdmans, 2005), 11–66.

27. Robert Kolb, *Luther's Treatise on Christian Freedom and Its Legacy* (Lanham, MD: Fortress Academic/Lexington, 2019), 17–87.

28. Marius Timmann Mjaaland, *The Hidden God: Luther, Philosophy, and Political Theology* (Bloomington/Indianapolis: Indiana University Press, 2016).

29. H. Richard Niebuhr, *Christ and Culture* (New York: Harper, 1951); cf. Robert Kolb, "Niebuhr's 'Christ and Culture in Paradox' Revisited," *Lutheran Quarterly* 10 (1996): 259–79.

30. Bernd Wannenwetsch, "The Simultaneity of Two Citizenships: A Theological Reappraisal of Luther's Account of the 'Two Regiments' for our Times," in *Simul* 80 (2021): 177–91, https://doi.org/10.13109/9783666565526.177.

31. Martin Luther, *On Temporal Authority* (1523), *WA* 11:245–80; *LW* 45:81–129.

32. Brett Muhlhan, *Being Shaped by Freedom: An Examination of Luther's Development of Christian Liberty, 1520–1525* (Eugene: Pickwick, 2012), 194–233.

33. Cf. Jane C. Strohl, "The Framework for Christian Living: Luther on the Christian's Callings," in *The Oxford Handbook of Martin Luther's Theology*, eds. Robert Kolb, Irene Dingel, and Lubomir Batka (Oxford: Oxford University Press, 2014), 365–69; and Gustaf Wingren, *Luther on Vocation*, trans. Carl C. Rasmussen (Philadelphia: Muhlenberg, 1957).

34. *BSELK* 892–99; *BC* 365–67.

35. Robert Scribner, "The Reformation Movements in Germany," in *The New Cambridge Modern History, Volume II, The Reformation 1520–1559*, ed. Geoffrey Elton (Cambridge: Cambridge University Press, 1990), 86–87; Tom Scott, *Town, Country, and Regions in Reformation Germany* (Leiden: Brill, 2005), 3–188. Cf. Robert Kolb, "Luther on Peasants and Princes," *Lutheran Quarterly* 23 (2009): 125–46.

36. Scott H. Hendrix, *Martin Luther: Visionary Reformer* (New Haven: Yale University Press, 2015), 168–69, 182; Christoph Volkmar, *Catholic Reform in the Age of Luther: Duke George of Saxony and the Church, 1488–1525*, trans. Brian McNeil and Bill Ray (Leiden: Brill, 2017), 453–513.

37. *WA* 44:665, 3–7, 436, 27–31; *LW* 8:118, 7:185. Cf. Robert Kolb, "Die Josef-Geschichten als Fürstenspiegel in der Wittenberger Auslegungstradition: 'Ein verständiger und weiser Mann' (Genesis 42,33)," in *Christlicher Glaube und weltliche Herrschaft. Zum Gedenken an Günther Wartenberg*, eds. Michael Beyer, Jonas Flöter, and Markus Hein (Leipzig: Evangelische Verlagsanstalt, 2008), 41–55.

38. *WA* 44:667, 32–35; *LW* 8:121.

39. *WA* 44:670, 28–671, 18; *LW* 8:125.

40. *WA* 44:417, 33–418, 6; *LW* 7:159–60.

41. *WA* 44:416, 13–17; *LW* 158–59.

42. *WA* 44:451, 40–452, 5; *LW* 7:206.

43. *WA* 31, 1:196, 19–198, 18, esp. 197, 3–198, 2, and 198, 12–13; *LW* 13:47–51.

44. *WA TR*: 4:238, 12–15, 240, 39–45, §4342.

45. On Calvin's adaptation of Luther's thinking on natural law and the "two kingdoms," cf. David van Drunen, *Natural Law and the Two Kingdoms: A Study in the Development of Reformed Social Thought* (Grand Rapids: Eerdmans, 2010).

Chapter 8

Lesslie Newbigin's Idea of a Christian Society

George R. Hunsberger

I was there at Duke University in Durham, North Carolina, USA, in 1994 when Lesslie Newbigin said, midway through the last of his three Hickman Lectures at the Divinity School,

> I think, therefore, that we are at the point where we have to ask the question, "Can we think of a Christian society?" If a secular society is, finally, not viable and if we do not wish to accept the tremendous and increasingly powerful challenge of Islam, can we escape the necessity of asking ourselves, what would it be to work for a Christian society?[1]

Having thus arrived at the announced theme for that lecture ("What Kind of Society?"), and after first presenting in the first half an extensive portrait of the emergence of the post-Enlightenment culture that we in the West inhabit, he suggests that there are six things he wants to say about "a Christian society." First, noting our rightful sense of guilt about the sins of Christendom, he warns that "while we must be aware of the immense dangers involved in talking about a Christian society, we must not allow these, I think, to prevent us from seriously discussing them."[2]

The second of the "six things" was perhaps his most focused concern:

> I believe—and it may sound paradoxical to say so—that it is in fact only a Christian society which can, finally, safeguard religious freedom. Islam, as we know, cannot do so. . . . The secular society is only able to admit religious freedom provided the religions keep out of the public square; provided that religion is regarded as a private opinion which cannot control that which goes on in the public square, in the universities, and so forth.[3]

The remaining four "things" expressed what would be required of the church for such a Christian society to be imagined and sought: that it would actually believe its creed; that there would be a sufficient number of Christians sufficiently articulate in their faith to exercise real influence in the public square; that there would be agencies for equipping lay people to explore and explicate the implications of Christian faith for their respective areas of public life; that the church would be actively evangelizing.[4]

To those six things, he added a final note: "It would be clear that to speak of a Christian society is not to impose upon society by any kind of coercion a particular set of beliefs but to offer to society the one message that can liberate us from all the powers that so manifestly enslave us today."[5]

I was taken by surprise by this mid-lecture move to assert that Christians should not only "think about the possibility of a Christian society" but "work for" it. I simply couldn't imagine such a deliberate attempt, at least not within my American context (which also happened to be *where* he was commending it). Was this a distinctly British thing, both in the context for it and in the predispositions to imagine such an aim? It certainly had little resonance with my own context. And it seemed a bit at odds with all I had previously learned from Newbigin. I was tracking with him in the two prior lectures in the Hickman series ("The Gospel as True" and "Scripture as the Locus of Truth") and the first half of the third one, as he offered his extensive analysis of the post-Enlightenment modern Western culture and a critique of that culture in light of its contrast with a biblically narrated vision for human life and society. The forms of Christian public action and witness he espoused for the churches resonated as well. But none of that had prepared me for this notion of "a Christian society" as a motivating and guiding aim for the public witness of Christians in modern Western society(ies). If there had been hints of it before in what I had heard and read from Newbigin, it remained startling to hear him make this (to me) sudden turn, one which my American ears found puzzling, if not wrong-headed. Whatever was possible to imagine in the UK, here it seemed very odd to consider it.

Maybe it was simply my inner American that had to wonder: How would, how could, a society like that of the USA shift to a consciously Christian sense of its social order? Who would decide that? How would it come to be embraced? And what would it look like if it were? What would it solve? How long would it last? This would not be the last occasion on which I would hear from fellow Americans that at least for our situation this did not make sense.[6] Or was this, after all, simply a British thing?

Or were there failures on Newbigin's part to make the connections he was presuming, whether for Britain or other modern Western societies? Clarity of definition was in short supply, as was also a coherent theory of societal change, it seemed to me. Re-examining the Duke lecture and two other major statements of Newbigin's thesis may help resolve such questions and enable us to grasp what Newbigin means and discern the contributions and limitations of his thesis. But first it will be helpful to note earlier signs that the idea was becoming an important one for him.

ANTECEDENT HINTS AND CLUES

In Newbigin's published work in the decade previous to the Duke lecture, there does not appear the kind of full-blown vision for seeking "a Christian society" that was presented at Duke. There were, however, some occasional remarks that indicate the idea was beginning to brew. Ubiquitous in that body of work, certainly, is a critical assessment of the nature of the post-Enlightenment culture and social order and an accounting of the missionary engagement with it to which Christians are called. But even these hints of the Christian society theme are few and muted.

The project that occupied Newbigin for the last decade and a half of his life started in the simple way that characterized much of his life: he was placed on a committee that was planning (feebly, he thought) a conference for the notorious year 1984; he challenged the effort as failing to get at the real issues that were at stake for the public witness of the churches; and so they assigned him to write a pamphlet to spell out what he meant. Much of it was sketched out on his train ride home from the meeting, and within three weeks he had produced a draft for a few others to review. As the first step in a longer process of study that unfolded, his draft was published by the British Council of Churches (BCC) and then by the World Council of Churches (WCC) with the title *The Other Side of 1984: Questions for the Churches*. The heart of the challenge the book made was this: "What I am pleading for is a genuinely missionary encounter with post-Enlightenment culture. We have too long accepted the position of a privileged option for the private sector."[7] That challenge was the heart of an extended BCC programme which took for itself the name "The Gospel and Our Culture" (GOC). Its plan, under the leadership of Newbigin and a few colleagues, included establishing a series of study groups, hosting local conferences for discussion, publishing the fruit of the study group process, and hosting in 1992 a National Consultation.

The Missionary Encounter

As that initiative was getting underway, Newbigin had in hand an invitation from Princeton Theological Seminary to deliver its Benjamin B. Warfield Lectures in March of 1984. That gave Newbigin an ideal opportunity "to develop more fully the message of that [earlier] booklet."[8] While I had heard and read these lectures many times, the glimmers of a "Christian society" proposal had not struck me to be as full-blown and directly argued as the later Duke lecture was. Nonetheless, it is present in the conversation of chapter 6, "What Must We Be? The Call to the Church," which he earlier said was where he would take up the question of "how the Christian witness is to influence the public life in a post-Enlightenment society." (118). In the midst of his discussion in chapter 6, comments such as these indicate a sense of the questions emerging for him.

> The church as a truly universal supranational society is the bearer of the vision that alone can give to each nation a true unity of purpose. (123)

> The church today cannot without guilt absolve itself from the responsibility, where it sees the possibility, of seeking to shape the public life of nations and the global ordering of industry and commerce in the light of the Christian faith. (129)

> Can there be such a thing as a Christian state or a Christian society, and ought we to seek it? (131)

On the heels of that last direct question, Newbigin notes that in the 1930s there were people on the European continent (Jacques Maritain and Hermann Dooyeweerd) and in the British Isles (John Baillie and T.S. Eliot) who "were sketching their views of a Christian society. . . . They asked themselves whether it could not be possible for Christians . . . to give the rudderless democracies a sense of direction and purpose, yet without the repression and intolerance that marked the totalitarian movements" (131). He adds caution when he later asks, "If we are to think of a Christian society, can we ensure that the same sins are not repeated when and if Christians are in a position to impose their views on others? . . . If there were a Christian state, would it not necessarily be intolerant?" (137). But finally, he affirms, "We can envision a state (whether or not such a thing is a present political possibility) that acknowledges the Christian faith as true, but deliberately provides full security for those of other views" (140).

When, in the last part of chapter 6, Newbigin suggests he will offer a list of seven "essentials" or "requirements," it is important to note the way he introduces the list: "We must ask what the conditions are for the recovery by the church of its proper distinction from, and its proper responsibility for, this secular culture. . . . I want to close by listing seven essentials for the answering of this question" (134). In other words, the list is about the church's responsible action, not about what the society may become as a consequence. This is sustained in the way he begins each item. Numbers 1 and 7 simply state the required element. Four of the others (3–6) state what they are essential for. Each is identified as a requirement (or condition) "for a missionary encounter with our culture." The only one that differs is number 2, introduced in this way: "Second on my list of essentials for the quest of a Christian social order . . . " (137). Here something is bleeding through from the other current in Newbigin's thinking, the idea of a Christian society. And it is especially noteworthy that it happens with respect to the essential of "a Christian doctrine of freedom," which, as noted above, was second on his list in the Duke lecture and by my assessment "his most focused concern" in the Christian society thesis.

In summary, I suggest that the weight of his interest in chapter 6 of *Foolishness to the Greeks* is the church's "missionary encounter with our culture," but the undercurrents of his emerging interest in "the quest of a Christian social order" lie close at hand.

The Character of the Christian Community

Another lectureship afforded Newbigin the opportunity to further expand his contribution to the Gospel and Our Culture agenda. He spent three months in the autumn of 1988 as the Alexander Robertson Lecturer teaching in the Divinity Faculty at Glasgow University. A regular routine of hour-long lectures, followed by small group discussions with interested students, provided the material for another published volume, **The Gospel in a Pluralist Society**.[9]

The phrase "Christian society" occurs a couple of times in the book as a description of the nature of Western civilization in prior periods or in reference to colonial presence in the South Pacific.[10] More pertinent to this current study are specific uses of the phrase in the chapter entitled "The Myth of the Secular Society." In this chapter Newbigin depicts and critiques the idea of a secular society as it was presented in an influential book by Denys L. Munby by that same title.[11] The phrase "Christian society" enters the discussion through the back door since Munby's 1963 book was "a deliberate rebuttal of the book by T. S. Eliot written twenty-three years earlier, *The Idea of a Christian Society*."[12] Newbigin comments about Eliot's work, as he had done in *Foolishness to the Greeks*, that:

> It was the rise of the totalitarian ideologies of the 1930s which prompted T. S. Eliot and others to ask about the possibility of a society which would not be neutral but would be a Christian society. That question has not been seriously followed up. We have settled for what seemed the easier option—a secular society within which Christianity would be a permitted option.[13]

Newbigin's critique of Munby's proposals is not simply to use him as a whipping boy or as a scapegoat. Newbigin had found early on that Munby's treatment helped him to understand secularization, particularly as it yields a particular form of society, and to discern its advantages as well as its detriments. Many years before *The Gospel in a Pluralist Society* was written, Newbigin had made a similar, and perhaps more thorough, critique of Munby.[14] In that earlier context, there is one interesting and important comment he made that relates to the concern of this present study:

> Can a truly secular economic order survive the disappearance of a religious motivation? In putting these questions, let me repeat, I am not trying to prepare the way for a reassertion of the idea of a Christian society. I do not think that Christians should be trying either to preserve or to restore the 'Christendom' situation.[15]

By 1989 he is not so eager to make such a disclaimer. In fact, in the following chapter in *The Gospel in a Pluralist Society*, on "The Congregation as the Hermeneutic of the Gospel," there are clues that while he is not yet fully following Eliot's lead, aspects of such an argument are emerging for him. He asks, "What could it mean for the Church to make once again the claim which it made in its earliest centuries, the claim to provide the public truth by which society can be given coherence and direction?"[16] For the moment, however, his primary concern was to understand the nature and importance of the local congregation as it seeks "a Christian impact on public life." The major thesis of the chapter starts with a question:

> How is it possible that the gospel should be credible, that people should come to believe that the power which has the last word in human affairs is represented by a man hanging on a cross? I am suggesting that the only answer, the only hermeneutic of the gospel, is a congregation of men and women who believe it and live by it.[17]

What follows is another list, similar to and yet distinct from the list with which *Foolishness to the Greeks* ends. He presents what he calls "six characteristics" of such a congregation as he has called a "hermeneutic of the Gospel." Noteworthy is that each begins "a community of" (or a community "that" or "where").[18]

The Gospel as Public Truth

What continued to focus Newbigin's thought during the late 1980s and into the 1990s was his sense that the gospel is true and that it is decidedly public truth. And there were important antecedents in his thought about that. Three chapters in *The Gospel in a Pluralist Society* illustrate that forcefully: ch 6, "Revelation in History"; ch 8, "The Bible as Universal History"; and ch 9, "Christ, the Clue to History." In the second of these (ch. 8), he begins with the complaint he had often heard from a "learned Hindu friend":

> As I read the Bible I find in it a quite unique interpretation of universal history and, therefore, a unique understanding of the human person as a responsible actor in history. You Christian missionaries have talked of the Bible as [if] it were simply another book of religion. We have plenty of these already in India and we do not need another to add to our supply.[19]

Newbigin concurs. And his accents on "the Gospel as public truth" (and later on "a Christian society") must be read in terms of such a perspective.

Alongside numerous speeches and published articles on this theme, there was a particular set of lectures that gave Newbigin an opportunity to play out his argument in a more extended way. I refer to the Osterhaven Lectures given in the fall of 1990 at Western Theological Seminary in Holland, Michigan. These were published in 1991 as **Truth to Tell: The Gospel as Public Truth**.[20] The titles of each lecture/chapter show the story he is telling: "Believing and Knowing the Truth," an epistemology for Christian belief; "Affirming the Truth in the Church," an ecclesiology for a church that believes; and "Speaking the Truth to Caesar," a public missiology for the church in the public square. The territory he engages is certainly background for the Christian society thesis he will propose later, but that phrase is nowhere used in the lectures. The only close cousins to it are to be found in his efforts to respond to the questions, "What might be involved in the attempt to prove the validity and power of the Christian faith in the public life of a nation?" and "Is it possible to say anything that could help the Church . . . to bear genuine gospel witness in face of the great public issues of society?"[21] To the latter he responds in part by saying, "The most important contribution which the Church can make to a new social order is to be itself a new social order."[22] In his exposition of that assertion on the pages that follow, there is important grounding for his later work.

As the GOC programme approached its culminating event, the National Consultation planned for 1992 at the Hayes Conference Centre in Swanwick, UK, it was determined that its organizing theme would be "The Gospel as Public Truth." In its announcement of the event, the aim of the Consultation was identified to be "to test the thesis that the Christian Gospel can provide a positive critique of contemporary Western culture, the basis of unity and coherence, and the possibility of a hopeful future for the public life of our society."[23] The idea that the Christian Gospel can or could provide "the basis of unity and coherence for the society" caught my eye from the beginning. In reactions much like those I would have later in response to the Duke lecture, I found it "hard to imagine such as the form of any serious proposal in the American setting." In my report on the Swanwick Consultation, which I had attended, I went on to add,

> [T]he American [GOC] movement . . . does not posture itself around the thesis that the Christian faith ought to provide "the basis of unity and coherence" for the society. That lingering hope for a restored Christendom arrangement does not strike us as either possible or preferable. We are more oriented toward learning new patterns for our "after Christendom" life in a pluralist society.[24]

In the event of the consultation itself, it is fair to say that the accent guiding the discussions was the affirmation that the gospel is public truth. The "basis of unity and coherence" notion had hardly any play. Even Newbigin's opening address did not give it any notice, nor did it raise the prospect of thinking about "a Christian society."[25] But its presence in the thesis to be tested signaled a shift yet to come in Newbigin's thinking.

DEVELOPMENT OF THE "CHRISTIAN SOCIETY" THEME

Shortly after the Duke lecture, Newbigin published a brief column in *Leading Light*, calling for this theme to be the agenda for the Gospel and Our Culture program he led in the UK going forward.[26] That was followed by a lecture in December 1995 at King's College, London, entitled "Can a Modern Society Be Christian?"[27] It was similar in style and argument to the Duke lecture but uniquely expressed. Newbigin's focus on this issue culminated in a book written in collaboration with two friends who shared his basic vision and brought special expertise to the topic. One was Lamin Sanneh, a scholar of Islam and World Christianity, and the other was Jenny Taylor, a journalist intimately acquainted with Muslim concerns in Britain. The culminating chapter, written by Newbigin, was entitled "Activating the Christian Vision."[28] This final articulation of the thesis, set alongside the Duke and King's lectures, will form the basis for the reflections that follow.

An important historical note should be made here. An international consortium of a couple dozen Neo-Calvinist scholars invited Newbigin to dialogue with them on the Gospel and Our Culture agenda he had been pursuing. They selected two of his recent papers—the not-yet-published manuscripts of the Duke and King's lectures (noted above)—to be read in advance in order to focus the conversation. Members of the group prepared responses for discussion at the colloquium, which was held in June 1996 at Leeds in the UK.

Following the colloquium, Newbigin prepared a fairly lengthy response to the conversations.[29] Among his comments were a couple that are pertinent to the present study. He reports that "I have now come to the conclusion that [using the phrase 'a Christian society'] was a mistake and that I must avoid completely the use of this phrase." His reasons were two-fold: "It is almost inevitable that this phrase evokes in the minds of the hearers the concept of Christendom in its medieval sense" and these discussions "have convinced me this phrase implies or suggests a stable equilibrium within a society, which is in fact impossible." These comments are obviously important for assessing the final essay of the three we are engaging here.[30]

WHAT IS A "CHRISTIAN SOCIETY"?

What would such a society be like? Is Newbigin talking about an idea, a vision, a hope, an aim? Where do we find hints and clues?

The three essays all develop a sense of the shaping of the post-Enlightenment, modern "secular society" that is dominant at the present time. All raise the question of "a Christian society," all using that phrase (with varying frequency). And all provide a list of . . . well, that's where there is ambiguity within each and amongst them. What kinds of items are these that appear in his several lists? Are they priorities, features, prerequisites, tasks?

We begin by looking at the language used by each essay to set up the topic of "a Christian society" and frame the list of proposed features that follows. And we will watch what language is used in reference to the items themselves that are on the lists, allowing us to gain clarity about Newbigin's vision of "a Christian society."

THE DUKE LECTURE[31]

"Can we think about the possibility of a Christian society? What would that imply?" (55). "Can we escape the necessity of asking ourselves, what would it be to work for a Christian society?" (57). "Imply" and "work for" are the key words here. Among the six listed "things" he wishes to say about it, four refer to something about the presence and character of the church. The church is implicated, but in what way? In a couple of cases, the word "required" is used. Number 3 says that "a Christian society would require a church which actually believes its creed" (58). Number 6 says a Christian society "will require a church which is evangelizing" (60). There is ambiguity in such "require" language. Does it mean these are things required as pre-conditions in order for a Christian society to come about? Or are these beliefs and practices required to be a part of any society that is a Christian one? Are they inherent in what such a society would be? Which are they: features that create (work for) a Christian society or features that define (in part) what it is? In this lecture it seems the tilt is in the latter direction, given the way numbers 4 and 5 on the list are expressed: "A Christian society would be one where there were a sufficient number of Christians sufficiently articulate in their faith to exercise a real influence in the public square" (59) and "A Christian society would be one where there were agencies which made it possible for Christian lay men and women in all the different sectors of public life . . . to explore and explicate the implications of the Christian faith for that particular area of public life" (60). In his concluding comments, he summarizes, "Can we not look for a Christian society which would have at least those characteristics that I have tried to describe?" (61). His list, in other words, attempts to define what he thinks a Christian society would be like.

THE KING'S LECTURE

The word "required" occurs here as it did in the Duke lecture, but it has in a sense been turned on its head. At Duke it was about what a Christian society would require to be true of the church. Here the church is the active agency of whom something is being required. The list comes to many of the same features but from a different angle. "What would be required of a church which acknowledged the obligation to seek here in Britain for a Christian society?" (105). Because a Christian society would be one "whose public life is shaped by the Christian beliefs about the human person and human society" (105), the character of its life is required to nourish such a society.

The first three items echo the Duke lecture, using for each one the language of requisite, or requirement. It is required of the church "that we recover the belief that the gospel is true . . . that it is the public truth" (105–6), "that the Church becomes an evangelising community" (106), and that "it will be required of men and women in all areas of secular responsibility that they are theologically equipped to discern the bearing of the Gospel upon the matters with which they have to deal in their secular work" (106–7). The fourth and fifth items on this list are more general. One (number 4) is about what a Christian society would be, and here Newbigin moves closer to defining his terms.

> Since a Christian society, as I am trying to imagine it, would be a society where those in authority both affirm explicitly their allegiance to the Christian faith as their guiding light in all the decisions they have to make, and affirm the right of others to hold and express different beliefs, such a society would have to be one

in which opportunities for discussing the business of the public square would have to be maximised. (107)

The other (number 5) makes specific that "such a vision for society implies a Christian community equipped for vigorous controversy" (107).

Newbigin finishes this section of the lecture where it began: "What I have tried to suggest . . . is a call to the churches of this country [Britain] to the possibility of a new vision for our nation and to have the courage to affirm it in the public square for all to hear and see" (108).

THE "ACTIVATING THE CHRISTIAN VISION" CHAPTER

This rendering of Newbigin's "Christian society" agenda is forthrightly particular to Britain. For the British society, as for modern Western societies generally, he concludes, "We must look afresh at the idea of a Christian society." When he asserts that, Newbigin immediately knows that using the phrase precipitates the need to distance the notion from Christendom connotations. After struggling briefly to argue that such an idea is not a return to the territorial principle (admitting that its demise is irreversible), he pivots to the need "to address Christians about their understanding of the relation of the gospel to the public square" (150). Thus, the topic is reset. And with only a couple of exceptions, the language of "Christian society" tends to be avoided in the chapter and instead gives way to the language of "a Christian vision for society."[32] He is again directly addressing the church as he had done in the King's lecture. But now it is not about what is required of it but rather about the church's consequential action that effectuates the Christian view for society, as the chapter's title also suggests. It is about "speak[ing] realistically of a Christian vision for society" (154), about that vision becoming "effective in practice" (155), and about Christians exerting "a preponderant influence on public life" (153).

"The first step," he says, "in approaching the idea of a Christian society is a negative one. We have to question the assumption that a secular state is neutral." This is a summary of all he has argued in the lengthy analysis portion of the chapter (as was also the case in the Duke and King's lectures). This "negative" step quickly yields to a positive one. He observes that "society is being continually shaped by a set of beliefs which have a privileged position as against other beliefs." He posits that "a Christian society, if such were possible, would be one in which the Christian faith has this privileged position" (152–53). This is no longer singularly about a basis for freedom, which much of his argumentation asserts. Rather, it is about a sweeping displacement of post-Enlightenment secular foundations. This accent on a "privileged position" lingers through the chapter and comes back full-throated in the brief "Conclusion" chapter that follows it (162–65). There Newbigin presents an extended argument that "there is no need for us to be timid or embarrassed about seeking a privileged position for the Christian faith in the public life of the nation" (163). Hard as he labors to make that case, I find it harder still to square it with previous affirmations such as this one: "It is this unique event of cross and resurrection that must govern Christian action in the public realm" (148). Or again, in an earlier published statement, Christian mission "cannot mean an attempt to restore the hegemony of the church over public life."[33] As I recall it, the cross is about relinquishing privilege, not seeking it.

SUMMARY REFLECTIONS ON THE THREE TEXTS

Several summary comments would be in order.

First, while there are some hints and clues throughout these texts about what Newbigin thinks "a Christian society" actually is, and while at several points he states a few of its features in a more direct way, there is insufficient clarity about what he understands a Christian society to be. He obviously believes it would mean something has changed the current secular order into something more compatible with the gospel's logic and order. He is very clear about a change in the basis for religious freedom, liberating religiously held "truths" from their consignment to the realm of "private opinion" and providing safeguards for everyone's right of dissent. He hints that there is more that comes with that: restoring the question of purpose, for the individual person and for human society; conceiving of human freedom as both freedom *from* restriction and freedom *for* responsibility; and properly balancing the right of an individual with that of the common good. But it is not clear in the end what exactly would need to be true of a society for it to be called Christian. How much of the Christian narrative must be embraced? Can a few aspects of its logic be brought on board, cut loose from other essential dimensions of it? Newbigin has not presented a coherent answer to such questions. Further, Newbigin's reflections do not account for the difference between a society and a state. His proposals seem to vacillate between what we might take to be referring to one or the other.

Second, each of the essays works hard to be very particular about Christian beliefs and practices that have something to do with the possibility and/or emergence of a Christian society. Newbigin implies throughout that these are things that are necessary in order to bring about a shift from the present social order to a new one called "Christian." But he doesn't trace the way this causation works or how, exactly, it will bring to fruition the society he envisions. He doesn't connect the dots. Nor does he put forward any clear theory of societal change that would suggest these activities hold promise toward that end. The change he envisions is enormous and would amount to a considerable cultural re-working and re-formulation! The analogy of the historical formation of the present post-Enlightenment secular society would suggest that what he envisions would require a comparably lengthy period of time and would depend on numerous historical events or social moods that lie outside the range of conscious action by a company of committed agents of change. James Davison Hunter has warned of too facile an intention "to change the world" or attempt to achieve pervasive culture change.[34] Lacking a credible theory of cultural and societal change, Newbigin's use of the idea of a Christian society as a motivation and aim for Christian public witness and mission is more likely to frustrate than enliven the churches.

This is not an argument for inaction or withdrawal from public life. The agenda Newbigin portrays has its own rationale and force, quite apart from its attachment to the goal of fostering or creating a Christian society. On other grounds his agenda is fully warranted and necessary for the church's mission of bearing faithful witness to the reign of God in shared life, in deeds of mercy, and in words of grace.[35] Newbigin has called for these things in a myriad of ways throughout his lifetime and has sharpened their focus in more recent times around the challenge of a missionary encounter with our modern Western culture. They stand on their own, quite apart from the hope that they may play some role in bringing about "a Christian society."

Third, each of the three essays we have explored includes a list of things that are viewed as needed or required for a Christian society to emerge and sustain itself. Aside from their potential bearing on a Christian society agenda, they offer important guidance for the church's public witness generally.

There is a shared sense on the lists that a Christian society would require "a sufficient number of Christians sufficiently articulate in their faith."[36] *Sufficient* is not defined, other than to say enough to exercise real influence in public life. But, as Newbigin and others concur about their British context, Christian churches and their membership appear to be in decline. A great turnaround would thus be necessary. While it is not clearly said, it is perhaps assumed that the other elements of Christian action listed will turn the numbers around to produce a sufficient number or proportion of the population. And is it further presumed that such new growth in the Christian community will be of the "sufficiently articulate" sort? There are long games of catechesis and disciple formation implicated to undergird such a hope.

There are a couple of items that are recurrent on the lists and would appear to be interrelated. One is that the Church would believe its creed, which is to say that it will believe that the gospel is true and is public truth. The other is that the Church becomes an evangelizing community. Holding and commending a gospel that is true should ride together. But in both cases, a steep growth curve is implicated for the churches.

Building on these, there is another cluster of notions bound together. "It will be required of men and women in all areas of secular responsibility that they are theologically equipped to discern the bearing of the gospel upon the matters with which they have to deal in their secular work."[37] This is what Newbigin says he has "elsewhere called the de-clericalization of theology."[38] The so-called laity *are* the church, present in the warp and woof of daily public life, in their arenas of work, of commerce, of home, and of civil discourse. This is what Newbigin describes as "the ordinary life of the congregation." To support this public vocation of the laity, Newbigin calls for "agencies" which would make it "possible for Christian lay men and women in all the different sectors of public life . . . to explore and explicate the implications of the Christian faith for that particular sector of public life."[39] Taking people's daily work life seriously is long overdue. This is a desperately needed growth area for the churches.

I conclude this section by noting something Newbigin did not include in these three lists which I believe is of primary importance, given the precipitating concern of his Christian society project. He believed that "it is in fact only a Christian society which can, finally, safeguard religious freedom."[40] I take my cue for an addition to Newbigin's lists from his oft-quoted statement in *Truth to Tell*: "The most important contribution the Church can make to a new social order is to be itself a new social order."[41] So, if the secular society has shown itself ineffective to guard true freedom, and Islam hasn't the foundations to provide it, then one would want to say, as a requisite, "The church needs to embody in its own life the kind of true freedom, and tolerance of dissent, that it seeks to offer the society."

A SINGULAR CHRISTIANITY?

Whatever Newbigin confessed to his friends at the Leeds Colloquium that he had learned from them about implying or suggesting a stable equilibrium within a society, he should have applied in his references to the Church, churches, Christians, the Christian view of society, or Christianity itself. He speaks throughout as though the Church is homogenous, as though the churches comprise a unified whole, as though Christians live and move as a singular force. The fact that none of these things are demonstrably true, whether in Britain or in other Western societies, mitigates any possible connection between what he calls Christians to do and the bearing that may have on a Christian society. Surely the question has to arise, which churches? Which Christians? Which Christian vision for society? The outlined task is daunting enough without having to resolve the differences that hinder a concerted approach. This is a recognition not only of the diversity of denominational and traditional heritage but of vast differences of imagination and identity among Christians.

Even in the details of Newbigin's call to the church, large ideological divides open wide. I offer two examples.

When Newbigin indicates that a Christian society "would require a church which actually believes its creed," he means one that "has the courage to believe in its own gospel and to proclaim that gospel as truth."[42] The gospel of which he speaks is from the beginning a public announcement. It is public truth, proclaiming that "the power which has the last word in human affairs is represented by a man hanging on a cross."[43] This qualifier distinguishes the gospel as Newbigin saw it from the gospel of personal salvation that many Christian communities see it to be. The same difference plays out with respect to the meaning and method of evangelism as well. On the ground all of this is contested territory.

One item on the "Activating" chapter's list is about how the church sees its mission. He says that "part of our Christian obedience is the acceptance of our share of responsibility for the life of our city, our nation, the world."[44] Newbigin rightly connects that to eschatology, but of a particular sort. He roots this responsibility for public life in a wholistic biblical eschatology oriented to "the consummation of God's universal purpose for his whole creation" over against "a privatized eschatology which thinks only of the destiny of the individual soul."[45] The latter yields a different sense of mission. Contested eschatologies breed contested missiologies.

A public sense of the "evangel" and the "eschaton" are two of Newbigin's most important theological contributions. They form the bedrock of his encouragements to engage the public square. But the continuing strength of privatized versions of gospel and destiny cautions against presuming a united front. The reality of a multitude of co-existing Christianities, as it were, is itself a fruit of the post-Enlightenment secular world. This thickens the challenge of the path ahead for fellow Christ-learners.

A CONCLUDING PROSPECTUS

If Newbigin's account of "the idea of a Christian society" is in the end unclear, and if his sense that it provides a proper motivation and aim for the church's action is not fully convincing, we may yet find that the force of Newbigin's proposals, combined with the force of their limitations, frame important territory for public missiology and public theology to engage. Both the prophet Jeremiah's "seek the welfare of the city where I have sent you into exile" (Jer. 29:7) and Jesus's "strive first for the kingdom of God and his righteousness" (Matt. 6:33) disallow turning blindly or blandly away from the questions raised by "the idea of a Christian society."

Newbigin's example more than demonstrates that the project needs the kind of rigorous missiology, ecclesiology, and eschatology he lends it. His claims about "the gospel as public truth" and the congregation as the "hermeneutic of the gospel" are good places to start. His earlier reluctance and later embrace of the challenge in T. S. Eliot's phrase "the idea of a Christian society" may provide a clue about where such a project must begin. What circumstances in the social fabric of the 1930s in Britain and western Europe moved Eliot and others to move toward such an idea?[46] And how do those compare with the circumstances in Britain which moved Newbigin to take it up in the 1990s? Likewise, what circumstances in the present time may be reigniting a return to serious consideration of this theme, a return evidenced, for example, by the recent book by R. R. Reno, *Resurrecting the Idea of a Christian Society* (2016)?[47]

NOTES

1. Lesslie Newbigin, "What Kind of Society?," *Trinity Journal for Theology and Ministry* IV, no. 2 (Fall 2010): 56–57; cf. 55. As noted by the editor of the *Journal*, this article was transcribed from the audio recording of Newbigin's 1994 lecture by Martha Chambers (vol. IV, no. 2, p. 7). Already in 1994 Newbigin's normal practice of lecturing from a fully typed manuscript had become modified due to his increasing blindness in the 1990s. In this case he lectured using only a note card with a few verbal cues for the points he intended to make.

2. Newbigin, "What Kind of Society?," 57.

3. Newbigin, "What Kind of Society?," 57.

4. Newbigin, "What Kind of Society?," 58–61.

5. Newbigin, "What Kind of Society?," 61.

6. I experienced such conversations in the context of the Duke lectures and again when, on his last visit to the USA in June 1997, he gave a lecture at the Beeson Divinity School, Samford University in Birmingham, Alabama. The lecture was entitled "The Gospel in a Pluralist Society," and in it he reiterated his thesis about a Christian society, asking, "Is it not what we ought to be envisioning?" This lecture is available from Beeson in audio and video recordings.

7. Lesslie Newbigin, *The Other Side of 1984: Questions for the Churches* (Geneva: WCC Publications, 1983), 31–32. For Newbigin's description of the origins of this "pamphlet" and the programme that followed, see Lesslie Newbigin, *Unfinished Agenda: An Updated Autobiography* (London: SPCK Publishing, 1993), 251–54.

8. As noted by Newbigin in the published version of the lectures; see Lesslie Newbigin, *Foolishness to the Greeks: The Gospel and Western Culture* (Grand Rapids:

Wm. B. Eerdmans Pub. Co., 1986), iv. To unclutter the footnote apparatus, material drawn from this book in this and succeeding paragraphs will be cited by page number in parentheses within the body of the text.

9. Lesslie Newbigin, *The Gospel in a Pluralist Society* (Grand Rapids: Wm. B. Eerdmans Pub. Co., 1989).

10. Newbigin, *Gospel*, 190, 222.

11. Denys L. Munby, *The Idea of a Secular Society, and Its Significance for Christians* (London: Oxford University Press, 1963). Newbigin had engaged Munby's argument in a similar, and in some ways more extensive, way in Newbigin's much earlier book, *Honest Religion for Secular Man* (Philadelphia: Westminster Press, 1966), 126–37.

12. Newbigin, *Gospel*, 216; see also T. S. Eliot, *The Idea of a Christian Society*, First American Edition (New York: Harcourt, Brace and Company, 1940).

13. Newbigin, *Gospel*, 221.

14. Newbigin, *Honest Religion*, 126–37.

15. Newbigin, *Honest Religion*, 134.

16. Newbigin, *Gospel*, 223.

17. Newbigin, *Gospel*, 227.

18. Newbigin, *Gospel*, 227–33.

19. Newbigin, *Gospel*, 89.

20. Lesslie Newbigin, *Truth to Tell: The Gospel as Public Truth* (Grand Rapids: Wm. B. Eerdmans Pub. Co., 1991).

21. Newbigin, *Truth to Tell*, 66–67.

22. Newbigin, *Truth to Tell*, 85.

23. As reported in *The Gospel and Our Culture* newsletter (NA) 4, no. 1 (January 1992): 5.

24. George Hunsberger, "British and American Comparisons," *The Gospel and Our Culture* newsletter (NA) 4, no. 3 (December 1992): 2–3.

25. Lesslie Newbigin, "The Gospel as Public Truth: Swanwick Opening Statement," https://newbiginresources.org/1992-the-gospel-as-public-truth-swanwick-opening-statement/ (accessed October 1, 2021).

26. Lesslie Newbigin, "Leading Off: A Christian Society?" *Leading Light* 2, no. 1 (1995): 4, 18.

27. Lesslie Newbigin, "Can a Modern Society Be Christian?," in *Christian Witness in Society: A Tribute to M. M. Thomas*, ed. K. C. Abraham (Bangalore: Board of Theological Education—Senate of Serampore College, 1998), 95–108.

28. Lesslie Newbigin, "Activating the Christian Vision," in *Faith and Power: Christianity and Islam in 'Secular' Britain*, Lesslie Newbigin, Lamin Sanneh, and Jenny Taylor (London: SPCK, 1998), 144–61.

29. Lesslie Newbigin, "On the Gospel as Public Truth: Response to the Colloquium" (unpublished manuscript), https://newbiginresources.org/?s=response+to+the+colloquium.

30. Determining whether or not Newbigin stuck with his declared "avoidance" of the phrase has to keep in mind the chronology of the first presentation/transcription of each one, not their formal print publication. Neither of the first two, the lectures, were

published until well after their presentation—the Duke lecture, sixteen years later; the King's lecture, three years later.

31. Here and in the two sections that follow, page numbers for the essay being described are indicated within the text instead of unnecessarily piling up footnotes.

32. For comparison purposes the phrase "a Christian society" is used nineteen times in the Duke lecture, eight times in the King's College lecture, and only four times in the "Activating" chapter. For the new language, see Newbigin, "Activating the Christian Vision," 154, 157. In the latter instance, it can be documented that a conscious shift of language took place between a pre-publication draft and the published text. Cf. 157 with a quotation from the earlier draft in Lamin Sanneh, "The Church and its Missionary Vocation: The Islamic Frontline in a Post-Christian West," in *Mission in the Twenty-first Century*, ed. Andrew Walls and Cathy Ross (Maryknoll, NY: Orbis Books, 2008), 136.

33. Lesslie Newbigin, "Mission in a Pluralist Society," in *A Word in Season*, ed. Eleanor Jackson (Grand Rapids: Wm. B. Eerdmans Publishing Co., 1994), 172.

34. James Davison Hunter, *To Change the World: The Irony, Tragedy, and Possibility of Christianity in the Late Modern World* (New York: Oxford University Press, 2010).

35. See, for example, Lesslie Newbigin, "Evangelism in the Context of Secularization," in *A Word in Season*, ed. Eleanor Jackson (Grand Rapids: Wm. B. Eerdmans Publishing Co., 1994), 152–55.

36. Newbigin, "What Kind of Society?," 59.

37. Newbigin, "Can a Modern Society be Christian?," 106–7.

38. Cf. Newbigin, *Foolishness*, 141–44.

39. Newbigin, "What Kind of Society?," 60.

40. Newbigin, "What Kind of Society?," 57.

41. Newbigin, *Truth to Tell*, 85. Cf. Newbigin, *Foolishness*, 137–41.

42. Newbigin, "What Kind of Society?," 58–59.

43. Newbigin, *Gospel*, 227.

44. Newbigin, "Activating the Christian Vision," 153.

45. Newbigin, 153–54. Cf. Newbigin, *Foolishness*, 134–37.

46. Among these others, Newbigin has noted, were Jacques Maritain, Hermann Dooyeweerd, and John Baillie; see Newbigin, *Foolishness*, 131. Curiously, Newbigin nowhere mentions the similar effort of his own mentor, J. H. Oldham, in J. H. Oldham, *The Resurrection of Christendom* (London: The Sheldon Press, 1940).

47. R. R. Reno, *Resurrecting the Idea of a Christian Society* (Washington, DC: Regnery Faith, 2016).

Chapter 9

Love in Luther

Beyond Thesis 28

John R. Stumme

Gary Simpson calls love "the only virtue of Christian life together."[1] He refers to Paul, Augustine, and Martin Luther to support his claim, and one could add Jesus. Love is the preeminent and comprehensive virtue and norm that gives unity to the Christian moral life. The church throughout the globe, as it has done throughout its history, carries on an ongoing conversation about the meaning of love. Luther's writings on love in the Christian life continue to be a vital part of this conversation.[2]

Simpson describes a crucial feature of Luther's understanding of Christian love: "Love issues from faith in Christ, which is created by the Spirit."[3] Love does not stand alone since faith precedes love. Christian love follows from and depends on faith in the gospel promise. We are not justified by love. We are justified before God by faith in Jesus Christ alone without the works of the law. Luther's most important contribution to the church's conversation on love—in the sixteenth century and today—is his insistence on the priority of faith in our relation to God.

Christian ethics, affirming this priority, has the task to reflect normatively on the meaning of human love in light of faith in God's self-giving love for us, as summarized, for example, in the church's creeds. Among various possibilities I approach "Love in Luther" from this Christian ethics perspective. My focus is on his concept of love in a single statement.

"Thesis 28" in the title refers to the last thesis of Luther's *Heidelberg Disputation* (1518). In this thesis Luther asserts what divine love and human love are. Going "beyond" thesis 28 indicates that I do not consider that it is a good stopping place for Christian ethics. My critical appraisal revolves around what I find missing in the thesis, namely, the doctrine of creation. The phrase is also meant to convey my observation that Luther himself in other writings on love goes beyond thesis 28 and points toward a different concept of love. Throughout I make references to texts where Luther speaks of love in ways that do not fit into the conceptual strictures imposed by thesis 28. I am not persuaded by interpretations that assume Luther's writings on love are basically of one piece, perhaps with different emphasis in places but presenting a coherent whole.

Thesis 28 deserves careful attention because during the last hundred years or so it has been a decisive text in interpreting love in Luther and in Christian ethics. This is the case even though the *Heidelberg Disputation* may properly be considered a "pre-Reformation" text.[4] Its contemporary importance is largely due to Andres Nygren's impressive book *Agape and Eros*.[5] Since its publication in English in the 1930s, his book has been the most important text on love in Luther and for many its accepted interpretation.

Luther's significance for Nygren is that he recaptured the New Testament meaning of agape and challenged the church's unwarranted mixture of Greek notions of eros with agape. Nygren claims that for Luther there are two opposed kinds of love: God's self-giving, creative agape and humans' acquisitive, self-seeking eros. God's agape descends to sinners in contrast to eros that strives to ascend to the highest good. Christians recognize eros as sinful and in faith become instruments of God's self-giving love.

Nygren finds thesis 28 to be a validating source for his dualistic concept of love. He quotes it in Latin at the beginning of the second part of his book, and he later spells out its significance: although the thesis doesn't use the words, Nygren writes, "Yet the passage may be said to contain one of the clearest delimitations of Eros and Agape, and the most apt description of the deepest characteristic of each."[6] For Nygren and many others, this thesis defines what Luther means by love. Praise and criticism of Nygren often apply also to thesis 28.

THESIS 28: TWO KINDS OF LOVE

Thesis 28 states, "God's love does not find, but creates, that which is pleasing to it. Human love comes into being through that which is pleasing to it."[7]

Luther speaks in categorical terms: there are two loves, divine love and human love. There is one kind of divine love, and there is only one kind of human love. In both kinds love describes the relationship of a subject with an object, of a lover with what is loved, which is the only thing the two loves have in common. The two differ profoundly in how they view the subject-object relationship. In the one, God's love creates its object, which makes the object pleasing to the subject. In the other, human love emerges from the attractive power of the object that pleases the subject. In naming the two kinds of love as divine and human, Luther is asserting that everything that can be said theologically about love fits into these two categories. Interpreters should not soften his bold thesis.[8]

In elaborating on the thesis, Luther traces his understanding of human love to Aristotle in which "the object of love is its cause," which assumes "that each power of the soul is passive and material and active only in receiving something." He judges this love unfavorably "since in all things it seeks those things that are its own and receives rather than bestows something good."[9] Luther identifies human love as sinful self-seeking: it is motivated by what the object gives to the subject and does not benefit the person who is its object.

God's love turns all this around, Luther argues. Instead of the goodness or attractiveness of the object luring the subject (the human being) to love it, the subject (God's love in the cross) creates the object, which otherwise is without being and goodness, and makes it attractive. Christian love for others is this same divine love. "The love of God, which dwells in human beings, loves sinners, evil persons, fools, and weaklings in order to make them righteous, good, wise, and strong." Nor is divine love self-centered: "Rather than seeking its own good, the love of God flows out and bestows good." Therefore, "sinners are attractive because they are loved; they are not loved because they are attractive." Such a love is the opposite of human love that "avoids sinners and evil persons." God's love in Christ seeks sinners, not the righteous. "This is the love of the cross, born of the cross, which turns in the direction where it does not find good, which it may enjoy, but where it may confer good upon the evil and needy person."[10]

Nygren's paraphrase of Luther's thesis captures its meaning: "Human love is acquisitive love, and so is created by the desirable nature of its object. God's love is itself creative—i.e., it makes something of that which is nothing."[11] The thesis means that divine love is "unmotivated" (by any object), indifferent to value; it does not recognize value but creates it, and all human love is always egocentric and acquisitive.[12] Nygren rightly understands that thesis 28 supports his agape-eros dualism.

OTHER CONCEPTS

The concept of love in thesis 28 differs from other common understandings of love in the Christian tradition. The tradition speaks, of course, of "good" and "bad" loves. 1 John, for example, contrasts love of the world with love of the Father (1 John 2:15). Augustine incorporates a similar approach in his description of the "two cities" that "have been created by two loves: that is, the earthly by love of self-extending even to contempt of God, the heavenly by love of God extending to contempt of self."[13] These concepts of love speak of a single human love whose goodness or badness depends on what is loved. For thesis 28 all these loves—of Father and of God as well as of world and of self—fall under the category of "human love" insofar as their value is given by the object that pleases them. For Luther's thesis, "good" love depends entirely on the subject, on the lover, be it God or humans. Only divine love is good love.[14]

Thesis 28 also differs from Christian concepts of ordered love (*ordinata caritas*), which depend on the object of love.[15] Ordered love holds that people order their loves properly when they are in accord with God's ordering of creation's goods. It seeks to identify these goods and the manner in which faithful people should love them in a world with multiple goods where human loves are wrongly ordered due to sin. Jesus's double commandment provides the basic structure of ordered love, instructing humans to order their loves to love God above all and the neighbor as one's self (Matt. 22:34–40; Mark 12:28–34; Luke 10:25–28). Thesis 28 is at odds with ordered love since divine love (also Christian love) creates what is pleasing to it, which means there are no goods outside that creative act to order, and human love, pleased by what is good or what it views as good, is held to be selfish love.[16]

CREATION IN CHRISTIAN ETHICS

Christian ethics in my normative sense depends on the church's scriptural teachings on creation to make sense of love and the Christian life. That is hardly a controversial affirmation. Love in the Christian narrative belongs to creation as well as to sin and to redemption. That is, love did not originate in sin or in redemption but in creation. God created and sustains a good and orderly creation to be loved, capable of communicating its goodness, and made humans to be lovers of God's good works, giving them the creational vocation to live in mutual love. Christian ethics must build creation into the ground floor of its account of love if it is to avoid a partial, incoherent, and distorted concept of love.

Thesis 28 is about sin and redemption, about God's love that saves sinners. Creation, in the sense of the First Article of the Creed, is not mentioned; neither do I find that it has an essential influence on what it says about divine and human love. In terms of God's love, its absence means that the thesis makes redemption creation and thereby fails to incorporate the necessary distinction between God's creative love and God's saving love. For human love, the absence of creation means that the thesis presents human love itself as sinful and thereby fails to incorporate the necessary distinction between God's good creation and sin.

THE CROSS IS CREATION

Thesis 28 speaks the language of creation: "God's love does not find but creates," and what is created pleases God. This is true. The thesis expresses well the meaning of the Genesis account of creation "in the beginning" that God called "very good" (Gen. 1:1, 31): God's overflowing love does not find but alone creates the good creation, which is pleasing to God.

Luther, of course, is not referring to that creation but to the redemptive love of the cross as creation. In denying that God's love "finds" sinners, Luther strengthens the idea that he understands redemption to be *creatio ex nihilo*, not re-creation, not giving new life to the dead. The cross finds nothing since the sinner is nothing, not even, it seems, God's good creature. Since human creatureliness is non-existent, wiped out by sin or without significance, the cross creates the object of its redemptive love.

"Finding" and "creating" represent two understandings of redemption, which Luther presents as an either/or, one that he rejects without qualification and one that he affirms. "Finding" presupposes God's creative work, and "creating" does not. In redemption as creation, the Redeemer has no prior history with or commitment to humanity and so creates from nothing; there is nothing else but the act of redemption. In redemption as finding, the Redeemer acts with purpose to restore a prior relationship with the lost, a beloved creature of his own making.

God's redemptive "finding" is a broad and deep biblical tradition. "I have gone astray like a lost sheep," the Psalmist confesses, and then he cries out for help: "Seek out your servant" (119:176). Jesus announces, "The Son of Man came to seek out and to save the lost" (Luke 19:10). The woman who seeks the lost coin, the shepherd who seeks the lost sheep, and the father who waits for his wandering son all know the value of what is lost and the longing to find it. They, like God, act with purpose to recover and to return, to restore, the loss of a previous relationship (Luke 15:3–32). Luther's assertion that God's love in the cross "does not find" its object is striking.

Luther, however, does not remain bound by his rejection of "finding," and in his *Small Catechism*, for example, he goes beyond thesis 28. He recognizes that God's redemptive love in Christ finds "a lost and condemned human being," whom he has created, who is not nothing, who is "freed" from "all sins, from death, and from the power of the devil."[17] Luther in his catechisms knows the difference between the cross and creation, which Augustine expresses well: "For Christ did not die for human beings in order that they might be created but for sinful human beings in order that they might be justified."[18]

If redemption is creation, as thesis 28 envisions, then "every act [of redemption] has to be *ex nihilo*, presuppositionless." So claims Oliver O'Donovan in his critique of Nygren (and by extension of thesis 28). O'Donovan understands that "the creative work of God allows for teleology, and so for a movement within creation," which "presuppose[s] the fact of creation as a given starting point, to a destiny which 'fulfills' creation by redeeming it and by lifting it to a new level." Therefore, he argues, "Between that which is and that which will be there must be a line of connection, the redemptive purpose of God. We cannot simply say that agape has no presuppositions, for God presupposes that which he himself has already given in agape. . . . We confess that our being-as-we-are and our being-as-we-shall-be are held together as works of the One God who is both our Creator and Redeemer."[19]

A Luther beyond thesis 28 makes O'Donovan's point in biblical language: "The human being was created in the image of God and for life eternal; he forfeited this life through the fall of Adam in the Garden of Eden and became subject to death; but he will be made alive again through Christ (1 Cor. 15:22)."[20] Redemption presupposes creation, and Christ fulfills God's redemptive purpose for creation. Luther calls Christ "Co-Creator," an affirmation that underscores both creation and redemption as works of love of the one Triune God. We humans "were created by Him without our own aid and agency," which means that our created goodness is not meritorious or salvific.[21] Rather it is God who is faithful to what he has created. God's character is such that, as Athanasius said, "It was impossible . . . that God should leave man to be carried off by corruption, because it would be unfitting and unworthy of Himself."[22]

HUMAN LOVE IS SELF-SEEKING

Love in human experience is also of two kinds according to thesis 28: either it is human love, or it is Christian love. Human love is nothing more than self-seeking love. Christian love, the love of Christians, is nothing less than God's own creative, self-giving love. Love is either selfish or selfless. As Nygren interprets Luther, "Christian love is by nature wholly other than human love, and its protype is nothing else but God's agape. Like this, it is spontaneous, unmotivated, groundless, creative."[23]

First, human love. In describing human love as what "comes into being through that which is pleasing to it," the thesis correctly points to the pull of an object to bring forth bonds and acts from an affective disposition. Luther and Aristotle agree that's how life is. Our encounter with a person, an idea, a cause, an activity, a place, a food, a sunset, or a piece of music is able to evoke in us love for that reality.

The thesis is problematic not because of its description but because of its judgment: Human love is equated with sin. Whenever people are moved to love because they are pleased by someone or something, their conduct is always and entirely self-centered. The thesis targets not certain acts of love but the structure of human love, of loving the good. Any love that binds a person with a good that she or he may enjoy falls under its judgment.

The thesis is sweeping. The entire range of peoples' ordinary loves, joys, pleasures, and desires are dismissed as self-serving. When they attend to, admire, appreciate, seek, or yearn for someone or something that attracts them, they are in every case demonstrating their egoism. There are no "innocent" loves; enjoying a cool breeze on a hot afternoon is selfish. There is no "natural" or good self-love. The bonds of family and of friendship are self-centered. All love of what is beautiful, good, or true is acquisitive. If a person of faith loves God because his loving goodness is pleasing also to her, she is, it seems, only seeking her own.[24]

In other writings, however, Luther steps away from his negative judgment on all human love and affirms a positive, non-selfish connection between love and a created good. He gives a simple yet telling example in commenting on the Gospel of John. "Light," he writes, "is a glorious thing. In fact, nothing surpasses it. Everybody loves the sun, and all creatures rejoice when it rises so resplendently early each morning."[25] One may want to qualify his statement if crossing the desert, but most, especially if living in Wittenberg, would agree: "Everyone loves the sun."

Enjoying God's gift of the sun is not sinful. Luther celebrates that people appreciate, admire, delight in, and desire the sun, its splendor, and its benefits. Luther does not even hint that peoples' love of the sun is self-serving or acquisitive. If one wants to use "eros" to identify such love of the good, then Luther's affirmation might appropriately be called "non-possessive eros."[26] Neither does love of the sun belong to Luther's category of divine love. Christians' love of the sun is hardly self-giving; it is not directed to the needy or unrighteous; and it does not create the sun and its goodness and beauty. Luther's comment on the sun illustrates a familiar reality in ordinary taken-for-granted human experience—people loving a good in a non-acquisitive way. A Christian account of love needs to uphold such love as good and proper in creaturely existence, but thesis 28 does not allow one to do so.

Thesis 28 is able to condemn human love without qualification because it does not integrate creation into its basic assertions about human love. Without the doctrine of creation, it is unable to draw any distinction between God's creative work and human sin. The Christian tradition has wisely rejected Manichean tendencies that deny creation's goodness. The very first article of the *Formula of Concord* ("Concerning Original Sin") reaffirms the difference "between original sin and human nature": "Even after the fall this [human] nature still is and remains a creature of God. The difference is as great as the difference between the work of God and the work of the devil."[27]

The "yes" of creation comes before the "no" of sin. Creation is good, not evil or neutral; what pleases God is meant also to be pleasing to humans. We are to know and love its goods, especially other humans who are like us and alongside us.

"The work of the devil" is always and variously and seriously present. The devil's work does not destroy creation, but it does disrupt, distort, and corrupt its goodness and our loves. The sun is worshipped as God instead of being received as a gift from God. Humans in their self-centeredness seek to absorb all into their own sphere and to call it love. Human loves stand under God's judgment, and Christians confess that they do not love God above all and their neighbor as themselves. The cross of Christ, they believe, promises forgiveness to sinners, freedom from their self-centeredness, and the faith that moves them to order their loves to God and neighbor.

In giving us new life, the Holy Spirit does not take away the creaturely call and ability to love. The Holy Spirit's gifts instead affirm, restore, and convert human creaturely love to be in accord with God's intention for his creatures. Thesis 28 views the relationship differently. Since creation is absent, God's love in the cross creates a totally new love, Christian love. Instead of renewing it, Christian love replaces human love. To paraphrase the thesis, "God's love does not find any created human love to redeem, so it must create from nothing a love that is pleasing to it."

CHRISTIAN LOVE IS DIVINE LOVE

When Christians love, their love is God's love. Christian love is God's indwelling love, coming from God and flowing through Christians to others. It is a new, powerful, exceptional, heavenly love. It does what God does—making evil persons good, fools wise, the weak strong, the unattractive attractive. So claims thesis 28.[28]

If Christian love is divine love, how then do God the Creator and human creatures differ? This difference is especially important when speaking of love since "God is love" (1 John 4:16) and we human beings are not. Christians too love as creatures, and our love necessarily differs from God's love. "Of God alone can it be said that his love needs no faith to afford a competent subject for it, no hope to carry it forward into action. God's love is its own subject, its own enactment." In God "to be and to love and to act are one and the same." Since "God is not who we are, 'love' can be predicated of God and man not univocally, but only by analogy."[29]

Since it does not articulate any difference, thesis 28 means, according to some interpreters, that just as God's love creates its object, so Christian love creates its object and its value. Such a claim, however, ignores that God and Christians relate differently to the object they love. While God's love bestows value on creation, Christian love recognizes and gratefully receives its goodness. In loving others, Christians are acknowledging the neighbor's dignity and worth given by God. Christian ethicists mislead and baffle when they echo thesis 28 and assert, "The Golden Rule demands a divine love that not only discovers but actually creates its object."[30] Christian ethics does well to leave aside the pretentious idea that Christian love is so God-like that it creates the value of that which is without value.

Thesis 28's concept of Christian love, untethered from creation, is all about the subject, the one who loves. Christian ethics done in its framework would evaluate actors and actions by looking only to the subjects, to their loving motivation. It would have no reason or need to attend to the objective (outside the self) goods in the world. It would not appeal to creation to know what is to be loved, what goods are to be protected, and what goods are to be sought. Loving subjects alone would determine what it means to act in love.

Discussion about abortion illustrates how questions about subject and object influence a concept of love. Some say, "The unborn is valuable because I love it (if I decide to do so)." Others say, "I love the unborn because she is valuable." In the one, subjective love confers dignity and worth on the unborn; in the other, the objective dignity and worth of the unborn as God's creature calls forth love. What the second person says seems to be what is condemned in thesis 28, namely, that human "love comes into being through which is pleasing to it." The first person seems to express divine love—not finding but creating what is pleasing to it.

Luther's thesis defines the recipients of Christian love by what they lack—they are unattractive or "sinners, evil persons, fools, and weaklings." Yet recipients of love are always more than that. They share the same created human nature with those who love them. They all—givers and receivers of compassion alike—are sinners, whose roles may change. The recipients' needs, failures, or evilness are occasions to love, but they are not the final reason for Christians to do so. They are to be loved, and are lovable, because they are God's good creatures. Without this conviction compassion for people who are in need, for which the thesis calls, easily becomes hierarchical, demeaning, and dominating.

Thesis 28 conceives love as a one-way affair. In its human love, the object controls the "passive" subject; in its Christian love, the subject is in control, changing the recipient from valueless to valuable. There is no recognition of the possibility or the desirability of mutual love, which is our creational vocation. We humans, finite and needy creatures, equal before God, receive life from others and give life to others. Love in its many manifestations, including self-giving love, takes place within, not above or outside, the social bonds and communications of receiving and giving life.

CREATION AND LOVE, LOVE AND GOOD

Luther in his *Lectures on Galatians* (1535) demonstrates the significance of creation for a concept of love. In affirming the created value of the neighbor, he links neighborly love and the good. Sinners are attractive and to be loved because of their created nobility. Luther speaks of some objects of love as being more worthy of our love than others and thereby points to the need for our loves to be ordered. He sets out elements for a Christian ethical perspective that recognizes the authority of the goods given in creation to direct our action so that the subjectivity of the lover is not the only concern of ethics.

Luther does not conceive love as indifferent to value or as creating the neighbor's value. He views the neighbor as one worthy of love, indeed, more worthy of love than any other creature, for there is "no creature . . . nobler than your neighbor." Our neighbor "is not a devil, not a lion or a bear or a wolf, not a stone or a log. He is a living creature very much like you." Luther praises God's human creatures: "There is nothing living on earth that is more pleasant, more lovable, more helpful, kinder, more comforting, or more necessary. Besides, he is naturally suited for a civilized and social existence. Nothing could be regarded as worthier of love in the whole universe than our neighbor."[31]

Although the devil obscures the neighbor's goodness, the devil is not able to destroy the nobility God has bestowed on humans. This nobility that gives dignity and value to all people is the reason why Christians should be concerned about those in need. He connects Christ's teachings on love to our common human nature created by God.

> Now our neighbor is any human being, especially one who needs our help, as Christ interprets it in Luke 10:30–37. Even one who has done me some sort of injury or harm has not shed his humanity on that account or stopped being flesh and blood, a creature of God very much like me; in other words, he does not stop being my neighbor. Therefore as long as human nature remains in him, so long the commandment of love remains in force, requiring of me that I not despise my own flesh and not return evil for evil but overcome evil with good (Rom. 12:21).[32]

In insisting that the doctrine of creation and the commandment to love the neighbor as one's self belong together, Luther provides the basis for Christians to affirm the universal character of love—all are neighbors—and, along with it, human equality and human solidarity, especially with those most in need. Luther, of course, has more to say about creation and love in other writings.

"EVERYONE KNOWS" LOVE'S MEANING

It is surprising and refreshing to hear Luther say "everyone knows" what love means, as he does in a sermon on 1 Timothy 1:5–7. "It is really not so complicated," Luther in effect is saying. "Just listen to how people use and understand the word in their ordinary human relationships." Instead of claiming that love in Paul or in the New Testament has a special meaning or instead of appealing to Aristotle, Luther turns to everyday life, to the created order, and offers a common-sense definition that tells us much about love's meaning: "But 'love' in German, as everyone knows, means nothing else except to be favorably and affectionately disposed toward a person from the heart and to offer and show him all kindness and friendship."[33]

Luther views love as one, into which a variety of loves may fit. He does not oppose two kinds of love, and he says nothing about love creating its object. Before talking about love as action, he presents love as the affectionate disposition of the heart. He does not define it by a particular act (e.g., create) but sees it open for all kinds of acts of kindness. Luther captures the unitive character of love—a bond of mutual affection whose attitudes and action bring people together in friendship—a theme that is absent in thesis 28.

Most significant is that in his *Treatise on Good Works*, Luther uses the language of "kind disposition" to describe both God's love of humans and human's love of God. "For I could not have faith in God if I did not think he wanted to be favorable and kind to me. This in turn makes me feel kindly disposed toward him, and I am moved to trust him with all my heart and to look to him for all good things." Human love of God is not disinterested; it recognizes that God's kind disposition is good for the self. In a paraphrase of John 3:16, Luther speaks of God's love for humans as being "so kindly disposed toward you that he even gives his own Son for you," so that "your heart in turn must grow sweet and disposed toward God."[34] God's affectionate bond with the world leads to God's self-giving in the cross, which calls forth love for God. Luther's understanding of love as kind disposition embraces a spectrum of ways of loving—from self-giving, to having mutual love, to loving God, the Good who is the source of all goodness.

Christian ethics, when it turns to Luther, should go beyond his understanding of love in thesis 28 of the *Heidelberg Disputation*. That in any case is the argument I have attempted to make. In so doing I have also been challenging the hold that Nygren's interpretation of love in Luther and in the Christian tradition continues to exert. By brief references to a few other of his writings, I have been suggesting that there are other ways into love in Luther that incorporate creation and offer more promise for Christian ethics today.

NOTES

1. Gary M. Simpson, "Fruit of the Spirit," in *The New Testament and Ethics: A Book-by-Book Survey*, ed. Joel B. Green (Grand Rapids, Michigan: Baker Academic, 2013), 94. During the first two decades of the ELCA, I enjoyed some wonderful conversations with Gary Simpson. We were together for annual meetings of Lutheran ethicists and the Society for Christian Ethics and for gatherings of study task forces in the ELCA's Church in Society unit. We, in studies, could always count on Gary's personal support and his contributions to the church's reflection on society from the depth of his theological knowledge. I know him as a person of the church and as a friend, an experience for which I am grateful.

2. For two historical overviews, see Robert Kolb, *Luther's Treatise on Christian Freedom and Its Legacy* (Lanham, MD: Fortress Academic/Lexington, 2019), and Carter Lindberg, *Love: A Brief History through Western Christianity* (Oxford: Blackwell Publishing, 2008).

3. Simpson, "Fruit of the Spirit," 94.

4. Oswald Bayer writes that in *On the Babylonian Captivity of the Church* (1520), "what is 'reformational' in Luther's theology is thus set forth with a specificity that is unequaled in any other of his writings." The treatise "articulates the way to understand the relationship between *promissio* and *fides*, between promise and faith." Here Luther's own position "is stated in an unmistakable way—which cannot be said of writings such as the *Heidelberg Disputation* with its articulation of the *theologia crucis* (theology of the cross)." See Oswald Bayer, *Martin Luther's Theology: A Contemporary Interpretation*, trans. Thomas H. Trapp (Grand Rapids, MI: William B. Eerdmans Publishing Company, 2007), 46. What the *Heidelberg Disputation* does do is to criticize forcefully the scholastic tradition of his day for giving saving significance to human moral ability.

5. Anders Nygren, *Agape and Eros*, Parts I and II, trans. Philip S. Watson (Philadelphia: The Westminster Press, 1953). First published in Swedish in 1930 and 1936. William Werpehowski provides an excellent overview and appraisal of Nygren's book in "Anders Nygren's *Agape and Eros*," in *The Oxford Handbook of Theological Ethics*, eds. Gilbert Meilaender and Werpehowski (New York: Oxford University Press, 2010), 433–48. A collection of twenty-one essays by theologians and philosophers about love in the Western tradition shows Nygren's continuing influence: see Frederick V. Simmons with Brian C. Sorrells, eds., *Love and Christian Ethics: Tradition, Theory, and Society* (Washington, DC: Georgetown University Press, 2016). For more

on Nygren and Luther, see my bibliography at https://www.academia.edu/40245968/Annotated_Bibliography_on_Luther_on_Love.

6. Nygren, *Agape and Eros*, 724–25. The Latin of the thesis is found on page 233: "Amor Dei non invenit sed creat suum diligibile, Amor hominis fit a suo deligibili."

7. Martin Luther, *Heidelberg Disputation* (1518), in *The Annotated Luther: 1*, ed. Timothy J. Wengert (Minneapolis: Fortress Press, 2015), Kindle edition, loc. 1380. There Dennis Bielfeldt places the *Heidelberg Disputation* in context and overviews its content. Gerhard O. Forde provides a commentary in *On Being a Theology of the Cross: Reflections on Luther's Heidelberg Disputation, 1518* (Grand Rapids, MI: William B. Eerdmans Publishing Company, 1997). See also Steve Paulson, "An Introduction to the *Heidelberg Disputation*," and Wade Johnston, "Reflection on Theses 27 and Theses 28," in *Theology of the Cross: Luther's Heidelberg Disputation and Reflections on Its 28 Theses*, eds. Kelsi Klembara and Caleb Keith (Minneapolis: 1517 Publishing, 2018), Kindle edition. Christopher D. Jackson presents a critical view: "Luther's Theologian of the Cross and Theologian of Glory: Distinction Reconsidered," in *Pro Ecclesia* 29, no. 3 (August 2020): 336–51.

8. Tuomo Mannermaa, *Two Kinds of Love: Martin Luther's Religious World*, trans. and ed. Kirsi I. Stjerna (Minneapolis: Fortress Press, 2010), Kindle edition, loc. 189. Like Nygren, Mannermaa begins with thesis 28 of the *Heidelberg Disputation* and makes its contrast between divine and human love his key for interpreting love in Luther. He softens thesis 28 by arguing that it does not really consider all human love as self-seeking.

9. Luther, *Heidelberg Disputation*, loc. 1685–88.

10. Luther, *Heidelberg Disputation*, loc. 1688–99.

11. Nygren, *Agape and Eros*, 725.

12. See Nygren's chart contrasting agape and eros and his interpretation of Luther: Nygren, *Agape and Eros*, 210, 725ff.

13. Augustine, *The City of God Against the Pagans*, XIV, 28, ed. R.W. Dyson (Cambridge: Cambridge University Press, 1998), 632.

14. Although out of line with thesis 28, Luther too speaks in terms of one love whose value is determined by what is loved. It is difficult not to do so when dealing with Johannine writings. One example is Luther's endorsement of Christ's lament "that though the light had come into the world, men had loved the darkness rather than the light" (John 3:19). Martin Luther, *Sermons on the Gospel of St. John: Chapters 1–4*, in *Luther's Works*, eds. J. J. Pelikan, H. C. Oswald, and H. T. Lehmann (Saint Louis: Concordia Publishing House, 1957 [henceforth *LW*]), 22:377.

15. See Risto Saarinen, *God and the Gift: An Ecumenical Theology of Giving* (Collegeville, Minnesota: Liturgical Press, 2005), 53–58. Saarinen draws in part on thesis 28 for his critique of *ordo caritatis*. He summarizes, "The Lutheran alternative to the 'order of love' is thus nothing else than the perspective of God as giver. God's agape is God giving love to a world that is lacking it. Our rationalistic account of love is rather an evaluation of some already existing goodness. But this evaluation finally only reflects some self-interest" (56). For Luther, Christians, in imitating divine love, are called to fulfill the needs and wants of others. In so doing, they become givers.

16. However incompatible it may be with thesis 28, Luther does speak of properly ordering one's loves. Christians love Christ as their chief love and as the key to order their loves. Luther writes what this means: "To be sure, I do love my wife and child, my house and home, and my friends; but I do not love them more than I love Christ; I do not love them so much that on this account I would deny Him and His Word. No, I would much rather surrender everything the world loves and, instead, suffer what it shuns and avoids" (*LW* 24:163). Oswald Bayer gives another example from a Luther sermon on the rich young man. Humans cannot live "without having space, air, a place to belong, a body, and time." Balancing life in the world and discipleship to Christ "requires obedience to the First Commandment, honoring and loving God above all things and placing trust in him." As cited by Bayer, Luther affirms a proper self-love: "You should love your own life" but nothing more than God. "God grants you gladly your wife, your child, your possessions and indeed your very life," and they are to be left "only if the things of God are at stake." See Oswald Bayer, "Luther's Ethics as Pastoral Care," *Lutheran Quarterly* 4, no. 2 (1990): 131, 134, 135. Luther interprets the Ten Commandments in his *Small Catechism* in terms of ordered love. The First Commandment means, "We are to fear, love, and trust God above all things," and the other commandments begin that "we are to fear and love God, so that" we do not do and we do what the commandment requires. In these and other texts, Luther understands that love has an order. Martin Luther, *The Small Catechism*, in *The Book of Concord*, eds. Robert Kolb and Timothy J. Wengert (Minneapolis: Fortress Press, 2000), 351ff.

17. Luther, *The Small Catechism*, 355, 354. It is appropriate to remember how Luther begins his explanation of the First Article of the Apostles Creed: "I believe that God has created me together with all that exists" (354). Lutherans learn early that the Christian narrative is one of creation, sin, and redemption.

18. Augustine, "Letter 194," in *Letters 156–210*, Augustine Heritage Institute (Hyde Park, N.Y.: New City Press, 2004), 292. The context for the quotation in the text is Augustine's dispute with Pelagius over grace and merits. Augustine is insisting that our created human nature does not give humans merits. After the sentence quoted in the text, Augustine writes, "The man, of course, already existed who said: *Wretched man that I am! Who will set me free from the body of this death? The grace of God through Jesus Christ our Lord* (Rom 7:24–25)."

19. Oliver O'Donovan, *The Problem of Self-Love in St. Augustine* (New Haven: Yale University Press, 1980), 13, 158–59. O'Donovan in this study of Augustine is criticizing Nygren, who is echoing Luther.

20. Luther, *Sermons on the Gospel of St. John: Chapters 1–4*, *LW* 22:30.

21. Luther, *Sermons on St. John*, 26.

22. Athanasius, *On the Incarnation* (Christian Classics Ethereal Library), Kindle edition, loc. 138. Athanasius summarizes his perspective: "We will begin, then, with the creation of the world and with God its maker, for the first fact that you must grasp is this: *the renewal of creation has been wrought by the Self-same Word who made it in the beginning.* There is thus no inconsistency between creation and salvation, for the One Father has employed the same Agent for both works, effecting the salvation

of the world through the same Word Who made it in the beginning" (37–38, italics in text).

23. Nygren, *Agape and Eros*, 726.

24. See Ilmari Karimies, "Can Luther's Doctrine of God as the Giver and God as the Highest Good be Reconciled? A Critique of Tuomo Mannermaa's Two Kinds of Love," *Pro Ecclesia*, XXIV, 4 (Fall 2015): 475–84. Karimies challenges Mannermaa's claim that Luther's theology requires rejecting any theology that views God as the highest good. Instead, he argues, for Luther God as giver and as *summum bonum* are not "mutually exclusive but rather complimentary" (476). He finds five texts in the early Luther where he speaks of God as the highest good. God is "infinite goodness, who can never be exhausted," according to Luther. Antti Raunio refers to Karimies's article and writes that clarification is needed on "how Luther understands the traditional view of God as the highest good." See Antti Raunio, "Love," in *The Oxford Encyclopedia on Martin Luther, II* (Oxford: Oxford University Press, 2017), 217. In reference to the *Heidelberg Disputation*, Raunio writes, "The difficulty of combining the love of God as the highest good with this differentiation between human and divine love would appear to be a genuine problem in Luther's conception of love" (209). Raunio does not deal with other criticisms of Luther's concept related to creation (205–19).

25. *LW* 22:406.

26. For more on "non-possessive eros," see Werpehowski, "Anders Nygren's *Agape and Eros*," 442–3.

27. "Formula of Concord," *The Book of Concord*, 488.

28. I do not know what happens to human agency when Christian love is God's love, and the thesis does not offer a creation-based concept of human agency. Nygren, however, gives one plausible interpretation: he calls the Christian agent an "instrument" or a "tube" of God's love (*Agape and Eros*, 734–35).

29. Oliver O'Donovan, *Self, World, and Time: Ethics as Theology*, 1 (Grand Rapids, MI: William B. Eerdmans Publishing Company, 2013), 126–27. O'Donovan is criticizing Nygren's "famous concept of agape, 'creating value in its object.'"

30. Antti Raunio, "Natural Law and Faith: The Forgotten Foundations of Ethics in Luther's Theology," in *Union with Christ: The New Finnish Interpretation of Luther*, eds. Carl E. Braaten and Robert W. Jenson (Grand Rapids, MI: William B. Eerdmans Publishing Company, 1998), 108. Raunio adds "not only" to modify "discovers" in Luther's text; Luther, however, does not qualify his rejection of God's love "finding" an object.

31. Martin Luther, *Lectures on Galatians, 1535, Chapters 5–6; 1519, Chapters 1–6, LW* 27:58.

32. Luther, *Lectures on Galatians*, 58–59.

33. Martin Luther, "Sermon on the Sum of the Christian Life, 1 Tim. 1:5–7, Preached in Worlitz, November 24, 1532," in *Sermons 1, LW* 51:267.

34. Martin Luther, "Treatise on Good Works," in *The Christian in Society, I, LW* 44:30, 38.

Chapter 10

Citizenship as Co-Creation

Theological Foundations for Democratic Renewal

Marie-Louise Ström

It is widely observed that democracy is in crisis. The church has potential to reframe the problem in ways that generate civic energy and hope.[1]

Gloomy commentaries about democracy appear all across the world, as much in the "old" democracies of the West as in the "new" democracies of the ex-Soviet region and the Global South. Brazenly autocratic leaders have taken the helm in countries that previously valued democratic principles. Nationalism is on the rise, accompanied by hostility toward immigrants and refugees. Dishonesty in elections along with delegitimization of state electoral machinery have proliferated. Voters are easily swayed by misinformation campaigns via social media. Systemic corruption cripples democratic states and delivery of basic services. From France and Sweden to Poland and Hungary, from India and the Philippines to Tunisia and South Africa, from Brazil and Venezuela to Haiti and the United States of America, the refrain is the same: the norms and institutions of democracy are in peril.

The structural crisis is accompanied by a human and civic crisis: not only are the vertical relationships between citizens and their governments more distrustful and fractious, but also horizontal relationships between citizens are increasingly frayed.[2] In America a culture of individualism, competition, and consumerism poses a threat to relationships at every level. Among both rich and poor, the rat race to *have more* pits citizens against each other in zero-sum battles that produce growing inequality and powerlessness. Identity politics add new dimensions to the competition for resources and power, feeding growing polarization. Citizens increasingly retreat to corners with others like themselves while turning their backs on those who are different. Knowledge elites in government, academia, and the professions are considered society's "winners," able to hold sway over the "losers." As Michael Sandel has argued:

> Today, the common good is understood mainly in economic terms. It is less about cultivating solidarity or deepening the bonds of citizenship than about satisfying consumer preferences as measured by the gross domestic product. This makes for an impoverished public discourse. What passes for political argument these days consists either of narrow, managerial, technocratic talk, which inspires no one; or else shouting matches, in which partisans talk past one another, without really listening.[3]

Democracy rarely conveys possibilities for empowering citizens to do the shared work of building a better society. Instead, it drives more and more of them to despair.

Faced with such a litany of problems, Americans differ deeply about causes and solutions. In a recent edition of *The Atlantic*, George Packer observes:

> The 1970s ended post-war, bipartisan, middle-class America, and with it the two relatively stable narratives of getting ahead [Republicans] and the fair shake [Democrats]. In their place, four rival narratives have emerged, four accounts of America's identity. [. . .] They reflect schisms on both sides of the divide that has made us two countries, extending and deepening the lines of fracture.[4]

Packer calls the four camps Free America (libertarian capitalists), Smart America (cosmopolitan technocrats), Real America (patriotic working-class folks), and Just America (groups mobilized against oppression). The first two convey positions broadly associated with Republicans and Democrats respectively, while the last two categories point to vociferous sub-groups on each side. Today polarization among all these groups descends frequently to the level of hatred. No matter what issues one considers to be most important, without addressing the crisis in civic life, political stalemate is inevitable and collective capacities will further erode.

Part of the problem is that conventional understandings of democracy, citizenship, and politics have shrunk. For most people today, democracy is primarily about elections. The good citizen is an informed voter. Political parties play an outsized role, and government becomes the focal point of politics, displacing the agency of citizens. People may express concern about the democratic crisis but don't see themselves as part of the solution. This government-centered understanding of democracy leads a growing number of people to distance themselves from public life and focus rather on individual pursuits and private life. Others retain a commitment to the public good but choose rather to live this out through personal expressions of neighborliness. From this point of view, the good citizen is someone who attends to the needs of others, particularly those less fortunate, and dedicates time to volunteering. This communitarian understanding of democracy counters the dog-eat-dog dynamics of partisan politics and can in some instances foster relationships across differences, but it is inattentive to questions of power. Efforts to address society's big problems tend to be piecemeal, and citizens continue to be sidelined and feel powerless.

With the call to service that permeates the gospel, many churches feel most comfortable focusing on supportive ministries to those in need. Others feel compelled to get involved in hot issues through more overtly partisan channels. Some Christians identify with Packer's Real America (the stereotype of evangelicals) and others with Just America (the stereotype of mainline churches). The crisis in democracy and civic life polarizes churches too.

There is a third way of understanding democracy as everybody's work, every day, in multiple settings, including the workplace.[5] This alternative paradigm stresses citizens (including citizens in government) as co-creators of a good society. People have sought to practice this kind of democracy in different parts of the world, and I experienced its possibilities firsthand.

I grew up in South Africa, experiencing racial segregation and polarization at its worst. I was active in the struggle against apartheid, and for twenty years I worked for a large non-partisan NGO, the Institute for a Democratic Alternative in South Africa (Idasa),[6] that played a crucial but largely unsung role in the country's transition to democracy. Throughout its thirty-three years of existence, Idasa wrestled with what it meant to build a democratic *society*, not merely establish a democratic government. It did not take too long after the first democratic elections in 1994 before most citizens, operating in consumer mode, expressed frustration about poor service delivery from government. In response, Idasa initiated a citizen leadership training program that aimed to equip people with skills to organize their communities to solve problems and work together for change. They learned many practical civic and political skills, such as discerning people's interests, mapping power, negotiating differences, and holding each other accountable. Tapping into each other's talents and resources while also collaborating with government, they tackled a large array of problems, including care for AIDS orphans, water shortages, housing, high funeral costs, and many more. The results were sometimes incredible. In some of the poorest and most neglected parts of the country, people developed agency and glimpsed what could happen when they recognized each other as co-creators of better communities.

Co-creation shifts the identity of the citizen from consumer to civic producer, from protestor to joint problem-solver, from armchair critic to active collaborator in building the commonwealth. This "public work" approach to democracy is counter-cultural. Elected officials do not willingly share power. Polarizing politics proves to be strangely seductive. The idea of co-creation challenges deeply entrenched patterns in society. Exploring co-creation through a theological lens offers resources for the church to take a lead in practicing a different kind of democracy and rebuilding civic life.

HUMAN BEING AS CREATED CO-CREATOR

This chapter explores two theological ideas that can inspire Christians to embrace the concept of citizens as co-creators and become involved in public life in constructive ways. Philip Hefner coined the phrase "created co-creators," spelling out his basic idea as follows:

> Human beings are God's created co-creators whose purpose is to be the agency, acting in freedom, to birth the future that is most wholesome for the nature that has birthed us—the nature that is not only our own genetic heritage, but also the entire human community and the evolutionary and ecological reality in which and to which we belong. Exercising this agency is said to be God's will for humans.[7]

Hefner explores the idea of humans as created co-creators as part of a broader theological interaction with evolutionary science and related questions of genetic and cultural conditioning. It is an impressive project, but the extensive scientific aspect is not of direct relevance to this essay. However, the intersection of the idea of the citizen as co-creator and the human being as created co-creator holds much potential for public theology and also potential to animate broader democratic renewal.

The question of what we, as human beings, were created to be like and to do is anchored in the biblical narrative that God created humankind in God's image, as *imago Dei*. Hefner, in an overview of the doctrine of creation in Carl Braaten and Robert Jenson's survey of Christian dogmatics, notes that the *imago Dei* has formed a foundational element of Christian anthropology from the time of the church's earliest theologians. He identifies two major categories of interpretation of the *imago*, with the more prevalent focusing on particular human attributes. The second category, he observes, includes those theologians who interpret the *imago* from a relational angle: "[They] consider the image of God to refer to the fact of relationship to God, of co-responding to God, of being God's counterpart."[8] Hefner combines the two approaches in his novel concept of the created co-creator. He writes:

Homo sapiens is distinctive in terms of six important characteristics: consciousness, self-consciousness, the ability to make assessments, the ability to make decisions on the basis of those assessments, the ability to act freely on those decisions, and the ability to take responsibility for such action. Such self-aware, free action becomes a kind of creating activity, a co-creating, with God. Humans can claim no arrogant credit for being co-creators; they were created co-creators.[9]

Christians often recognize human creativity as reflecting the image of God the Creator. Hefner takes this further, asserting that co-creation—a relationship based on shared work and shared responsibility for creating the world's future—forms the foundation of God's relationship with men and women. The *imago Dei* is not a passive reflection, as if in a mirror; it is about *agency*.

It is commonly noted that God's statement in Genesis 1:26, "Let us make Adam in our image," points to plurality within the very being of God. Humanity's diversity is one way of understanding this aspect of the *imago Dei*. For Christians, of course, the doctrine of the Trinity also throws particular light on this statement in Genesis. Jürgen Moltmann's treatment of the "social Trinity" stresses the *relationality* that springs from this plurality. Putting the idea of the social Trinity in conversation with Hefner's theme of the created co-creator further expands our understanding of the *imago Dei* and the co-creative relationship between humans and God.

Moltmann presents the social Trinity as an alternative to the hierarchical, monotheistic logic that shapes traditional thinking about the Trinity as "One in Three." This logic applies in the debates among early Patristic theologians about God as one "substance" in three Persons, just as it does in later trinitarian proposals such as God as one "subject" in three "modes of being." For Moltmann, with the "One" as the starting point, there is "not only . . . undue stress on the unity of the triune God, but there is also a reduction of the triunity to the One God."[10] He proposes a reverse logic, beginning with the three Persons of the Trinity to arrive at a new conception of the One. The self-differentiation of the three Persons illuminates their relationality—relationship cannot exist without differentiation—and thus forms the basis of a *social* doctrine of the Trinity. The relationship between Father, Son, and Holy Spirit is understood to be one of unending, self-emptying love and mutual indwelling—*perichoresis*—an eternally dynamic union rather than a unitary subject in three expressions. This emphasis on perfect, equal sharing—*communio* within the inner life of God—presents a different understanding of God's power from the traditional conception of God's sovereignty. Rather, God's power is relational and horizontal, extending also to God's relationship with humankind. Moltmann stresses that the Trinity becomes open and all of creation is drawn into this dynamic relationship.

The plurality and relationality of the Trinity extends into the world through the *work* of the three Persons. This life of love is not merely a rapturous dance of perichoretic reciprocity.[11] God engages with the world through a dynamic "trinitarian co-working," as Moltmann observes, with Father, Son, and Holy Spirit working distinctively, and also equally and inter-relatedly. This work has been from the beginning, is ongoing, and is always new. Moltmann elaborates:

> In the historical and eschatological testimony of the New Testament, we do not merely find one, single form of the Trinity. We find a trinitarian co-working of Father, Son and Spirit, but with changing patterns. We find the order Father—Spirit—Son; the order Father—Son—Spirit; and finally the order Spirit—Son—Father. Up to now, however, dogmatic tradition has only worked with a single pattern. And in the West this pattern has always been Father—Son—Spirit.[12]

Theologians have paid much attention to the fellowship of love—*communio*—within the life of the Trinity. The argument here is that a shift in focus to the life of the Trinity as *cooperatio*—the collaborative work of Creator, Son, and Spirit—expands the meaning of relationality within the Trinity. Thus, the idea of human beings as God's created co-creators means that they are drawn into the open Trinity at work.

The ongoing work of God is trinitarian *and* co-creative in every respect—creating, redeeming, and re-creating the world. This captures the full panorama of God's action in the world and God's relationship with all of creation. Bringing forth the *imago* in God's created co-creators is the work of the Trinity. The Father's work as Creator is recognized in the *created* co-creators, whose created status means they are not God's equals although they bear the likeness of God. In Moltmann's trinitarian reading of the *imago Dei*, he emphasizes that the *imago* is not a *fait accompli*, but rather a work in progress with an eschatological orientation: "The true likeness to God is to be found, not at the beginning of God's history with mankind, but at its end."[13]

The *imago Christi* fully anticipates the *imago Dei* in humankind. The Son's work liberates humanity from sin and death—from finitude—and enables men and women to be God's *co*-creators. Redeemed, they are drawn out of isolation and brokenness into fellowship, becoming part of the Son's body, the church, and entering into renewed relationships with each other. Jesus the Son redeems the imperfections, ambiguities, and contradictions of human creativity, making it possible for human beings to participate together in the new creation.

The Spirit endows men and women with agency to fulfill their role as created co-*creators*. The Spirit begins the work of new creation in this life, gradually transforming human beings into the Son's likeness, *imago Dei*, in anticipation of the Kingdom of God. Moltmann elaborates how this process of transformation is both part of the present and the future: "So likeness to God . . . is charge and hope, imperative and promise. Sanctification has justification as its presupposition, and glorification as its hope and its future."[14] In Moltmann's scheme, becoming *imago Dei* and becoming fully human are one and the same process. Both are part of the Holy Spirit's work of sanctification, beginning in this world and pointing toward the Kingdom. If, as Moltmann puts it, the *imago* is not only "hope" but also "charge," this implies that human beings themselves have a role to play in their "becoming." God's created co-creators are called to assume their role by doing concrete, world-building work with others in the here and now. In the power of the Spirit, they take on the likeness of God, however falteringly, as they work together to transform the world and shape a common future.

Accepting the charge of being the *imago Dei* opens the possibility of becoming the *imago Dei*. In faith Christians understand this to be the calling and potential of every human being. This belief in a high destiny for humanity stands in stark contrast to the widespread negativity that prevails in the world today about human beings. However promising the idea of being made in the image of God might seem, it is a promise that is difficult to accept, especially when we struggle to recognize the *imago* in others and ourselves. All around we are directly confronted with the inadequacy of our ideas and actions, our failures of judgment, the unforeseen negative outcomes of our words, behavior, and projects in the world, even when well-intentioned. As Hefner points out, "Many critics have charged Christianity with an essential *ecological* irresponsibility, whether with respect to the natural and physical ecosystem or with respect to the intrapersonal network of relationships. Christian anthropology has been charged with a concern to dominate . . . and with a sense that nothing has value outside the human."[15] It is not difficult to see how today's bleak outlook on humanity and the future arises. The *co*-dimension of the concept of the created co-creator is particularly important and also challenging, in the church and the world.

Hefner's theory of the created co-creator stirred up a fair deal of controversy, and many Christians remain uncomfortable with the idea. Critics concerned about the seeming hubris of the *co*-element—the danger that human beings might consider themselves to be on the same level as God—proposed alternative formulations such as "creative creatures" and "co-creative creatures." Beyond the Christian community, the idea would no doubt strike many as too limiting. Hefner remained insistent that "created co-creator" conveyed a vital and unique truth:

> These positions, critical of the created co-creator imagery, nevertheless recognize one of its most important dimensions—its tremendous dynamism and

energy. Those who raise the first objection fear that this energy will get out of hand; the second, that it will be wasted on ends too small. Precisely because of this enormous energy, the created co-creator concept is a dangerous one.[16]

Similarly, the citizen as co-creator is a dynamic and "dangerous" proposal. It is also one that the world badly needs and the church needs to claim.

TOWARD A CIVIC ECCLESIOLOGY

While the idea of the created co-creator makes theologians nervous, there is widespread caution about the idea of citizen as co-creator too. Even though people sense that its generative power offers a way out of political paralysis, it is difficult to embrace. Some fear that it lets government off the hook and expects too much of citizens. Demanding things from government is easier than being part of the solution. From government's point of view, the idea of citizens as co-creators is usually not welcome either. Government employs experts who know how to do work with predictable outcomes; involving lay citizens brings unforeseen consequences. The agency of citizens is also plainly threatening to those in power. It cannot be scripted. Politicians no longer hold center stage.

Yet the world urgently needs a new democracy paradigm. Today's complex, often interrelated problems are far too big for governments and experts to solve on their own. In order to deal with massive challenges, from climate change and pandemics to political misinformation and the growing problem of loneliness, we need much more widespread engagement in democracy as "public work." This is different from "public works," provision of large-scale public infrastructure, although there is an important constructive dimension. Public work is collaborative effort by a mix of people, working across their differences, to address common problems and create public goods, both material and cultural—a commonwealth.[17] Importantly, the idea of citizens as co-creators goes beyond the legalistic categories of citizenship to include young people under voting age and migrants who begin making a new life in a new place. Anyone who is able and willing to roll up their sleeves and co-create the common life is a citizen. This identity is honed through open democratic politics that Luke Bretherton describes as:

> the relational practices through which a common world of meaning and action is created and cultivated.... Or, to put it another way... the craft of maintaining commonality by recognizing and conciliating conflict with others in pursuit of goods held in common. It involves discovering a shared vision of human

flourishing in the face of the inevitable and intractable disagreements and differences that emerge in any form of life with others.[18]

The political idea of citizens as co-creators and the theological idea of human beings as created co-creators can be integrated into what is presented here as a civic ecclesiology. The most widespread model of the church today is "church as servant," rooted in a commitment to embody Jesus's example of how we are to love one another by washing one another's feet, both in the church and in the world.[19] Churches perform service in two main ways. First, they focus on meeting the needs of the poor and the distressed through concrete, life-giving actions that range from soup kitchens and prison visits to addiction counseling and financial loans. Second, some efforts also strive to address causes of problems, which leads Christians to engage in more explicitly "political" work (here politics is usually understood in conventional partisan terms), such as writing letters to elected representatives, participating in protest marches, and facilitating conversations about issues roiling the society from racism and LGBTQ rights to abortion and climate change. Service in this vein is seen as prophetic critique of the unjust structures of society and acts of solidarity with those who suffer.

A core aspect of Christology is that the suffering of Jesus is made visible in the suffering of the poor. This is another dimension of the *imago Dei*. Moltmann writes about the "messianism of the poor," arguing that the redemption of the rich and powerful members of society lies in the transformative encounter with Christ in the poor. This leads Moltmann to call the church the "messianic fellowship of service," a church that seeks fellowship with Jesus in proclaiming freedom to those who live "in the shadow of the cross: the poor, the handicapped, the people society has rejected, the prisoners and the persecuted."[20] This is an urgent and rousing call, but the servant metaphor for the church, like all metaphors, has a "yes" and a "no."[21]

The human being as created co-creator points toward an understanding of the church as the "messianic fellowship of co-creation," to modify Moltmann's phrase. Here the basic metaphor is that of "church as citizen," with an essential emphasis on citizen as co-creator, not simply voter, consumer, or volunteer. The citizen, in a civic ecclesiology, works with others across lines of difference in multiple settings spanning church, work, and the broader community to build our common world. The church adopts a public role as a full participant in what Bretherton calls the politics of the common life. This understanding of the church requires new habits of mind and new skills for doing public work. It also requires a different kind of leadership, oriented toward empowering members to work collectively on common concerns. It means creating a culture of agency inside the church that can be spread into the world.

The problem with the servant metaphor is that it skews the focus toward people's deficits and weaknesses. This applies to professionals in service industries such as health, welfare, and education as well as in the church. Instead of seeing human beings as created by God, uniquely gifted and filled with the power of the Holy Spirit, the expert focus is on what people lack and how they can be fixed. The poor and oppressed are too often regarded with pity. Such service is riddled with complex power dynamics, creating dependency and self-doubt as people internalize an image of themselves as helpless victims. Moltmann acknowledges this problem fleetingly: "The dialectic of lordship and servitude in society is many-faceted. There is dominion through the enslavement of others. But there is also dominion through service, and through taking on the burdens of others."[22] Critically interrogating the model of church as servant does not suggest that Christians should fail to take human suffering seriously, but rather that they respond to the weak and the needy in ways that recognize the *imago Dei*, striving to catalyze their potential.[23]

Today, in the servant church's acts of solidarity, the problem is not so much patronizing as polarizing behavior. Even an injunction as concrete as Luke 4:18—proclaiming good news to the poor, freedom to captives, sight to the blind—can be interpreted in ideological ways, embroiling Christians in the cultural and partisan wars that divide society.[24] In highly polarized environments, people on different sides of a fight demonize and dehumanize each other, making assumptions about each other's motivations and positions, refusing to listen, and using extreme language that boils over into hatred and even violence. The *co*-dimension of our calling as created co-creators demands of us that we work *with* others who are different and make us uncomfortable.

In a plural world, even within church communities, conflicts are inevitable. Countering polarization does not imply that people should strive to agree on everything. Disagreements can be deep, but they need to be respectful, and we need to remain open to learning from the other side. In the broader world of politics, seeing our fellow citizens as co-creators demands first and foremost that we recognize their dignity as human beings and believe that they have an important role to play in solving the problems we face in our local communities and nation. The philosophy of nonviolence as developed by theologians like Howard Thurman[25] and Martin Luther King[26] adds profound resources for accomplishing this. If entered into deeply as a philosophy, not simply treated as a menu of confrontational tactics, nonviolence is redemptive, enabling people on both sides of a conflict to reveal the *imago Dei*.

A civic ecclesiology focuses on productive public work, that is, the tangible work of building a good society that involves every citizen. It provides a counter to the consumerism that is ravaging our planet and, in particular, the consumer view of the citizen whose role is to demand more benefits.

Moltmann describes this as a "kindergarten mentality" into which citizens retreat too eagerly, "quite content to be secure and safely provided for, and to make over their freedom to 'Big Brother' and 'Mother Church.' Protests against their authority and retreats behind their sheltering cloak are often not very far removed from one another."[27] While government has important work to do, figuring out how these duties should best be distributed is a question that should never overlook or undermine the agency of citizens. The stakes are too high. To deal better with the problems facing the world, it is essential to tap into the knowledge, wisdom, talents, and energies of as many people as possible. This is political work in the older, non-partisan sense of the word, requiring ongoing negotiation of different interests and ideas. It offers the possibility of sustainable solutions, supported by diverse groups and not undermined or reversed by some as soon as they get the chance.

A church that focuses on its civic role nurtures the vision and skills that enable created co-creators to be agents of hope, cultivating new dispositions, "re-learning" how to recognize the likeness of God in each other and even in ourselves. Bretherton reminds us that this is the deep work of democracy, beyond the state-centric approach, and notes some of the key practices involved:

> Democracy as a political relation through which to generate and sustain a just and generous common life involves certain practices and commitments, each of which has its own point of connection to and resonance with scripture and theology. These entailments include: the need to listen and talk to each other; the need to assemble so as to form a people or demos; a moral commitment to the institutionalization of plurality; and the need to organize.[28]

The church can become a site of civic empowerment where people learn the skills for creating a democratic culture. While my experiences in this area have taken place in secular settings, I have found myself longing for the church to become central to such work.

For five years I was part of a grassroots popular education initiative in Burundi, one of the world's poorest and most conflict-ridden countries. In partnership with an NGO called the Burundi Leadership Training Program (BLTP) and the Netherlands Institute for Multi-Party Democracy (NIMD), I worked with Burundian educators to adapt Idasa's citizen leadership training program to their context and to familiarize them with the public work theory of democracy that infused the curriculum. Most Burundians felt that constitutional democracy made no difference to their lives; in fact, it only provoked new waves of conflict and violence. But learning the concept of citizens as co-creators and acquiring skills for co-creative public work was often transformative. In rural villages people worked across deep divisions to address common problems, from poor crop yields and tensions among livestock farmers and crop growers to alcoholism and teenage pregnancy.

After seeing the impact of the citizen leadership training program, the Burundi National Police negotiated with BLTP to adapt the program to help address security problems at the grassroots level in collaboration with a newly created category of community-based police men and women. "Security is everybody's business" became the slogan. Police and community leaders in equal numbers were trained to understand democracy as an integral part of their daily lives and work. They learned to see themselves and their fellow citizens as co-creators of safer communities, becoming empowered and navigating their differences by thinking and acting politically in the broader sense of the word. They began to draw on each other's resources and exercise accountability both vertically and horizontally. In short, they became community organizers. The program made a tangible difference in the places where it was implemented. Police and community members were astonished to discover what they could achieve together.

My direct involvement in the program ended once my Burundian partners felt confident that they could run it on their own. I knew this was true but was much less confident that BLTP would continue to receive the financial resources it needed from international partners. The program was not terribly expensive to run. I became convinced that it would be a lot more sustainable and have greater reach if it could be adopted by local churches, with support from their larger church bodies. I believe this provides but one example of the kind of work that churches with a civic mission could and should do everywhere, all the time, in rural and urban settings, among the rich as well as the poor.

Public theologians apply their minds to a wide range of issues. This volume engages urgent problems from racism, migration, and pandemics to injustice and repression in Asia, Africa, and elsewhere. But without working to renew democracy and repair the civic fabric, efforts to address any of these are severely hampered. Citizens' energies are diminished and the potential contributions of "undesirable" groups (however they may be defined) are sidelined. A publicly oriented "citizen church" can model empowering, citizen-driven ways of working to solve difficult problems while also developing capacity for building a shared life among people from diverse backgrounds and of diverse views. In today's irreducibly plural world where public discourse is scripted by partisan positions and identity politics that increase the distance between "us" and "them," churches can offer a radical, democratic alternative.

NOTES

1. This chapter distills key arguments from the master's thesis that I wrote with Gary Simpson as co-advisor. Gary was one of my main interlocutors as I explored the field of public theology while learning to think theologically about my work as a democracy educator. I am deeply grateful for all he has taught me both inside the classroom and out.

2. The concept of citizenship is understood throughout this chapter to entail more than legal status. See, for example, Peter Levine, "The Case for Civic Studies," in *Civic Studies*, eds. Levine and Karol Soltan (Washington D.C.: Bringing Theory to Practice, 2014), 3.

3. Michael J. Sandel, *The Tyranny of Merit: What's Become of the Common Good?* (New York: Farrar, Strauss and Giroux, 2020), 29.

4. George Packer, "How America Fractured into Four Parts," *The Atlantic* (July/August 2021).

5. Harry C. Boyte, *Everyday Politics: Reconnecting Citizens and Public Life* (Philadelphia: University of Pennsylvania Press, 2004), 93.

6. Later, simply the Institute for Democracy in South Africa but still known by the original acronym.

7. Philip J. Hefner, *The Human Factor: Evolution, Culture, and Religion*, Theology and the Sciences (Minneapolis: Fortress Press, 1993), 27.

8. Philip J. Hefner, "The Creation," in *Christian Dogmatics*, vol. 1, eds. Carl E. Braaten and Robert W. Jenson (Philadelphia: Fortress Press, 2011), 331.

9. Hefner, "The Creation," 326.

10. Jürgen Moltmann, *The Trinity and the Kingdom: The Doctrine of God* (Minneapolis: Fortress Press, 1993), 17.

11. For example, George Cladis states that "perichoresis means literally 'circle dance.'" See George Cladis, *Leading the Team-Based Church* (San Francisco: Jossey-Bass Publishers, 1999), 4.

12. Moltmann, *The Trinity*, 95.

13. Jürgen Moltmann, *God in Creation: A New Theology of Creation and the Spirit of God* (Minneapolis: Fortress Press, 1993), 225.

14. Moltmann, *God in Creation*, 227.

15. Hefner, "The Creation," 338.

16. Hefner, *The Human Factor*, 237.

17. See Institute for Public Life and Work, www.iplw.org.

18. Luke Bretherton, *Christ and The Common Life: Political Theology and the Case for Democracy* (Grand Rapids, MI: Eerdmans, 2019), 34.

19. Avery Dulles, *Models of the Church* (Garden City, NY: Doubleday, 1974), 95. The theory of "servant leadership" has proved hugely influential in business and other organizational settings, building on the seminal text by Robert K. Greenleaf, *Servant Leadership: A Journey into the Nature of Legitimate Power and Greatness* (New York: Paulist Press, 1977).

20. Jürgen Moltmann, *The Church in the Power of the Spirit: A Contribution of Messianic Ecclesiology* (Minneapolis: Fortress Press, 1993), 97.

21. I am indebted to Prof. Terence Fretheim for ingraining this in me.
22. Moltmann, *The Church*, 103–4.
23. For over thirty years, the Asset-based Community Development Institute (https://resources.depaul.edu/abcd-institute) has called for such a shift in practice in the broader world of community development.
24. See Amanda Ripley, *High Conflict: Why We Get Trapped and How We Get Out* (New York: Simon and Schuster, 2021). Ripley shows the almost irresistible pull of conflicts that bring out the worst in human beings and how difficult it is to escape them.
25. Anthony C. Siracusa, *Nonviolence Before King: The Politics of Being and the Black Freedom Struggle* (Chapel Hill: University of North Carolina Press, 2021), 48–77.
26. Martin Luther King, *Stride toward Freedom: The Montgomery Story* (New York: Harper & Brothers, 1958), 77–95.
27. Jürgen Moltmann, *The Spirit of Life: A Universal Affirmation* (Minneapolis: Fortress Press, 1992), 104.
28. Luke Bretherton, "Democracy," https://www.saet.ac.uk (forthcoming). For extensive illustration, see Luke Bretherton, *Resurrecting Democracy: Faith, Citizenship, and the Politics of a Common Life* (New York: Cambridge University Press, 2015).

Chapter 11

Pandemic Politics

Critical Social Theory and Societal Chaplaincy

Robert O. Smith

This chapter includes two of my blog entries from early 2020, at the beginning of the Covid-19 pandemic.[1] Through these attempts at social analysis, I intended to start conversations with fellow pastoral leaders. The short introductory essay preceding those blog entries is a retrospective introduction and assessment of those efforts. Throughout I have been informed by both the specific content and general commitments modeled by Gary Simpson.

Since late 2018 I have worked in the offices of the Northern Texas–Northern Louisiana Synod (NT-NL) of the Evangelical Lutheran Church in America (ELCA), both as an Associate to Bishop Erik Gronberg and as the director of Briarwood Leadership Center. Briarwood has gone through several phases of its life as an NT-NL ministry. It started nearly thirty years ago as a church campground; soon afterward it transitioned to being a retreat center. With the construction of a new building housing the NT-NL offices and providing space for educational efforts, the initial vision of Briarwood Leadership Center was realized.

Things were moving along well through the first part of 2020. Then, along with every individual, group, and institution experiencing the onset of the Covid-19 pandemic, Briarwood's world changed. Although Briarwood is a ministry, it is also a business squarely within the hospitality sector. We immediately faced the reality that our entire business model—gathering people together to experience God's love—was evaporating before our eyes. The time had come to fully develop our emerging priority of being a leadership center, providing resources to communities so they could flourish within rapidly changing societal conditions.

Given my service in the office of a synodical bishop, I sensed that pastors throughout the United States would need accompaniment and assistance as they shepherded their communities through this emerging crisis. We were convinced at the time that we were well-equipped to name and address the pastoral needs congregations would be facing. My theological training has always been inflected with political and social analysis, from my time studying with Simpson and other prominent thinkers at Luther Seminary as well as my doctoral studies in political theory and religious sociology. I was convinced that our pastors would need to utilize tools to comprehend the society-wide challenges of the pandemic moment, challenges that would directly affect congregational life.

CIVIL SOCIETY

Those thoughts were coming together in late March 2020 when, on March 23, Texas Lieutenant Governor Dan Patrick, speaking on Fox News, told Tucker Carlson that he, along with other senior citizens, would prefer death over the United States suffering the economic costs of pandemic restrictions, including the "social distancing" encouragement to stay home.

"No one reached out to me and said, as a senior citizen, 'Are you willing to take a chance on your survival in exchange for keeping the America that all America loves for your children and grandchildren?'" Patrick said. "And if that's the exchange, I'm all in . . . I just think there's lots of grandparents out there in this country like me—I have six grandchildren—that what we all care about and what we love more than anything are those children. I want to live smart and see through this. But I don't want the whole country to be sacrificed and that's what I see."[2]

I considered Lt. Gov. Patrick's messaging harmful, especially since he was allowing market-based concerns to override epidemiological evidence. As people in US states such as Texas and my home state of Oklahoma were receiving inconsistent messages from government leaders, the question of how community-based religious leaders should navigate the pandemic came to the fore. How could church leaders navigate these complex thickets without contributing to the rapidly growing trend of politicization?

My response was to communicate with the pastors of our synod, employing Simpson's reading of Jürgen Habermas's notion of "civil society" into conversation with what Simpson calls the "Christian prophetic imagination." Not wanting to name Lt. Gov. Patrick directly, I instead focused on the more analytical notion of "the economic sphere's colonization of both governance and people's lives."[3]

The blog entry utilized figures from Simpson's 2002 book, *Critical Social Theory*,[4] since it continues to be not only the clearest exposition of Habermas's ideas but also the clearest application of those ideas from a church-based perspective. My conclusions were that President Trump's statement that "'our country wasn't built to be shut down' ignores the fact that human bodies (American or not, documented or not) were not built to withstand coronaviruses against which they have no immunity."[5]

Although invoking President Trump, I asserted that "the present American reality in which Civil Society and the Political State are utterly colonized by the Market Economy is not a partisan issue."[6] The problem is that "this ideology of acquiescence to the market moves beyond 'Let them eat cake' to 'Let them die.'" In such a political moment, the notion of "necropolitics," theorized by Cameroonian philosopher and political theorist Achille Mbembe in conversation with Foucault and Agamben, forces us to ponder "the power and the capacity to dictate who may live and who must die, the power to kill or to allow to live."[7] Necropolitical dynamics and conditions, both within "normal" times and in states of exception, are undoubtedly matters of church concern.

SOCIETAL CHAPLAINCY

Those efforts to promote societal analysis catalyzed a new series of thoughts toward vocational responsibility. My next blog post, this time published on the NT-NL website, introduced the concept of "societal chaplaincy" as we pondered church actions in the coming weeks and months. At that point nobody was thinking, or at least publicly communicating, that the pandemic would stretch into the coming years.

Building on the foundation of critical social theory presented by Simpson, I first sought to comprehend the scope of the unfolding Covid-19 crisis. At that point, in early April 2020, the United States had just surpassed three thousand Covid deaths; Dr. Deborah Birx, President Trump's White House Coronavirus Response Coordinator, suggested that the United States could see a hundred thousand deaths "if we do things almost perfectly."[8] At the time some models were projecting "a potential American death toll between 1.6 and 2.2 million."[9] The present writing in late 2021 has just seen the death toll exceed 800,000, indicating that those upper-end numbers aren't out of reach.

In response to what at the time seemed like "eye-popping numbers," I suggested that Americans would have a difficult time coping with the challenges ahead. No experience with a magnitude close to Covid-19 had ever occurred within the United States, at least since the Civil War. My sense was that national leadership—far more occupied with economic rather than human loss—was not preparing "the American people for the national trauma to come."[10] Even religious leaders were "not yet looking at the broader implications of this crisis" and were focused instead on "not being able to gather in person" and the resulting effect on financial support. "While those concerns are real," I said, "they pale in comparison to the societal trauma for which local governmental and public health leaders are actively preparing."

In response to these epochal developments, I urged development of something like "societal chaplaincy," a vocational stance that "involves broadening comprehension of our call to include community-wide and societal well-being" extending far beyond our primary, often congregational, communities. Building implicitly on the need to critically restructure the relationship between civil society and the governmental and economic spheres, I urged proactive engagement with medical professionals, funeral home directors, first responders, local policymakers, and communities of color, including Indigenous communities.

LET THEM DIE: COVID-19, CIVIL SOCIETY, AND THE MARKET ECONOMY
MARCH 24, 2020

Recently, President Trump again changed his central message to Americans regarding the COVID-19 coronavirus pandemic. After first downplaying the severity of the pandemic, comparing it to the common flu, Trump transitioned to a more somber tone,[11] suggesting that American lives would not resemble "normal" until months from now. Today, the same day Surgeon General Jerome Adams warned that "this week, it's going to get bad,"[12] the President said[13] that "America will again and soon be open for business. Very soon. A lot sooner than three or four months that somebody was suggesting."[14]

From a science-based public health point of view, this rhetoric is deeply irresponsible. Science, however, is not the main determinant of the President's political strategy. As he said in the March 23 press conference, "If it were up to the doctors, they'd say let's shut down the entire world."

This flippant rhetoric indicates an even deeper defect in present American culture: the economic sphere's colonization of both governance and people's lives. This colonization, although long in the making, promises to produce disastrous results if President Trump's current thinking is allowed to shape public health policy.

Although I analyze this situation from a theological and ethical viewpoint, I am influenced by German philosopher Jürgen Habermas's[15] work on social and political theory, especially his understanding of "Civil Society" as the sphere of democratic possibility. Civil society is the collection of organizations and institutions developed by people to organize and represent the traditions, values, and interests that shape their lifeworld.

The ideal relationship between Civil Society, on one hand, and the Political State and Market Economy, at least from the perspective of regular, everyday people, looks something like this (both figures drawn from Gary Simpson's *Critical Social Theory*[16]):

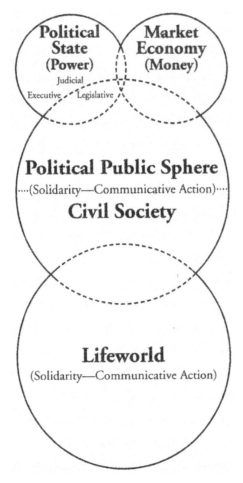

Figure 11.1. Civil Society between Lifeworld and Political State/Market Economy. *Critical Social Theory: Prophetic Reason, Civil Society, and Christian Imagination, Guides to Theological Inquiry* (Fortress Press, 2002), p. 121.

In this figure one's lifeworld feeds into Civil Society, which then informs the State and the Market Economy, with their mediums of governmental systems and money. While that chart may show the actual contours of American lives, it in no way reflects the messages and priorities received through American media consumption. What we are told we should care about (national party politics and the economy, represented by little more than the Dow Jones Industrial Average) looks a lot more like figure 11.2.

In this figure we see the Lifeworld and Civil Society squashed under the impinging weight of the Political State and the Market Economy. Rather than those systems serving the needs of the people, the people are perceived within those systems as serving their interests.

The present COVID-19 crisis provides example after example of how this colonization informs policymakers' decisions. Is this a public health crisis or an economic crisis? In truth, of course, it is both. But it is an economic crisis within the Lifeworld of regular people—a crisis within the *real* economy— rather than primarily a crisis of the stock market. That fact has been confusing for policymakers concerned primarily with corporate liquidity; they are used to letting corporations make their own decisions regarding the well-being of workers.

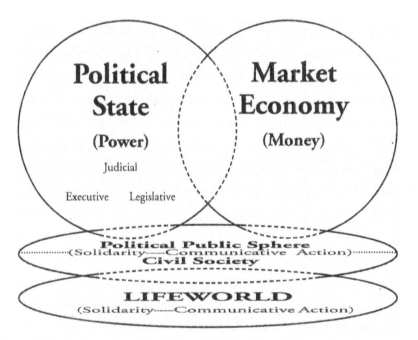

Figure 11.2. Colonization of the Lifeworld. *Critical Social Theory: Prophetic Reason, Civil Society, and Christian Imagination, Guides to Theological Inquiry* (Fortress Press, 2002), p. 114.

The Market Economy has colonized the Political State as well as Civil Society to the extent that the President of the United States has been pulled back from recognizing the seriousness of this health crisis for people's lives and has placed the well-being of the Market Economy in direct competition with the wellbeing of American citizens. Saying "our country wasn't built to be shut down" ignores the fact that human bodies (American or not, documented or not) were not built to withstand coronaviruses against which they have no immunity.

The present American reality in which Civil Society and the Political State are utterly colonized by the Market Economy is not a partisan issue. These values are promoted by neoliberal Democrats no less than Log Cabin Republicans. In the midst of American struggle with this pandemic, this ideology of acquiescence to the market moves beyond "Let them eat cake" to "Let them die." At present, there is no starker example of contemporary American domestic necropolitics[17] and no greater illustration of why this crisis could be leveraged to produce a renewal of American political culture.

SOCIETAL CHAPLAINCY: PREPARING FOR THE STORM TO COME
APRIL 4, 2020

As the magnitude of the COVID-19 crisis is revealed, religious leaders—at every level, national to local—will be challenged to respond to the needs of their communities and society at large. The magnitude and scope of this disaster will fundamentally challenge American society, shaping the callings and responsibilities of all pastors, priests, imams, and rabbis.

The Scope of the Problem

On March 29 President Trump and the Coronavirus Task Force extended federal social distancing guidelines until April 30 and announced that a US death toll from the virus under a hundred thousand would be a success. The United States is well on its way toward that figure.

On March 2 the US had confirmed one hundred COVID-19 coronavirus infections. On April 2[18] that figure had increased to 244,678 cases. While infection rates aren't entirely reliable given problems in national testing procedures, the number of deaths is clear. On March 30 the US surpassed three thousand COVID-19 deaths. That number had doubled by April 2.

To put these numbers into the perspective of relatively recent American experience, 2,977 Americans, mostly civilians, died in the terrorist attacks of 9/11. The magnitude of the present challenge is clarified when we realize that the estimate of 100,000 to 240,000 deaths is the low end of a model projecting a potential American death toll between 1.6 and 2.2 million.

A hundred thousand deaths, according to Task Force coordinator Dr. Deborah Birx, is a best-case scenario "if we do things almost perfectly."[19] The problem, of course, is that the US response to this crisis hasn't gone "almost perfectly" at almost any turn. To compare with another American tragedy, the US Civil War killed an estimated 750,000.[20] If we lose a hundred thousand Americans in a one-month period, the US would be experiencing 9/11-level losses on every day of that month, spread throughout the country.

In addition to this high death toll, millions more will be infected with the virus, experiencing a range of symptom severity. As it has in Italy, this virus will fundamentally challenge aspects of American self-understanding. Without a doubt it is a generational moment. We will all remember Spring 2020 and its aftershocks.

Slowly Dawning Recognition

I share these eye-popping numbers not to provoke despondency or despair but to indicate the struggle that lies ahead for the United States. It is a challenge unlike any the US has ever faced. That may be why our national response to this crisis has been exceptionally inadequate,[21] especially in comparison to most other Western democracies.

In some ways President Trump himself embodies the process through which Americans have come to grasp the monumental nature of the challenges that lie ahead.

President Trump ended his March 29 press conference with an addendum, something he wanted everyone listening to hear. "I grew up in Queens, NY," close to Elmhurst Hospital, a facility that had been overrun in the days just prior to the press conference. "I've been watching that for the last week on television." The President described freezer trucks being brought in because the hospital morgue was full. And he was taking it personally. "I've seen things I've never seen before. I mean, I've seen them, but I've seen them on television in faraway lands."

For Americans, wars and massive human tragedies are events that occur "over there," as President Trump put it, "in faraway lands." For centuries America prided itself on having not been attacked by a foreign enemy on its mainland territory—Pearl Harbor and 9/11 are dismissed as cheap shots. For the most part, the United States has imagined the Atlantic and Pacific as buffers insulating it from a conflicted world.

As a result, Americans have never seen anything like this in the US mainland. The United States has not experienced famine or war in the last century. We are not accustomed to seeing a field hospital[22] set up in New York City's

Central Park—a structure most often set up by xenophobic televangelist Franklin Graham's organization, Samaritan's Purse, in faraway countries. As the national grief and trauma following 9/11 attested, Americans are not accustomed to considering thousands—or hundreds of thousands—of fellow Americans killed.

Preparing for the Storm

Because we have not had national experiences of suffering and loss, Americans may not yet have the capacity to comprehend the scope, scale, and magnitude of what lies ahead with COVID-19. Most Americans are, by now, aware of the shocking numbers listed above. Our primary response has been to seek the safety and comfort of our families, not anticipate broader societal impacts and implications. We have not yet responded collectively.

National leadership has not prepared the American people for the national trauma to come. Religious communities—as congregations, as regional bodies, as denominations, and within ecumenical and interfaith alliances—have a clear role to play. In the absence of national leadership from the governmental sphere, religious leaders can help name, address, and respond to this emerging societal need.

But we are not yet there. My sense is that many religious leaders—I am speaking to local, regional, and national levels—are not yet looking at the broader implications of this crisis. Congregational pastors, for instance, are focused on addressing the challenges created by their communities not being able to gather in person; online worship plans have been developed in short order. They are additionally worried about how the lack of gatherings will affect financial support. While those concerns are real, they pale in comparison to the societal trauma for which local governmental and public health leaders are actively preparing.

As this moment will define a generation, it has the ability to shape our pastoral vocations, calling us to an urgent sense of societal chaplaincy. Societal chaplaincy involves broadening comprehension of our call to include community-wide and societal well-being. This call includes our primary communities and congregations while extending far beyond.

As we consider the scope of this crisis, the societal chaplain takes seriously the ethical challenges and practical implications of medical professionals determining who receives access to life-saving medical care and who does not. These decisions will result in the need for mass palliative care and counseling for both patients and families. Such a situation demands rethinking how death and dying are viewed as both morgues and funeral homes[23] are stretched beyond capacity, individual funerals are impossible, and municipalities need to consider mass burial policies. Societal chaplaincy is made necessary when we are anticipating a scale of suffering and death beyond the scope of what most of us can even imagine.

Societal chaplaincy involves critical engagement with policymakers and governmental authorities, ensuring that policies are equitable and just. As hospitals implement ethical structures for rationing life-saving resources, marginalized communities—persons of color, immigrants, Indigenous peoples, the immunocompromised, and those living with disabilities—will potentially be denied services[24] at a greater rate. As in all moments of crisis, COVID-19 will exacerbate already existing social inequities. A societally minded religious leader will understand that elected officials and clinicians will seek the best for all persons in their communities while guarding against inequities and unconscious bias.

Each religious tradition has wells of spiritual resources and social critique to draw from in times of extreme challenge. The relative comfort of American society—especially apparent in predominantly white, mainline denominations like my own—diminishes our capacity to draw fully from those wells.

Faith leaders will need to be strong voices of support for local officials seeking the best for all persons in their communities. Local leaders seeking to implement social controls when national and statewide leaders lack courage need our vocal support. As healthcare providers and first responders are depleted due to ongoing infection and quarantine, those systems will begin to falter due to lack of personnel, in addition to the shortage of personal protective equipment (PPE). Medical personnel will be threatened when some families receive news of unwelcome clinical decisions regarding access to care. Faith leaders can be important voices to help maintain the bonds of civic trust, good order, and the structure of civil society.

My fellow faith leaders, the COVID-19 coronavirus crisis is expanding our vocation. We are called to look outward for the benefit not just of our own communities but for the good of society itself as we seek to promote the flourishing of human communities. This developing tragedy is also a time of potentially tremendous remaking.

What do you perceive is needed in such a time as this?

What global and communal wisdom can we draw upon for responding to this axial moment?

I invite you into this conversation so we can consider together what we might be able to accomplish for the good of all. Stay tuned for potential ways we can engage these and other questions collectively as faith leaders.

CONCLUSION:
EQUIPPING CHURCH LEADERS

Writing now in early 2022, it is apparent that the ideas I offered near the beginning of the pandemic, while drawing some interest, did not take hold in a way that transformed the ELCA's societal response to the (ongoing) COVID-19 pandemic.[25] That does not mean, however, that such efforts are in vain. Given their attempt to identify, confront, and reverse a colonizing process, they represent instead what Jewish philosopher Santiago Slabodsky might call a "triumphal failure of barbaric thinking."[26]

2020 and 2021 have seen efforts to mobilize civil society efforts to challenge governmental and economic systems. The intensification of the Movement for Black Lives following the murders of George Floyd and Ahmaud Arbery are pertinent examples. It is often the case, however, that these movements understand themselves to be organizing in spite of religious institutional authority rather than being inspired in any way by religious commitments.[27] It is no surprise, therefore, to have seen most "mainline" denominations and the constituent congregations turn in on themselves rather than engage the broader questions posed by concepts such as societal chaplaincy.

Indeed, 2021 has seen many efforts by entrenched establishments to push back on any effort to change virtually any status quo. All sides of American political equations have seen the pandemic as an opportunity to bring change. The massive effort among certain political leaders to foment and then to underplay the significance of the January 6, 2021, assault on the US Capitol is one example. Attacks against Critical Race Theory, as baseless as they are coordinated, is another.[28] The trend of politicization in local life (the "lifeworld" of civil society) has manifested itself in higher COVID death rates for people living in counties that voted for President Trump[29] and in the continued intrusion of national political parties into local elections.[30]

Rather than actively countering these trends, many congregations have been torn apart by conflicts over masking and social distancing practices. Churches have not found ways to adequately address the onslaught of disinformation encountered by their members. We are a thermometer registering political attitudes rather than a thermostat seeking to change the temperature of public debate.[31]

Many progressive Christians are understandably wary of claiming Christian power to influence societal change. Any hope we might have for renewing our social authority, however, will need to begin with revisiting theories and theologies of power, a study that will necessarily consider the possibility that such power is not ours to have.

A stance of societal chaplaincy is potentially useful not only for extraordinary circumstances like a global pandemic. The stance of listening and seeking comprehension of broad systems of life rather than addressing an isolated point of crisis could serve religious communities well as they demonstrate their holistic care and concern for society itself. It is possible that, in these reflections on political theology and critical social theory, we can revive interest in Dietrich Bonhoeffer's later reflections on the call to being "'religionless-worldly' Christians" who practice an "arcane discipline" for the sake of the world.[32]

My failure to transform American society with the preceding blog posts does not mean my efforts were wasted. Seminaries and divinity schools must continue to make room for both the well-defined disciplinary study of history, liturgy, and theology and for various forms of practical reflection and pastoral training alongside competencies in engaging various lenses and tools of social analysis. Without these various disciplines working side-by-side, we have no hope of producing leaders—lay, rostered, and ordained—who can discern God's will not just for leadership within churches but for the sake of a rapidly changing world desperately in need of the gospel.

NOTES

1. See Robert O. Smith, "Let Them Die: COVID-19, Civil Society and the Market Economy," *An Okie Abroad*, Wordpress, March 24, 2020, https://robertowensmith.wordpress.com/2020/03/24/let-them-die-covid-19-civil-society-and-the-market-economy/; and Robert O. Smith, "Societal Chaplaincy: Preparing for the Storm to Come," Northern Texas–Northern Louisiana Synod of the ELCA, April 4, 2020, https://www.ntnl.org/societal-chaplaincy-preparing-for-the-storm-to-come/.

2. Matt Stieb, "Texas Lt. Gov. Dan Patrick: 'Lots of Grandparents' Willing to Die to Save Economy for Grandchildren," *New York Post*, March 23, 2020, https://nymag.com/intelligencer/2020/03/dan-patrick-seniors-are-willing-to-die-to-save-economy.html. Patrick returned to Fox News close to a month later to defend and expand his rhetoric. See Alex Samuels, "Dan Patrick Says 'There Are More Important Things Than Living and That's Saving This Country,'" *Texas Tribune*, April 21, 2020, https://www.texastribune.org/2020/04/21/texas-dan-patrick-economy-coronavirus/.

3. Smith, "Let Them Die."

4. Gary M. Simpson, *Critical Social Theory: Prophetic Reason, Civil Society, and Christian Imagination* (Minneapolis: Fortress, 2002).

5. Trump quote from Kathryn Watson, "Trump says U.S. 'was not built to be shut down,' signaling eagerness to reboot economy," *CBS News*, March 24, 2020, https://www.cbsnews.com/news/president-trump-economy-back-to-work/.

6. Smith, "Let Them Die."

7. Achille Mbembe, "Necropolitics," trans. Libby Meintjes, *Public Culture* 15:1 (Winter 2003): 11. See also Mbembe, *Necropolitics* (Durham: Duke University Press, 2019), 11.

8. Ben Kesslen, "Dr. Birx Predicts Up to 200,000 U.S. Coronavirus Deaths 'If We Do Things Almost Perfectly,'" *NBC News*, March 30, 2020, https://www.nbcnews.com/news/us-news/dr-deborah-birx-predicts-200-000-deaths-if-we-do-n1171876.

9. Smith, "Societal Chaplaincy."

10. Smith, "Societal Chaplaincy."

11. Jill Colvin et al., "Trump Changes His Tone, Gets Real on the Coronavirus Threat," *Associated Press*, March 17, 2020, https://apnews.com/article/public-health-donald-trump-us-news-ap-top-news-virus-outbreak-138aee1ff66cd878c084731300ba529b.

12. Rebecca Shabad, "Surgeon General Has Coronavirus Warning: 'This Week, It's Going to Get Bad,'" *NBC News*, March 23, 2020, https://www.nbcnews.com/politics/white-house/surgeon-general-has-coronavirus-warning-week-it-s-going-get-n1166421.

13. Caitlin Oprysko and Quint Forgey, "'Our Country Wasn't Built to Be Shut Down': Trump Pushes Back against Health Experts," *Politico*, March 23, 2020, https://www.politico.com/news/2020/03/23/trump-coronavirus-lockdown-skepticism-143800.

14. Kathryn Watson, "Trump Says Coronavirus Crisis Could Last until July or August," *CBS News,* March 17, 2020, https://www.cbsnews.com/news/coronavirus-crisis-trump-july-august/.

15. James Bohman and William Rehg, "Jürgen Habermas," in *The Stanford Encyclopedia of Philosophy* (Fall 2017), ed. Edward N. Zalta, https://plato.stanford.edu/archives/fall2017/entries/habermas/.

16. Simpson, *Critical Social Theory*.

17. See Mbembe, "Necropolitics," 11–40.

18. Figures were drawn from Center for Systems Science and Engineering (CSSE) at Johns Hopkins University (JHU), "Covid-19 Dashboard," https://gisanddata.maps.arcgis.com/apps/dashboards/bda7594740fd40299423467b48e9ecf6.

19. Kesslen, "Dr. Birx Predicts."

20. Guy Gugliotta, "New Estimate Raises Civil War Death Toll," *New York Times*, April 2, 2012, https://www.nytimes.com/2012/04/03/science/civil-war-toll-up-by-20-percent-in-new-estimate.html.

21. Fareed Zakaria, "It's Easy to Blame Trump for This Fiasco. But There's a Much Larger Story," *Washington Post*, March 26, 2020, https://www.washingtonpost.com/opinions/the-us-is-still-exceptional--but-now-for-its-incompetence/2020/03/26/4d6d1ade-6f9b-11ea-a3ec-70d7479d83f0_story.html.

22. Janelle Griffith, "'It's Surreal,' Nurse Practitioner Says of Field Hospital Set Up in Central Park amid Coronavirus Pandemic," *NBC News*, March 30, 2020, https://www.nbcnews.com/news/us-news/it-s-surreal-nurse-practitioner-says-field-hospital-set-central-n1172376.

23. Jake Seiner and John Minchillo, "'Surreal': NY Funeral Homes Struggle as Virus Deaths Surge," *Associated Press*, April 2, 2020, https://apnews.com/article/virus-outbreak-us-news-ap-top-news-new-york-city-photography-4ecadae923cc6bf3db3cf38757e68d9b?fbclid=IwAR1ZeUD2_cBzQcj6gEpdFLXRMDcCwXJCDG3Z4JD-zu97TrG8PCL_dfWH6XA.

24. Blake Farmer, "The Coronavirus Doesn't Discriminate. U.S. Health Care May Be a Different Story," *National Public Radio and Nashville Public Radio*, April 1, 2020, https://www.wvpublic.org/2020-04-01/the-coronavirus-doesnt-discriminate-u-s-health-care-may-be-a-different-story#stream/0.

25. The ideas did gain some denominational traction. I was honored to provide a presentation for ELCA Coaching, an important new ministry within the ELCA churchwide organization. See Robert O. Smith, "Grief and Hope: Societal Chaplaincy for and beyond Covid-19," ELCA Coaching, April 22, 2020, recorded at https://www.elcacoaching.org/podcasts/media/2020-04-22-grief-and-hope-societal-chaplaincy-for-and-beyond-covid-19.

26. See Santiago Slabodsky, *Decolonial Judaism: Triumphal Failures of Barbaric Thinking* (New York: Palgrave Macmillan, 2014).

27. On this point, see Kelsey Dallas, "Where Are Churches in the Black Lives Matter Movement?," *Deseret News*, July 24, 2020, https://www.deseret.com/indepth/2020/7/24/21334268/black-lives-matter-protests-civil-rights-movement-john-lewis-race-religion-churches; Myriam Renaud and Lerone Jonathan Wilder, "Black Lives Matter: Where are the Black Clergy?" *Aljazeera*, February 24, 2021, https://www.aljazeera.com/features/2021/2/24/black-lives-matter-where-are-the-black-clergy; Christina Turner, "Where Does the Black Church Fit in Today's Black Lives Matter Movement?" *PBS NewsHour*, March 30, 2021, https://www.pbs.org/newshour/nation/where-does-the-black-church-fit-in-todays-black-lives-matter-movement.

28. See Adam Harris, "The GOP's 'Critical Race Theory' Obsession: How Conservative Politicians and Pundits Became Fixated on an Academic Approach," *The Atlantic*, May 7, 2021, https://www.theatlantic.com/politics/archive/2021/05/gops-critical-race-theory-fixation-explained/618828/; and Stephen Sawchuk, "What Is Critical Race Theory, and Why Is It Under Attack?" *EducationWeek*, May 18, 2021, https://www.edweek.org/leadership/what-is-critical-race-theory-and-why-is-it-under-attack/2021/05.

29. Daniel Wood and Geoff Brumfiel, "Pro-Trump Counties Now Have Far Higher COVID Death Rates. Misinformation Is to Blame," *National Public Radio*, December 5, 2021, https://www.npr.org/sections/health-shots/2021/12/05/1059828993/data-vaccine-misinformation-trump-counties-covid-death-rate.

30. Ross Ramsey, "Analysis: From Homegrown Culture Warriors to Tomorrow's Texas Leaders," *The Texas Tribune*, December 13, 2021, https://www.texastribune.org/2021/12/13/texas-republican-local-elections/.

31. Cf. Martin Luther King, Jr., "Letter from Birmingham Jail," in *A Testament of Hope: The Essential Writings of Martin Luther King, Jr.*, ed. James Melvin Washington (San Francisco: Harper and Row, 1986), 300.

32. See Dietrich Bonhoeffer, *Letters and Papers from Prison*, vol. 8 of *Dietrich Bonhoeffer Works*, ed. Christian Gremmels et al., trans. Isabel Best et al. (Minneapolis, MN: Fortress Press, 2010), 405–6.

PART III

Faith and Religion in Contemporary Society

Gregory Walter investigates the problems of a theology of the cross in our "forensically fraught world," as Gary M. Simpson called it. He pursues the implications of Simpson's alliterative phrase, which engages the theology of the cross by the communicative court of reason. Walter weaves Simpson's considerations into an outline of the theology of the cross in five propositions, whose truth is predicated on the promise of the crucified Jesus's resurrection. The world, taken up by the wisdom of the cross, depends upon hoping in these promises and God's faithfulness—hope which finds expression through confession, repentance, and prayer.

David E. Fredrickson asserts that astonishment and silence, not belief, constitute the existential attitude that seeks to be passed from the main characters in the Gospel of Mark to the readers of the text. Fredrickson provides a brief tour of "the astonishing world of the Gospel of Mark," supplemented by relevant philosophic texts and epic poetry, to reveal ways that Mark's Gospel preserves astonishment and overcomes attempts to dull its effects upon Mark's characters. Fredrickson asks—and purposefully does not seek to answer—what possible use might their forms of astonishment be for the public theologian in the Christian tradition.

While reason seeks to suture the contradictions and incompleteness of nature and history, Guillermo Hansen maintains that faith represents a counterstrike within the very processes that guide human evolution. Leaning on Luther's concept of faith in the light of contemporary cognitive theories, he argues that faith embodies a different representational state. In the Christian tradition grounded in the motif of the cross, promises emerge where incompleteness is not disguised or sutured but revealed as a short circuit that jolts the creature into a new mode of being. Thus, Hansen concludes, faith expresses a new imagination, a new metaphorical frame, and mental representation committed to the value of what is discarded and wasted—both in nature as well as in society.

Josh de Keijzer contends that Christianity, to retain some degree of relevance and prophetic effectiveness in late modernity, must replace the concept of revelation as imparted *knowledge* with revelation as a kind of *being* made manifest in Jesus. His essay is patterned along Bonhoeffer's argument for "religionless Christianity" in *Act and Being*, but he arrives at different conclusions. For de Keijzer, an important underlying assumption is that the secular is as religious as any religion that preceded it. He argues for "religionless theology" out of historical necessity and compelling theological arguments, particularly the theology of the cross.

Chapter 12

Problems of a Theology of the Cross

Gregory Walter

> It was a strange and dreadful strife
> When life and death contended.[1]

If someone were to earn the name of a theologian of the cross, Martin Luther has told us that they are able to do nothing less than call things by their right name.[2] These theologians are, further, to share in God's wisdom such that, though that wisdom is weak, they show all human wisdom to be absurd. What many reject as shameful, the theologian of the cross embraces with pride. No matter the price required to think about the weakness of God or reject concepts draped in divine visibility and glory, these theologies of the cross have paved the way forward for any number of modern theological concerns, connecting to existential, emancipatory, and secular projects, as well as being elevated to a meta-critical theories or fundamental theological commitments. Taking the cross as the motor, axle, and center of all thought echoes Martin Luther's gnomic utterance: "The cross tests all!"[3] Whether drawing from any of the dimensions of this tradition, theologians of the cross find God hiding under what appears to be the opposite of God, divested of glory.

Because of the remarkable claims and power of the theology of the cross, it merits close attention, especially since that though it pledges to topple idols, it can engender authoritarian habits. These habits can be equally termed epistemological or ethical kinds of authoritarianism beyond those that afflict political and social life.[4] To disclose reality as it is without any further appeal disables all of our further questions, justifications, or pleas. To state what things truly are runs terrible risks in a world of plural names, worlds, and perspectives, bringing about disrespect and injury by giving things their wrong names. If the cross bluntly turns away our inquiring spade, preventing it from excavating more, we no longer can call the cross and its theologians to account. The critical veto would then have vanished.[5]

Paul, of course, used the cross critically. The cross itself was a punitive and juridical tool, whose power was not lost on Paul when he made it a central criterion of life instead of something that was itself judged and used as an instrument of terror (Gal 3:13). It seems to go contrary to the theology of the cross to suborn it to examination by another. After all, the point, Paul states, is to make the cross a scandal and absurdity in others' eyes (1 Cor 1:23–25)! But since the cross is a promise, it is part of the trials of the world. In particular, how the cross engages human reason requires us to inquire how the cross joins reason's own trial with itself.

I. THE FORENSICALLY FRAUGHT WORLD

If the event of the cross puts God to trial, the cross should itself be exposed to the trial of reason and, in that contention, enter into the trial of human reason with itself. Fulfilling this demand means attending to what trials are: forensic domains which admit debate, plea, demand, and the whole range of conversation and communication. Gary Simpson points the way forward for developing the problems of a theology of the cross when he extends this sense of trial, debate, and plea to the entire world, calling it "the forensically fraught world."[6] If the cross avoids such a world of trial, reasons, and demands, it is no cross and certainly not God's. How this cross is God's cross, how it offers such a disclosure of reality—all these things require our investigation, especially since it seems that such a focus on the cross lacks an explicit discussion of the very resurrection of Jesus crucified.

This examination rests in articulating what sort of claims this weak divine wisdom allows us to make and, with that, what sort of reality it proposes in conjunction with thoroughly recognizing its forensically saturated world. Challenge, answer, question, or plea: forensics here denotes a broad characterization of life as shot through with demand, question, and reply. Such a life saturated with forensic forces especially shows in the question of whose cross and what suffering this theology concerns since many kinds of theologians extend or even replace the cross on which Jesus was executed with other analogical or metaphorical crosses. Taking these questions up will allow us to root out a nascent theological authoritarianism, always lurking in claims that offer what seems to be the final or only word on what things are, and truly make it a weak wisdom. We need to make our claims firmly from the cross even while we recognize their limitations: that others may object and that we might get our claims wrong.

This problem also has epistemological and procedural consequences since it has to do both with the way that the cross engenders claims to truth as well as how the wisdom of the cross interacts with people's particular perspectives and history. Gary Simpson, in the same seminal article in which he argued for the forensically fraught world, outlined this anti-authoritarian need as well as the crucial aspects of a theology of the cross, and his theses merit continued attention. Simpson's important proposal is the claim he makes about the forensically fraught world and the concomitant need for our reasoning, even as theologians of the cross, never to allow our theological claims to evade the communicative court of reason. Three needs come out of his work: the theology of the cross in connection to reason and rationality (188–91), its reparation as the theology of the resurrected crucified one (192), and, in consequence, clarity on the sorts of claims one can make as a theologian of the cross in light of this crucified wisdom and word as promise.[7] I will weave these considerations together by offering an outline of the theology of the cross.

II. THEOLOGY OF THE CROSS

In order to think through these problems, we need to get clearer on what the theology of the cross entails, especially since there seems to be no single theology of the cross but many. As articulated by Hubertus Blaumeiser and Michael Korthaus in their valuable studies, the theology of the cross comes in many kinds.[8] Rather than engage in the interpretation of texts in this tradition and weigh their reception, I outline elements of the theology of the cross as a way to articulate these problems. I offer comments on each proposition in the outline.

(I). The cross discloses a world in which its members and God may be called by their right names.

This proposition (I) combines the apocalyptic wisdom of Paul with the much-used thesis from Luther's Heidelberg Disputation: "Theologians of the cross call a thing what it is."[9] Paul's cruciform wisdom allows for contradiction of other rationalities and has an especially pragmatic and epistemological cast.[10] In Paul's hands the wisdom of the cross dwells in a person so that the speaker can disclose the world under a new age, a world disclosed by the cross itself. This apocalyptic orientation harbors enormous authoritarian potential because the disclosure of a whole world cuts off all possibilities alien to that new life unveiled. Speaking of a new world can consign all else to the dying old world. Luther's version of calling things by their names trades less in this apocalyptic motif but depends on a distinction between name and reality such that we could easily call things by their wrong names. It remains a question whether Luther intends this use of names to apply to all things or only to God hidden in the cross. This too is expressed in Luther's emphatic rejection of what he calls the theology of glory.[11] Though it may be that Luther does not require the unveiling of a new world to offer things their right names, both of these seem to be disclosive in their intent. Rather than articulating a singular claim within a larger horizon, the wisdom of the cross reveals and shifts the entire world, giving it as a new world rather than an item within it.

This disclosure can be epistemically authoritarian if it does not allow for the recognition of hesitations, doubts, or the critical veto. Allowing for such recognition means that this world is forensically fraught. Gary Simpson's usefully alliterative phrase teaches us about an important feature of our judgments: that every claim, even a claim about the disclosure of the world as a whole, is made within and among disputes of power, justification, and truth.[12] When we make a claim, we assert it to be valid, that is, justified according to our best lights and sense. Simpson, following Jürgen Habermas but expanding on him, holds that recognizing the plural kinds of validity claims that we make depends upon a common conversation in the play, encounter, and evaluation of each other's reasons (188). People have their own ways of justifying their claims or making sense of and evaluating the claims of others. Asserting the many kinds of validity claims that many make is a procedural commitment with substantive purpose: respect for ourselves and each other demands we take seriously other's claims, pleas, and laments. Such respect is the root of anti-authoritarian practice.

Justification in this sense points to the needs and demands each of us has to make the best judgments we can make given what we each know and where we are. Considering our varied epistemic resources and vantage points, it makes sense to invoke the notion of a standpoint or position to articulate the place each person occupies. Sometimes I am more able to perceive something given my experience or history just as often as I am blind to what I have never known. Justification focuses, in this sense, on ourselves and our claims and what we grant to each other out of respect.

Some of the most difficult problems facing theologians of the cross depend upon whether they rely solely on a form of justification fixed to theological suppositions or if the claims such a person makes may in some sense exceed the constraints of their position or standpoint to be justified in other positions, if not worthy of being called true. In short, if the power of cruciform wisdom helps us to see things as they are, that perception may depend only on those who have the presuppositions shaped by that wisdom. To those who do not share that wisdom, such naming proves alien and likely wrong. In such a situation, the cross has no justification. This means that those who do not suppose the world to be saturated with God's weak wisdom in Jesus's crucifixion may judge the theologian of the cross's claims to be wrong, misguided, harmful, or simply a matter of trivial personal commitment. If we persist in holding our claims justified and true in that situation without taking into account this dissent or indifference, we risk an authoritarian version of the theology of the cross.

An authoritarian version of justification poses two problems: either it pretends to a viewpoint purified of all history, culture, and power, or it utterly isolates that viewpoint from the questions, pleas, and inquiry of others. In both cases it collapses the justification of a claim with its truth. In the modern gerrymandering of life into religious and secular domains, religious claims could seem to make sense on their own, a version of William James's definition of religion as that what we do in our epistemic solitude.[13] The theologian of the cross may see fit to limit their judgments to their own vantage, to give up on the idea that their claims affect the world beyond their own, or may apply to those who do not acknowledge the particular background assumptions and beliefs that the theologian of the cross possesses.

Simpson notes about the forensically fraught world is one that "the human community can never get beyond[,] nor should it ever appeal or regress below the communicative courtroom" (181). Because of the specific promise borne by the wisdom of the cross, the claims that one can make exceed our own locales since a promise is temporally extended and God's promise addresses the whole world. But we have not yet addressed the idea that the cross discloses the world as it is, calling creatures by their true names.

(II). The cross itself is an event in which God entirely submits Godself to the forensically fraught world so that such wisdom (I) may be practiced.

The many important theological distinctions between creator and creature, between time and eternity, and between God and the world founder on the cross if the cross is itself to disclose a world in which God is rightly called God, creator and creature distinguished, and time taken into God's own life. Simpson describes this aspect of the cross this way: "God submits to and becomes dependent upon the forensically fraught world" (190). This point needs a starting point in the cross as an event since this proposition (II) articulates a particular meaning of the cross in and among the many meanings the cross may hold.

Taking the cross as an event allows us to recognize that it bears many different meanings and historical effects. The death of Jesus is one execution among many, one act of political spectacle and terror wrought by an empire.[14] Yet the death of Jesus is vested with hope and love. Some have tried to wreathe it with roses. The multiplicity of crosses is born in the single event of the cross. Simpson urges us to frame this cross in the communicative court of reason so that the cross is subject to reason's multiple trials. If we intend to take it as God's own cross, that the cross bears Jesus at the extreme of his fidelity to and despair of his mission, we have to argue for it. We cannot simply take the cross that enables this new world to be given. This event may bear this meaning, but it depends upon a convincing argument to justify it to others in ways that make sense to them. The theologians of the cross are caught up in the trial of the cross: they may give voice to its truth by attempting to justify it in the communicative court.

Communicative reason, as we learn from Jürgen Habermas, is not a specific model of reasoning but rather a way to think about the many kinds of rationalities humans employ in their interaction. Each kind of human activity has a different form of rationality proper to it. We employ deduction when needed, inference when possible, and evidential testing in others. Communicative reason offers a way to think about the unity and diversity of human reason. It does not replace practical, theoretical, religious, or cultural forms of reasoning but organizes this in a way to engender respect, born out of the justification each person's standpoint affords. These kinds of reasoning are the sort out of which communicative reason can be built.[15]

Seeking reasons, demanding them from oneself or another, or formulating an explanation can all occur in the service of ends that are alien to the reasoning itself: economic exploitation, accrual of social power, or someone making private what is indelibly public. The cross appears on many labels to make it saleable and valorizes suffering. Forms of reasoning that declare neutrality in matters of privilege, race, or gender may harbor practices that silence, eliminate, or diminish the participation of all thinkers and speakers, especially when those social matters are at stake. Reason, in all of its forms, needs to be put on trial for the sake of understanding and for respect.

Jürgen Habermas cautioned theologians against moving theology into the courtroom of reason. He has frequently argued that theologians who directly subject their claims to others in the form of an open inquiry undermine themselves. By making theological claims, theologians change religious discourse into secular meaning, and he has responded directly to Simpson's theology of the cross. Habermas, commenting on the central claim that Simpson makes, pointed out this problem, arguing that

> [Simpson] suggests that on the cross even God submits to this forum [of communicative action and validity claims open to critique]. Hence, none of the lifeworld's segments can immunize themselves against the demand for an argumentative justification, not even—as I understand the sentence—theology. If this, however, is the *common ground* of theology, what then still constitutes the distinctiveness of theological discourse? What separates the internal perspective

of theology from the external perspective of those who enter into dialogue with theology?[16]

What persists throughout Habermas's comments on the adoption of communicative reason by theologians is that he fears such a move will only salvage religious meanings by liquidating them completely as they migrate into the profane world. Habermas finds the complete translation of Christian experiences, doctrines, and idioms into secular ones compelling but does not recognize that they have anything to do with theology or religious life any longer. Rather than taking up the many ways theologians have responded to Habermas's project and his cautions about theology, one can address his worry through the introduction of promise into the theology of the cross.

Promise sustains the theologian of the cross in the communicative court of reason because it offers itself to continual testing and the trial of reason as much as it holds forth a future world in which reasons may play a different role. A promise is not tested all at once since it consists of a pledge made and a future fulfilment. We need to take time to test it. We should heed Habermas's warning that theological work dissipates without promise—the theology of the cross can be utterly nihilistic if we try to sustain it after it has proven empty or dangerous. Understanding how the cross is the place of God's promise that is the resurrection of Jesus keeps the theologian of the cross attentive to the present, critical in memory, and open in hope.[17] But promise has its home in the theology of the cross only because it is the promise of the crucified one, Jesus. This comes out of the most important theological claim that Simpson makes: God "submits to and becomes dependent upon the forensically fraught world" (190).

The theology of the cross sustains theological inquiry because it takes its place in the message that the crucified Jesus is raised from the dead. This message is a promise and so fits the forensic trial of reason, though it does so with all the risk that a promise is. Promises can be tested, queried, rendered empty, or trusted. The promisor can be questioned and addressed, and so can the one who promises the resurrection of the crucified Jesus. God, by promising, entirely shares in the communicative conflict of the world.

Though Simpson does not discuss promise in his paper, he does point to it in two ways: the need for theology to place solidarity within the larger task of reconciliation and the need for a conception of the resurrection of Jesus from the dead fit to the theology of the cross. Together Jesus's mission, preaching, and sagacity show a way to think through the importance of the cross as a demand for reconciliation, just as all injury is. These concerns point out important elements in understanding the resurrected Jesus in this forensic world.

(III). The cross is reconciliatory because God raised the crucified Jesus from the dead. By God's resurrection of Jesus from the dead, the cross has become communicable as a promise.

Certainly, much of Christian tradition has tried to take the crucifixion and death of Jesus as the sole locus of God's reconciliation of the world. As a consequence, the resurrection of Jesus does not often play much of a role in theological inquiry about reconciliation, despite its own saturation in forensic metaphor.

Instead, the commonplace problems of the resurrection of Jesus center on the sort of body or life Jesus has, the character of his appearances to his friends and disciples, and the tangled questions of history. All of these questions matter; they need to be integrated with questions of the crucified Jesus. A fundamental problem of the cross lies in its connection to the resurrection of Jesus. The cross might be nothing more than something to overcome, despite Paul's constant sense of their deep connection: "handed over for our transgressions, raised for our justification" (Rom 4:25).

Simpson attends to the important point in his theology of the cross. He warns of a raised Jesus who escapes the forensically fraught world in some manner. In his articulation of a theology of the cross, Simpson identifies the need for a concept of the resurrection appropriate to the world of demand, plea, and injury (192). The contours for this discussion lie in an important question that haunts those who ponder reconciliation or forgiveness, namely, whether there are injuries that can never be repaired. Max Horkheimer put it best in his influential debate over memory and redemption with Walter Benjamin: "Past injustice has occurred and is concluded. The vanquished are really vanquished."[18] Taking the cross for what it first is, a means of execution and public spectacle, no matter what else it may come to be, at least must be injury.[19] Benjamin summarizes Horkheimer's view in a quotation he seemingly takes from Henrik Ibsen's *Brand*: "Luck is born of loss / Only what is lost is eternal."[20] Some forms of injury last forever. Simpson somewhat endorses Horkheimer's view—that loss cannot be repaired on the cheap in an act of memory that mutes or softens the demands of past injury (179).

That the world is forensically fraught means that injury calls for repair. Woe demands weal. Abel's blood cries from the ground (Gen 4:10–11). Does the resurrection answer the demands present in Jesus's death? The resurrection of Jesus does not reverse his death. Such a reversal would eliminate the crucifixion, forgetting it, leaving the risen Jesus without any wounds! Though Jesus does appear in other forms, he is recognized by his address (John 20:11–18), Eucharistic action (Luke 24:13–32), or display of his wounds (John 20:24–29). Resurrection does not undo the past. Instead, it offers something different: a future for the past, a past made future in promise. This is the sense best given to Rudolf Bultmann's phrase, "The resurrection is the meaning of the cross."[21] God, we add to Bultmann, reinterprets the cross by raising Jesus from the dead, which is a promise made within the world. By this action God does not reverse the calamity of Jesus's execution but makes the cross as failure into the mark of a new world. To further elaborate what it is to raise Jesus, we need to briefly outline the Jesus who is crucified and raised.

In order to articulate Jesus's life to specify the promise of his resurrection, we need to consider that by raising Jesus from the dead, God opens up possibilities that are concluded in Jesus's death. The resurrection is not just one more stage in Jesus's life, just as Jesus's life cannot be cut off from his death. Everything Jesus did and was must pass through the narrow way marked by cross and resurrection. Jesus's fidelity to his mission, his sagacious teaching, his apocalyptic speaking, his identification with sinner and tax collector, all of these fail in his crucifixion since the cross is the meeting place of fidelity and abandonment. This fidelity belongs to God and to Jesus alike: abandonment in Jesus's cry of dereliction and in God's silence and seeming neglect. By itself the cross does not speak. What it does is silence Jesus's words and bring to ruin his actions.

Raising Jesus from the dead does more than vindicate Jesus's activity.[22] This act makes Jesus communicable as a promise. Jesus's proclamation of the coming reign of God, his identification with sinners, and his failure on the cross are all given to be a promise in God's resurrection of Jesus from the dead.[23] Raising Jesus from the dead does not return him to the life he lived before, from which he would presumably die again (on the model of Lazarus), but instead makes him a communicable promise. This we understand as a promise because the body and life Jesus now lives are the crucified body and life given new possibilities that did not exist before. Jesus raised from the dead means that his mission and its rejection are now made into a doubled and extended gift, which is what a promise is. Jesus's life is now given to the world in a new way such that his mission is now given in announcing his resurrection, paradigmatically in the Lord's Supper. In short, Jesus's life is now God's promise, part and parcel with God's promise to Sarah and Abraham.[24] In raising Jesus from the dead, the God of Israel is the God whom Jesus called Father. This life cannot step over the forensic world but can only look back to Jesus who lived and died and then promise that his mission is not in vain and that more of the world can become part of this body.

Taking Jesus's resurrection as promise does not remove its ambiguity or diminish the many meanings, effects, and events of the cross. Promise creates possibility, but it does not utterly exclude or permanently stabilize the meaning of any event to which it is subject. While promise may be trusted, and indeed trusted with all one's heart, a promise still depends upon the fidelity of the one promising. That God raised Jesus from the dead remains open to dispute, and if we follow Simpson's demands, it does not conclude or eliminate the forensically fraught world. A promise also remains unsettled because it is a promise.[25]

(IV). The cross remains ambiguous because it is a place of violence and rejection as much as the place where life and death collide. Whether or not it is a sign of God's love depends upon God's fidelity to the promise in the resurrected Jesus.

No one can permanently fix the meaning of the cross. Even taking it as God's promise of justice in the crucified Jesus does not settle any debate. As a promise, the cross points toward a future gift that it now gives only in weak and mundane ways. The cross gets fit to other schemes, made without resistance into an instrument of conquest and submission. Demagogues and saints let the cross fall from their lips. The cross does not survive buffered from the fields of power and history but is buffeted by them.

These observations follow from the claim that the world fraught forensically is also a world saturated by power. Here power means that which is an act of dominance, having power over others, but also the power to produce possibilities. Power is ambiguous because of these dual effects. Turning to reason seemed to expose situations of power, emancipation from convention, and just order in place of the arbitrary. Yet reason itself is often an instrument of power. Everyday life is rife with difficulties and dominations; a defeated reason offers no way out of these acute and chronic problems.

Reason may be impure, but it is, as such, not wholly defeated. The forensically fraught world is composed of many demands, of which reason is a part. It issues a plurality of pleas, cries, and claims. Thus, these calls, all of them, need to be tried. Many of them are ignored or unable to be detected. And our reasoning too must be subject to inquiry to distinguish between "a truthful consensus and a mere convention" (181). Recognizing the flux of power that creates and restricts, Rainer Forst has offered an important way forward: power is that which opens and closes the space of reasons, the kinds of justification people accept.[26] Announcing the resurrected Jesus opens possibility and so affects the space of reason. While we cannot extract ourselves from the web of judgments and power that saturate life, if the cross is where God has subjected Godself entirely to that world, then the power of the resurrection is a power that emerges from that world, opening the future. There may be good reason to think of the Spirit as coming (*adventare*) to the body of Jesus on the cross, but if God joins and submits Godself entirely to the forensic world, God does not go above or below its communicative court. If there is a way in which God remains above and beyond this world, it is "of no concern to us."[27] If theologians of the cross can stick to God as God is in this submission, they can gain a place for the kind of reflexivity at which Simpson aims: "the necessity of reflexive critique and repentance as a radical life of repentance for all parties . . . as well as . . . a universally inclusive community" (194). The judgment of the resurrection is God's, but it still occurs within this world. Reason's pathologies do not defeat it so long as critics continue to put reason to trial and attend to the plurality of claims made of and about it, pleas and cries that must be heard in this communicative and forensic paradigm. Disputing reason is the means to its repair.

Rather than requiring that theological statements lose their particularity or distinctive grammars in translation into the public, the demands of communicative reason require our claims about the cross to be de-transcendentalized but not purified of their theological character. Theologians of the cross cannot lay claim to a God's-eye view outside of the fraught world; the God they concern themselves with has submitted Godself entirely to that world. To take up a position that is transcendent or even has a transcendental fashion removes the risk of promise, eliminating both the need for trust in God's promise and the need for God's fidelity.

To put it in practical terms, the activities that best fit the kind of claims made as theologians of the cross are prayer, repentance, and confession. In the promise of the cross, we await its fulfillment and pray. Prayer that takes place within the promise takes many forms. We may pray that God would be faithful, we may lament loss and death, we might hope that the Spirit will come to grant new possibilities. Prayer makes claims about the world and its loss and asks God to act even as it is an action. Praying in this fashion is to ask God to be true in the practical sense: true to God's promise. Thus, it should be no surprise that the Eucharist is the primary way in which we give thanks for God's faithfulness, plead for its continuance, and, most importantly, return to God's promise in the cross: "As often as you eat of this bread and drink of this cup, you declare the Lord's death until he comes" (1 Cor 11:26). We need to think more about the practical forms of the theology of the cross.

(V). The world opened by the crucified wisdom of God is the single world shared by all in the confession of it by those marked by this cross. This wisdom takes practical shape in prayer, confession, and repentance.

The apocalyptic frame that Paul used to articulate God's contrarian wisdom seems to require either two worlds or the displacement of the forensically fraught world with an entirely pacific one. Both approaches harbor authoritarian theologies of the cross. Both render dissenting claims without validity or justification. They both cast the world disclosed to be immune to any criticism or revision, akin to a God's-eye view that none can occupy. By following the outline we have developed, we can identify a parallel between the unity of Jesus in cross and resurrection as well as the common supposition of a singular world that shows the connection between the truth of our claims despite their plural forms of justification. This way we can recognize the wisdom of the cross neither is incommensurable to all other kinds of reason nor does it make contrary claims into another world than the world disclosed by it. This permits us to recognize how world disclosure can be reworked to the forensically fraught world.

The act of confession directly takes up this problem, as evidenced by the central biblical example of this act: "I will also speak of your decrees before kings, and shall not be put to shame" (Ps 119:46).[28] Occupying the place of the cross, such a theologian is justified to make claims whose validity extends beyond that place. We have already seen that these claims are promissory in character and so not only are communicable but also are context-transcending. This alone does not show how confession might be considered true.

Let us take an example from Luther's *Heidelberg Disputation*. In order to demonstrate how God's actions are ignored by humankind, Luther uses a part of Isaiah's prophetic oracle: "He had no form or majesty that we should look at him, nothing in his appearance that we should desire him" (Isaiah 53:2). This he interprets as, "The works of God always appear unattractive (*deformia*), seeming to be bad."[29] They appear in unexpected ways. In its communicability the cross itself makes the strong weak and the rational absurd. God takes what is lowly and despised, the cross, and makes it lofty and beautiful. But this reversal can claim truth only if God raised Jesus from the dead, a claim that is continually contested, not merely by the forensically fraught world but also because it is a promise. That the lowly are lofty and the weak strong are claims that are ambiguous and to be tried. Theologians of the cross must assert this reality and contend for it. Doing so, they make the pragmatic supposition of a common world instead of an apocalyptically divided one in which new and old remain incommensurable to each other, radically unmixed.[30] They act toward reconciliation, and they seek to open the closed possibilities of the past which extends to the whole of the world, owing to the promissory character of the resurrection of the Crucified One. Supposing a common world belongs to the very activity of confession, from the practical character of working to reconcile. To attempt to speak truth is to attempt to speak something that is no longer merely the property of standpoints and positions. If it is truth about the world, it cannot be gained or lost. With the deep entanglement of the theologian of the cross in power, language, and the particular position from which they confess, the reflexive demand of this situation is to repent, pray, and confess. These activities presume a common world: if I have experienced harm, there is an "aboutness" my act of confession or repentance requires. To confront injury and offer respect requires the supposition of a singular world that we share, regardless of our epistemic differences. If I act to respect you and your specific justificatory position, I refer to your claims and share in them through my respect. Even if I claim a new world has dawned in the resurrection, I still share a world with those who address me because of the address, even as I confess or repent.

Making judgments in the promise of the resurrected Jesus means taking a melioristic approach to the common world. Contrasted with the pessimism of an apocalyptic dualism or the optimism of a singular world that both utterly liquidate contrary claims, we can recognize that the common world crucified is a world that is not yet concluded.[31] Since the truth of our claims is predicated on the promise of this crucified Jesus's resurrection, a claim itself that is open and demanding God's fidelity, meliorism alone seems to be the critical path open to a theology of the cross. This time we can cite William James favorably. His approach to plurality best states the openness of the cross: "All that my pluralism contends for is that there is nowhere extant a complete gathering up of the universe in one focus, either of knowledge, power, or purpose."[32] That this world is the world as taken by the wisdom of the cross depends upon the work of confession, repentance, and prayer, prayer which asks God to be faithful as the God who has gathered all the world up into the cross of Jesus. Or best, we may confess, hoping in the promise of the crucified:

> Then let us feast this Easter day
> On Christ, the bread of heaven;
> The Word of grace has purged away
> The old and evil leaven.
> Christ alone, our holy meal,
> The hungry soul will feed and heal;
> Faith lives upon no other!
> Hallelujah![33]

NOTES

1. Martin Luther, "Christ Jesus Lay in Death's Strong Bands," v. 2, trans. Richard Massie in *Lutheran Book of Worship* (Minneapolis: Augsburg Publishing House, 1978), hymn 134.

2. Martin Luther, Thesis 21 in *Heidelberg Disputation* (1518), *D. Martin Luthers Werke* (Weimar: Böhlau, 1883–1993 [henceforth *WA*]), 1:362.

3. Martin Luther, "Crux probit omnia," in *Operationes in Psalmos* (1519–1521), *WA* 5:176.

4. Maeve Cooke, "Avoiding Authoritarianism: On the Problem of Justification in Contemporary Critical Social Theory," *International Journal of Philosophical Studies* 13.3 (2005): 382–83.

5. "Reason must subject itself to critique in all its undertakings, and cannot restrict the freedom of critique through any prohibition without damaging itself and drawing upon itself a disadvantageous suspicion. . . . The very existence of reason depends upon this freedom, which has no dictatorial authority, but whose claim is never anything more than the agreement of free citizens, each of whom must be able to express his reservations, indeed even his *veto*, without holding back." See Immanuel Kant, *Critique of Pure Reason*, trans. and ed. Paul Guyer and Allan Wood (Cambridge, UK: Cambridge University Press, 1997), 643 (A738/B766).

6. Gary M. Simpson, "*Theologia Crucis* and the Forensically Fraught World: Engaging Helmut Peukert and Jürgen Habermas," in *Habermas, Modernity and Public Theology*, eds. Don S. Browning and Francis Schüssler Fiorenza (New York, NY: The Crossroad Publishing Company, 1992), 173–205. Parenthetical citations are to this edition.

7. Simpson articulates the *theologia crucis* and the praxis of reconciliation in Simpson, "*Theologica Crucis*," 193–94.

8. Hubertus Blaumeiser, *Martin Luthers Kreuestheologie: Schlüssel zu seiner Deutung von Mensch und Wirklichkeit* (Paderborn: Bonifatius, 1995); Michael Korthaus, *Kreuzestheologie: Geschichte und Gehalt eines Programmbegriffs in der evangelischen Theologie* (Tübingen: Mohr Siebeck, 2007).

9. Luther, Thesis 21.

10. Lois Malcolm discusses the apocalyptic wisdom of the cross in Paul's theology in Lois Malcolm, "The Wisdom of the Cross," in *Reason and the Reasons of the Faith*, eds. R. Hutter and P. Griffiths (New York City, NY: T&T Clark, 2005), 86–118.

11. Luther, Thesis 21.

12. Summarized by Maeve Cooke, "The problem of justification that confronts contemporary critical social theories can be traced back to certain key shifts in the Western social imaginary over the past 150 years. One key shift is the 'linguistic turn' of Western philosophy, which has meant that there is now widespread acceptance that ideas of knowledge and validity are always mediated linguistically, and that language is conditioned by history and context. Another key shift results from the dissemination and interpretation of the writings of Nietzsche, and subsequently Foucault, for this has led to widespread acceptance of the subjectivity and partiality of ethical judgements." Cooke, "Avoiding Authoritarianism," 382.

13. "The feelings, acts, and experiences of individual men in their solitude, so far as they apprehend themselves to stand in relation to whatever they may consider the divine," in William James, *The Varieties of Religious Experience*, eds. Fredrick Burkhardt et al. (Cambridge, MA: Harvard University Press, 1985), 34.

14. For an overview of recent historical investigation into the various practices that go under the name "crucifixion," see Felicity Harley, "Crucifixion in Roman Antiquity," *Journal of Early Christian Studies* 27:2 (2019): 303–23.

15. See Gary M. Simpson, *Critical Social Theory: Prophetic Reason, Civil Society and Christian Imagination* (Minneapolis, MN: Fortress Press, 2002), 87–94.

16. Jürgen Habermas, "Transcendence from Within, Transcendence in this World," in *Habermas, Modernity and Public Theology*, eds. Don S. Browning and Francis

Schüssler Fiorenza (New York, NY: The Crossroad Publishing Company, 1992), 230–31.

17. I have elaborated on the relationship among promise, memory, and hope in Gregory Walter, *Being Promised: Theology, Gift, and Practice* (Grand Rapids, MI: Eerdmans, 2013), 37–61.

18. Max Horkheimer, "Letter to Walter Benjamin, 16 March 1937," in *Gesammelte Schriften*, vol. 16, ed. Gunzelin Schmid Doerr (Frankfurt: Fischer Verlag, 1995), 83.

19. This is to make a Christological point of what Sebastian Castellio said of religious persecution: "To kill a person is not to defend doctrine but to kill a person." Reformulated: "To crucify Jesus is not to accomplish reconciliation but to crucify Jesus." It is only when the Crucified One is raised from the dead that the cross can come to mean more without erasing the horror of this event.

20. Walter Benjamin, "Letter to Max Horkheimer, 28 March 1937," in *Gesammelte Schriften*, vol. 16, 487. Neither Gunzelin Schmid Noerr, the editor of this volume, nor I have been able to locate this line in the text of Brand.

21. Rudolf Bultmann, "Ausdruck der Bedeutsamkeit des Kreuzes" in "Neues Testament und Mythologie," in *Kerygma und Mythos: Ein theologische Gespräch*, ed. H. W. Bartsch (Hamburg: Reich & Heidrich, 1948), 47–48.

22. This is one of Wolfhart Pannenberg's preferred ways of characterizing what God does in raising Jesus from the dead. See Wolfhart Pannenberg, "History and the Reality of the Resurrection," in *Beiträge zur systematischen Theologie*, vol. 1 (Göttingen, Vandenhoeck & Ruprecht, 1999), 319–27.

23. This drastic summary of the resurrection of Jesus as I develop it in this essay deserves further reflection. The state of the question has not advanced far beyond that stated in Eberhard Jüngel, "Jesu Wort und Jesus als Wort Gottes: Ein hermeneutischer Beitrag zum christologischen Problem," in *Unterwegs zur Sprache*, 3rd ed. (Tübingen: Mohr Siebeck, 2000), 126–44; and in Robert W. Jenson, *Systematic Theology*, vol. 1 (New York and Oxford: Oxford University Press, 1997), 165–78. Ingolf Dalferth articulates the groundwork for a fresh start in Ingolf Dalferth, *Radical Theology: An Essay on Faith and Theology in the Twenty-First Century* (Minneapolis, MN: Fortress Press, 2016). The key lies in three propositions: 1. The resurrection of Jesus by God is an act by which God "reinterprets" Jesus as God's own speech. 2. The particular subject of the church's proclamation ought to be this Jesus raised and so interpreted, informed by historical and literary inquiry so framed. 3. The speaker of this promise is the Triune God, who has submitted to and acts within this forensically fraught world. Jenson, Jüngel, and Dalferth contribute to the first proposition. Simpson's essay (see n. 6) offers the means to reframe hermeneutical theology to fit the world that the Triune God embraces.

24. See Walter, *Being Promised*, 14–36.

25. Walter, *Being Promised*, 75–76.

26. Rainer Forst, "Noumenal Power," *The Journal of Political Philosophy*, 23.2 (2015): 111–27. The term "space of reasons," as employed by Forst, stems from Wilfrid Sellars and Robert Brandom. It refers to the plastic character of our reasoning, able to be shaped by power and practice alike and recognizing the justification of our claims from specific positions or standpoints that we occupy. Sellars means this in

contrast to the "space of causes" which do not give us reasons or justify our claims but instead give us effects.

27. Martin Luther, "Quae supra nos, nihil ad nos," in *De servo arbitrio* (1525), *WA* 18:605. This is Martin Luther's use of the "Socratic dictum" that focuses our attention on God's life with us and refuses speculation about God outside of God's promise, an important theme of the entirety of the *Bondage of the Will*. This dictum does not block another way in which theologians may consider God in Godself: through Luther's articulation of the fulfillment of promise in his three lights doctrine at the end of *Bondage of the Will*. On this see Thomas Reinhuber, *Kämpfender Glaube: Studien zu Luthers Bekenntnis am Ende von De servo arbitrio* (New York, NY: Walter de Gruyter Verlag, 2000), 189–97.

28. Motto of the Latin edition of the Augsburg Confession in *BSLK*, 31; from Martin Luther, "Letter to Cardinal Albrecht of Mainz, 6 July 1530," *WA* 30/2:398.16. Confession in this sense differs somewhat from Luther's earlier formulation of confession as self-abnegation in response to the promise of the gospel. That sense of confession as correlate of justification by faith does have a public and political dimension but not as obviously as the use of Psalm 119 does. See Martin Luther, *Vorlesungen uber die Romerbrief* (1515–1516), *WA* 56:419.

29. Martin Luther, Thesis 4, *WA* 1:356. Luther does not mean deformed but in a form contrary to expectations. Translating *deformia* in that first way myopically focused us to think of divine works in an anthropocentric and ableist way.

30. Habermas makes this argument at length in Jürgen Habermas, "From Kant's 'Ideas' of Pure Reason to the 'Idealizing' Presuppositions of Communicative Action: Reflections on the Detranscendentalized 'Use of Reason,'" in *Truth and Justification*, ed. and trans. Barbara Fultner (Cambridge, MA: MIT Press, 2003), 88–90.

31. We might venture, *per impossible*, that this is a melioristic apocalypticism.

32. William James, "William James to Minot Judson Savage, January, 1910," in *The Correspondence of William James*, ed. Ignas K. Skrupskelis and Elizabeth M. Berkeley with Wilma Bardbeer, vol. 12 (Charlottesville: University of Virginia Press, 2004), 407.

33. Martin Luther, "Christ Jesus Lay in Death's Strong Bands," trans. composite in *Evangelical Lutheran Worship* (Minneapolis: Augsburg Fortress Publishing House, 2006), hymn 370.

Chapter 13

Stunned:

David E. Fredrickson

INFINITE DEFERRAL

Is the Gospel of Mark a friend of public theology? The answer depends, in part, on the definition of public theology. For the purpose of this essay, I define this endeavor as statements about God, or the holy, or the sacred, that are discussable outside of the restraints of denominational and religious affiliation—restraints that are nevertheless still respected by the discussants—and have the aim of ordering, or at least taming, the chaotic flux of human experience. With this definition in mind, I would have to answer the question with *I don't know, yet*. The answer, of course, ultimately depends on the definition of another term, *friend*, and whether a friend can bear to witness a friend's astonishment. Perhaps if public theology could meet Mark halfway and pick up a conversation that is open to the infinite deferral of agreement, like friends who can't stop talking, then there might, just might, be a future for the Gospel of Mark in league with public theology. Until then . . .

A SYNOPTIC PROBLEM

I want to be clear: I answer *I don't know, yet* not because Mark has a theology that intends to trump other religions and prevent public discussion of matters of ultimate concern. It doesn't. In this regard the Gospel of Mark is quite unlike the Gospel of Matthew where Jesus plays the role of the teacher of a righteousness higher than the latter text presumes can be found in Judaism. For Matthew, moral matters are not left up to public discussion informed by traditional wisdom but fall under Jesus's dictates. (See, for example, "You have heard it said . . . " sprinkled throughout Matthew 5–7.) Moreover, God (who, according to Matthew, carefully observes, accurately calculates, and reliably repays good and bad acts up to the end of time) is the name for the enforcement mechanism of the higher righteousness Matthew's Jesus teaches. Thus, Matthew's tendency to dominate discourse with the force of its moral clarity and attunement to God's watchfulness makes it no friend of public theology.

Neither is the Gospel of Mark like the triumphalist Gospel of Luke and its sequel, the Book of Acts. In this two-volume work, the history of Jesus as well as the history of the early church rests securely within the arms of historical necessity. Such rest reduces faith to belief in divine providence, a Stoic doctrine about monarchical control of both world and personal events that later Christian writers, following the author of Luke-Acts, welcomed as they furthered Stoicism's entanglement of religion and empire. If Mark is an unlikely friend of public theology, then, it is not for the reasons circulating through Matthew and Luke. How, then, might we understand Mark's hesitation to join the public conversation about God, the sacred, or the holy?

QUESTIONS

There is a question that the Gospels of Luke and Matthew make impossible to ask but Mark demands we wrestle with: what might Christianity have become had the women's silence in the final verse of the Gospel of Mark (16:8)—and the emotions inside that silence—captured the imagination of those who once formed the belief system bearing the name Christian? Evidently, the terrified silence of Mary Magdalene, Mary the mother of James, and Salome embarrassed the authors of Luke and Matthew. And neither could the writers of the Gospel-ending additions in Mark 16:9–20 endure it. Ridiculous, they all must have thought. Mark, with its ragged ending and without Jesus returning from the dead to control interpretation of his appearance, is useless. For this reason Matthew, Luke, and Mark 16:9–20, each in their own way a proponent of the omnipotence and sovereignty of God, had a different question. How could the crazed speechlessness of these women in flight be an inspiration for theology in an imperial age? And we, also the naïve inheritors of empire, might ask, how can the women's stunned silence make its way right now into publics that are no less imperial but ever so much cleverer at hiding it?

Christianity's essence, the author of Luke-Acts argued against the Gospel of Mark, must remain in the realm of the *sayable*, specifically in the doctrine of divine providence. Luke's Jesus and Jesus's angelic stand-ins appeal to this doctrine that one encounters also in the writings of ancient Stoic philosophers. Jesus and the angels explain three times how to read the Bible (24:6–7, 25–27, 44–47): you read the Bible like a Stoic reads history or nature. You look for the author's intention. (Whether the author is God, nature, Zeus, or fate, it makes little difference if the providence question "What is Zeus up to?" is the question.) With so much hermeneutical chatter, however, Jesus and his angels drown out the silence that might have helped Christians acknowledge another faith, the one that might have a slight chance of opening Mark and public theology to one another.[1]

The author of Matthew, however, silences the women's silence, not by talking over their ecstatic terror like Luke's Jesus does but by ignoring it. For Matthew's Jesus, a theology worthy of public recognition is all about morality. While agreeing with Luke (against Mark) that Jesus did indeed show up at his own resurrection scene, Matthew transfigures the crucified, desolate, and abominated Jesus of the Gospel of Mark into a moral teacher extraordinaire who does public theology indirectly through his disciples: "and teaching them to obey everything that I have commanded you" (Matthew 28:20). Matthew's Jesus offers a stringent and seemingly altruistic ethic. Yet as an underappreciated friend to Christianity—Jacques Derrida—once pointed out, the morality and theology of the Matthean Jesus is ultimately transactional: "But when you give alms, do not let your left hand know what your right hand is doing, so that your alms may be done in secret [that's the altruistic part and bravo!]; and your Father who sees in secret will reward you [that's the altruism-ruining, transactional part Matthew projects into God]" (Matthew 6:3–4).[2]

ASTONISHED, NOT AMAZED

The Gospel of Mark doesn't teach a rigorous righteousness as Matthew does. It doesn't grant certainty through hermeneutics as Luke does. What does it do? It astonishes. At every turn in the narrative, readers walk into scenes of wonder, ghosts, impossible events, erratic behavior, strange implications of the unthinkable, or madness of the melancholic and manic kinds. The first scene (1:1–2), for example, *seems* to be purposeful, calm, and straightforward; God speaks to an unidentified, singular "you" about a messenger who is clearly John the Baptist and who will prepare the way of the *you* (whom I take to be Jesus) in "your way." God is saying that John is charged with the responsibility of getting the people into a state of repentance in anticipation of the Messiah's arrival, and once the task of moral reformation has been accomplished, the Messiah will occupy his throne and begin to rule. But perplexity creeps into our minds, especially for those of us who have read the Gospel of Mark before. We are perplexed because we can't ignore John's fate. His "way" leads to an execution, the convenient and least embarrassing solution to a problem created by a politician's incompetence and impulsiveness.[3] And we know Jesus's fate: it is the same as John's.

Herod and Pilate are two peas in a pod. And it is for a good reason—that reason being the axe at Herod's reluctant command brought down on John's neck—that Herod thinks Jesus is John's ghost (Mark 6:14–16). For his part, Pilate is amazed that Jesus dies so quickly. The shocking questions thus arise: Is the "I" of "I am sending" even aware of the haunting irony inhabiting John's "way"? Does the death of Jesus at the end of his way come as a surprise to the divine speaker, whose vulnerability to stunning outcomes (or "comings out"; see below) has been widely denied for nearly two thousand years of theology, that is, when theology is written by the elite, who fancy themselves imitators of God (see, for example, Ephesians 5:1; 1 Peter 1:15–17; 2 Peter 1:3–4), selecting what can and what cannot rationally be said about God for the purpose of ordering non-elites in acts and in submissions of so-called love? Mark 1:1–2 records a voice saying more than it might know.

Now turn to the final verse of the Gospel, Mark 16:8. There is so much that is strange about this verse, not least of which is the unusual positioning of *gar* (for) as the last word of the entire Gospel. This odd non-concluding conclusion implies that Christianity itself is impossible, or at least that its possibility is unknowable like the blank space following the title of this essay is unknowable. *Stunned:* resists the urge to make meaning; helplessly, we stare at paper. First-century readers gazed at papyrus. Mary Magdalene, Mary the mother of James, and Salome—the three being the only link between Jesus and the church—say nothing to anyone about the young man's instructions on how to reconnect with Jesus in Galilee. That is astounding. And there is much more of the uncanny for us to stumble over in the final verses of Mark:

> When the sabbath was over, Mary Magdalene, and Mary the mother of James, and Salome bought spices, so that they might go and anoint him. And very early on the first day of the week, when the sun had risen, they went to the tomb. They had been saying to one another, "Who will roll away the stone for us from the entrance to the tomb?" When they looked up, they saw that the stone, which was very large, had already been rolled back. As they entered the tomb, they saw a young man, dressed in a white robe, sitting on the right side; and they were alarmed (*exethambēthēsan*). But he said to them, "Do not be alarmed; you are looking for Jesus of Nazareth, who was crucified. He has been raised; he is not here. Look, there is the place they laid him. But go, tell his disciples and Peter that he is going ahead of you to Galilee; there you will see him, just as he told you."

Pay no attention to the stone mysteriously rolled away. That is merely a matter of amazement—perhaps an angel lent a hand, who knows? Such a feat is not worthy of further discussion in light of the astonishment to come. No, it is the empty tomb that stuns the women, and being told not to be stunned by the young man dressed in white, a color that in the case of ancient textiles was associated with funerals and only very rarely with purity, does not reduce their fear.[4] While the NRSV has translated *exethambēthēsan* as "they were alarmed," I suggest the emotional impact of their discovery of a missing corpse they came to touch, a doubled absence, is more astonishment than alarm, although certainly fear plays a part in their emotional condition, as I will discuss below.

A passage early in the narrative, Mark 1:21–28, introduces readers to the theme of astonishment; it also illustrates the drive of some characters to think their way out of being stunned. Their drive is a major theme in Mark: how astonishment so quickly diminishes into amazement. Astonishment, as I use the term in this essay, refers to the utter bewilderment and paralysis of thought and feeling brought on by the impression of a terrifying (or perhaps exhilarating) other "out there" or "within" that exceeds measurement or distinction. Astonishment shares with trauma a sense of being overwhelmed. Amazement, in contrast, is a reaction to that which is possibly, even though with difficulty, explicable; amazement wears off as one seeks to account for the wonder one feels. Astonishment bears within itself no promise of easing its way into amazement.[5] Note, however, in the following passage how stunned characters seek to fill in blanks, thus turning astonishment into amazement (and also note the NRSV does not share my concern to distinguish astonishment from amazement):

> They went to Capernaum; and when the sabbath came, he entered the synagogue and taught. They were astounded [*exeplēssonto*] at his teaching, for he taught them as one having authority, and not as the scribes. Just then there was in their synagogue a man with an unclean spirit, and he cried out, "What have you to do with us, Jesus of Nazareth? Have you come to destroy us? I know who you are, the Holy One of God." But Jesus rebuked him, saying, "Be silent, and come out of him!" And the unclean spirit, convulsing him and crying with a loud voice, came out of him. They were all amazed [*ethambēthēsan*, more accurately translated "astounded" or "stunned"], and they kept on asking one another, "What is this? A new teaching—with authority! He commands even the unclean spirits, and they obey him." At once his fame began to spread throughout the surrounding region of Galilee.

The verb *ekplēssō* names the same emotion that *thambeō* does.[6] So twice in this passage astonishment occurs, but notice that in both instances "teaching" and "authority" take over almost immediately and turn those who are stunned into broadcasters of Jesus's amazing powers. This pattern of astonishment diluted to amazement continues through the rest of the Gospel, but there are two significant exceptions: Jesus at Gethsemane (14:32–42) and the women at the tomb (16:1–8). As we will see, in these two episodes the emotional state remains transfixed on the blank.

But first, let's take a brief detour through relevant philosophic texts and epic poetry to get an idea how Mary Magdalene, Mary the mother of James, Salome, the crowd (9:15), disciples (10:24, 32), and most significantly, Jesus himself (14:33)—all suffering *thambos* (*astonishment*)—might have appeared to first-century readers. First of all, *thambos* had a long, contentious history in Greek philosophical thought. The question was whether philosophy ought to encourage the experience of speechless, terrified wonder or whether the rational individual should take every measure to curtail it. Often cited on the matter, Democritus (c. 460–370 BCE) backed the later approach and promoted *athambia* as the wise person's desired goal, as Robert Hankinson writes:

> The ideal of the undisturbed life had a long philosophical history, stretching back at least to Democritus, who advocated *athambia*, freedom from wonderment . . . as well as the presumably equivalent *euthumia*. . . . The term *ataraxia* itself was attributed to him, and while that is probably an anachronism, what matters is not the terminology but the attitude and ideal it indicates. In Democritus's case, this seems to amount to an avoidance of excessive states of emotion, indeed of sensations in general.[7]

Much closer in time to the composition of Mark's Gospel than Democritus, Plutarch (c. 50–c. 125) takes a different approach to the state of being stunned. On the one hand, he quotes with approval some lines from Sappho, *Fragment* 31. Her words had acquired canonical status by the first century as a description of the shattering of the self in moments of unattainable desire: "My tongue breaks down, and all at once a secret flame throughout my body runs." Plutarch then takes Sappho's words in a peculiar direction, away from lovers, past mystical rituals, and finally on to the classroom: "Just as persons who are being initiated into the Mysteries throng together at the outset amid tumult and shouting, and jostle against one another, but when the holy rites are being performed and disclosed the people are immediately attentive in awe (*thambos*) and silence (*siōpēn*), so too at the beginning of philosophy."[8] On the other hand, in another passage Plutarch attempts to split the difference between acknowledging the experiential truth of *thambos* and its prohibition by making a distinction in the origin of wonder:

> For there are many who take that saying of Pythagoras wrongly and out of harmony with his meaning. He declared that he had gained this advantage from philosophy, to wonder at nothing; but these men think that their advantage gained is to commend nothing, to show respect for nothing, holding that immunity from wonder lies in disdain, and seeking to attain to dignity by means of contempt. Now it is true that philosophic reasoning, through knowledge and acquaintance with the cause in every case, *does away with the wonder and amazement that*

spring from blindness and ignorance, but at the same time it does not destroy our serenity, moderation, or human interest.[9] (My emphasis)

The *thambos* that "springs from blindness and ignorance" and leads to helplessness in Plutarch's put-down is in fact the *thambos* of tragedy, poetry, and the Gospel of Mark.[10] Unlike Plutarch's writings and other philosophic texts whose goal was to fill the blank space after *Stunned:* with strategies for calming down and thinking straight, other ancient literature dealt with *thambos* the only way it is possible to treat the dreadful, unnamable otherness exuding from beauty, gods, godlike humans, or death: by suffering it, by being silenced by its overwhelming blankness and certainly not by turning it to the purpose of self-formation, as Plutarch attempts to do.[11] As we will see below, it is this very "helpless wonder" that haunts Mark's characters, even Jesus.[12]

Sappho is not the only writer to help us read Mark. Consider another of Mark's literary forbears in the writing of that which stuns. Three centuries before the composition of Mark, Apollonius of Rhodes described the astounding effect of Apollos's appearance and provided a template for the presentation of stunned characters within the course of his narrative:

> His [Apollos's] golden locks flowed in clusters over both cheeks as he went; in his left hand he held his silver bow, and his quiver was slung over his back from his shoulder. Beneath his feet the whole island shook, and waves washed over the dry land. Helpless wonder seized them when they saw him (*tous d' hele thambos idontas amēchanon*), and no one dared to look directly into the beautiful eyes of the god. They stood with heads bowed to the ground, but he proceeded far out to sea through the air.[13]

Note that for Apollonius *thambos* does not well up within the astonished person as if were a fault of the soul. To be stunned is to feel grasped or washed over by someone or something infinitely other than oneself causing an infinite (in the sense of not able to be defined) astonishment.[14] It is one's feeling of being overwhelmed that even contests oneself as a point of reference.

And this contestation takes us back to the women who flee the scene of Jesus's non-appearance (even as a corpse). In calling their astonishment *madness*, I am not diagnosing from a distance but trying to convey the impression first-century readers might have had of Mark's final words. Philo of Alexandria sums up seven centuries of the invention of madness and the conceptions the first reader of Mark might have brought to 16:8:

> Now "ecstasy" or "standing out" [*ekstasis*] takes different forms. Sometimes it is a mad fury [*lytta maniōdēs*] producing mental delusion [*paranoian*] due to old age or melancholy [*melagcholian*] or other similar cause. Sometimes it is extreme amazement [*sphodra kataplēxis*] at the events which so often happen

suddenly and unexpectedly. Sometimes it is passivity of mind, if indeed the mind can ever be at rest; and the best form of all is the divine possession or frenzy to which the prophets as a class are subject.[15]

Having inherited a vocabulary of mental instability from medical writers, tragic and erotic poetry, and ancient comedy, first-century readers might have concluded from Mark's unsatisfying ending that the women were insane: "Trembling (*tromos*) and madness (*ekstasis*) had seized them; and they said nothing to anyone, for they were afraid" (NRSV, modified).[16] They would have been right, as George Kazantzidis's description of the ancient literary and social construction of madness confirms:

> Madness in antiquity is experienced, first and above all else, as a violent displacement. *Ekstasis* derives from Greek *existēmi*, which means to "be or stand out of oneself," and, as a state of mind and being, it is usually followed by wandering through open spaces in an erratic way. Wandering, in its turn, is typically associated with isolation. This isolation can either be forced by others (madness, as a consequence of divine anger, could potentially be a miasma, and therefore contagious, so the madman has to be expelled) or it can be deliberate, the madman's own choice (e.g., Bellerophon in *Il.* 6.200–2). The mentally insane avoid contact with people. In the Hippocratic texts we find a wide range of pathological behaviors in which the patient wishes to be left alone: this avoidance is either attributed to feelings of hatred and disgust . . . or, more commonly, fear: before the madman loses touch with society, he is described as being afraid of others, turning consequently into an object of dread himself.[17]

The idea now crosses our minds, perhaps, that the set of religious ideas and practices we call Christianity, from the Markan point of view—a view that unlike the other two Synoptic Gospels does not disregard the women's *ekstasis* and does not count their madness flowing from astonishment as irrelevant to Christian faith—has been a grand mistake. Perhaps the author would have been crushed to discover that Luke's and Matthew's cover-up of the women's stunned ecstasy, of Jesus's stunned ecstasy too, became the scriptural inspiration for mission statements, encyclicals, creeds, and bumper stickers. Might it be that Christianity, as it has publicly come to be known now, is the invention of Matthew and Luke, whose endings joined forces to eradicate the shocking gap between Jesus and the church, a yawning chasm that must stay open for Christianity to be Christianity according to Mark, who, very likely, did not even know the word *Christian*?

Welcome to the astonishing world of the Gospel of Mark where God might say more than God knows, where madness rules minds, and where fearful silence impossibly transmits a witness to a Jesus who does not show up at his own resurrection. Instead, "he is going ahead of you to Galilee" (16:7). Whatever that might mean.

COMING OUT

It is intriguing: the Greek word standing behind the women's mad flight from the tomb is the same word marking what appears to be Jesus's sane (if it is sane to think on the idea of omnipotence and to experience life as if sovereignty were the truth of divinity) and purposeful entry from the wilderness of John's preaching and the Spirit's expulsion (1:3–13) into the wilderness first and then into public proclamation:

> In the morning, while it was still very dark, he [Jesus] got up and went out to a deserted place, and there he prayed. And Simon and his companions hunted for him. When they found him, they said to him, "Everyone is searching for you." He answered, "Let us go on to the neighboring towns, so that I may proclaim the message there also; *for that is what I came out [exēlthon] to do.*" And he went throughout Galilee, proclaiming the message in their synagogues and casting out demons. (My emphasis)

Notice the glaring difference in this passage between Jesus's formulation of his public purpose—to preach the reign of God—and the narrator's telling of Jesus's story. Jesus conceives of himself as a preacher of the rule of God, not as a healer, exorcist, or wonder-worker, and certainly not what he will end up being: abandoned. Yet, as I will lay out in the rest of this essay, the narrator leads us to think Jesus too is mad, and not just in the sense of angry, although his cry accusing God of dereliction in 15:34 echoes ancient accusations leveled at the departed, who, as hundreds of gravestones tell us, by dying abandoned the living. No, the madness that shadows Jesus in the Gospel of Mark, first noticed by those close to him in 3:21, is rooted in his unwavering belief in divine omnipotence.

You, a generous reader and possibly a public theologian, you who have extended to Mark's Gospel (and to this essay, so far) the hospitality all good readers give to texts, you who perhaps have fallen out of love with the power of God as I have, are welcome to take refuge, if little comfort, in the company of Mary Magdalene, Mary the mother of James, and Salome as they flee from the tomb. There the text runs into blank openness in an abrupt end, but at the same time with open arms it awaits *your* coming out. Mark 16:8 once again: "So they came out (*exelthousai*) and fled from the tomb, for trembling (*tromos*) and madness (*ekstasis*) had seized them; and they said nothing to anyone, for they were afraid" (NRSV, modified). Is it just a coincidence that "come out" is the verb for 1) the women's crazed flight from the empty tomb and 2) Jesus's own term for his entry into public ministry? I don't think so. Jesus's public coming out is freighted with ambiguity just as the "way" John prepares for the coming Messiah takes on ominous overtones in Mark 1:1–2. On the one hand, in 1:14–15 Jesus makes himself public by proclaiming the good news of God, and he does so with great confidence. With strong, clear words he announces the nearness of God's ruling activity and demands his hearers repent and believe in the gospel of God's rule. On the other hand, consider his last words: what could be more pitiful? Immediately following his lament, a lament that questions the omnipotent God's abandonment of him (15:34), he speaks a language not composed of solid words: "Jesus gave a loud cry and breathed his last [*exepneusen*; literally, "he breathed out]" (15:37). My point is that Mark's Jesus does not end up a hero for the kingdom of God, although he starts that way. Nor does he reveal the divine mind, since after 9:7 God no longer visits the scenes of Jesus's life to praise his beloved Son. In the end, there is no mind to be revealed and Jesus becomes the presence of God's absence. The narrative arc of Mark's Gospel is not Jesus's exemplary obedience to God's will, nor does Jesus impart any saving knowledge (as if knowledge were salvific!). Rather, Jesus's coming out turns out to be his undoing, his entry into the trauma of infinite disappointment in the omnipotent God in whose name he began his public ministry. The women coming out, fleeing from the tomb in silence, pick up where Jesus left off, screaming in their fearful silence against the non-response of a God he/they thought is able to do all things.

Thus, the narrator of the Gospel of Mark contests Jesus's desire to keep public theology simple. If Mark has any relevance for public theology, it would be not a matter of commending to all the God who can do all things. The object of Jesus's desire, the omnipotent God whom Jesus preaches, will fail to come out to him when he prays at Gethsemane and when on the cross he accuses God of dereliction. In other words, the entire narrative presents a far more complex picture of Jesus's career than Jesus does in the beginning chapters. Reading Mark from beginning to end is a heartbreaking experience. Jesus is confident that God can do all things (10:27; 14:36) and that believers themselves become omnipotent by believing as Jesus does. If only they believe, then God will extend omnipotence to them (9:23; 11:23). The gap between "if" and "then," however, only salts the wound of his inevitable dying.

This heartbreak might become the readers' experience of Jesus at Gethsemane, though the disciples surely passed their chance of witnessing it, of confessing it. What if Gethsemane were the moment of a new approach to public theology? The disciples slept as Jesus (was he dying from grief?[18]) was seized by *thambos*,[19] and here his astonishment is compounded by his feeling of helplessness (*adēmonia*):

> They went to a place called Gethsemane; and he said to his disciples, "Sit here while I pray." He took with him Peter and James and John, and began to be astonished (*ekthambeisthai*) and forlorn (*adēmonein*). And he said to them, "I am deeply grieved, even to death; remain here, and keep awake." And going a little farther, he threw himself on the ground and prayed that, if it were possible, the hour might pass from him. He said, "Abba, Father, for you all things are possible; remove this cup from me; yet, not what I want, but what you want" (Mark 14:32–36, modified).

Forlorn and suffering an astonishment preserved from amazement, Jesus grieves the loss of the omnipotent God to whom he still prays, to whom he submits himself. And there is no response. No wonder Mark's Jesus was an embarrassment to Matthew, Luke, and the authors of the added endings in Mark 16:9–20.

Mark refuses to be a slap-you-on-the-back kind of friend to public theology. Mark's peculiar way to be a friend, if this is even possible, is to preserve astonishment. To confess it. What does this mean? Mark confesses astonishment by linking religion, God, the sacred, and the holy to that which cannot be thought or acted upon but shakes me loose from myself. To the shock of its readers—at least for those readers whom the Christian/Stoic doctrine of divine providence has not dulled the senses to the madness of Mark's Jesus and the absence of his omnipotent and omnipresent God—Mark contests every moral, hermeneutical, philosophical, or theological attempt to overcome the coming undoing of self nearly every character in the story feels when the astonishing shows up.

Will the public theologian mutter, with friends like the Gospel of Mark, who needs enemies?

NOTES

1. For the Gospel of Luke's effort to play down the Gospel of Mark's emphasis on astonishment, see David E. Fredrickson, *The Promise of Not-Knowing: A New New Testament Reading* (Minneapolis: Fortress, 2022), 43–54.

2. See Jacques Derrida, *The Gift of Death and Literature in Secret*, trans. David Wills, 2nd ed. (Chicago: University of Chicago Press, 2008), 88–108.

3. For "way" (*hodos*), see Anton Cornelis van Geytenbeek, *Musonius Rufus and Greek Diatribe* (Assen, Netherlands: Van Gorcum, 1962), 23. See also 2 Tim 4:7.

4. See Liza Cleland, "Not Nothing: Conceptualising Textile Whiteness for Cult Practice," in *Textiles and Cult in the Ancient Mediterranean*, ed. Cecilie Brøns and Marie-Louise (Oxford: Oxbow Books, 2017), 32.

5. See Aristotle, *Topica*, 106b9–14.

6. See Mark 6:2; 7:37; 10:26; 11:18. The term shares with *thambos* the element of fear of the unexpected. See Chrysippus, *Fragmenta moralia*, 409.7; Plutarch, *Phocian*, 28.3.

7. R. J. Hankinson, "Galen and the Sceptics (and the Epicureans) on the Unavoidability of Distress," in *Galen's Treatise Περὶ Ἀλυπίας (De Indolentia) in Context: A Tale of Resilience*, ed. Caroline Petit (Leiden: Brill, 2019), 160. For *athambia* and Democritus's rejection of astonishment, see Democritus, *Fragmenta* 4.215–16; Cicero, *de* Finibus, 5.8.23.

8. Plutarch, *Progress in Virtue*, 81D–E. See also Plutarch, *Demetrius*, 38.4–5.

9. Plutarch, *On Listening to Lectures*, 44B–C. See also Plutarch, *Fragments*, 178.

10. For other examples of Plutarch's denigration of astonishment, see Plutarch, *Pericles*, 6.1; Plutarch, *Numa*, 15.1; Plutarch, *Aratus*, 32.1–2.

11. For *thambos* as a response to beauty, see Homer, *Iliad*, 3.395–99; as a reaction to the appearance of gods or godlike humans, see Homer, *Iliad*, 24.483–84; Homer, *Odyssey*, 24.101.

12. For helpless astonishment, see Plutarch, *Brutus*, 15.7–8.

13. Apollonius of Rhodes, *Argonautica*, 2.676–84. Translation is found in William H. Race, *Apollonius Rhodius. Argonautica*, Loeb Classical Library 1 (Cambridge, MA: Harvard University Press, 2009), 167.

14. For astonishment without limit (*thambos apeiriton*), see Apollonius of Rhodes, *Argonautica*, 4.682.

15. Philo, *Who is the Heir of Divine Things?*, 249, in *Philo. On the Confusion of Tongues. On the Migration of Abraham. Who Is the Heir of Divine Things? On Mating with the Preliminary Studies*, Loeb Classical Library 261, trans. F. H. Colson and G. H. Whitaker (Cambridge, MA: Harvard University Press, 1932), 409–11. For other examples of *ekstasis* as madness, see Hippocrates, *De morbis i–iii*, 1.30.5–8; Ps.-Galen, *Definitiones medicae*, 19.416:7–8; Menander, *Aspis*, 305–9; Philo, *On the Cherubim*, 69.

16. For silence and madness, see Joannes Actuarius, *De diagnosi*, 1.35.16–24. Trembling is also a symptom of madness: Hippocrates, *Coa praesagia*, 92; Hippocrates, *Prorrheticon*, 1.14. For fear as a symptom, see Galen, *De locis affectis libri vi*, 8.192.6–7. For trembling, silence, and madness experienced together, see Posidonius, *Fragmenta*, 436. For trembling and astonishment "having" or "seizing" victims, see Homer, *Iliad*, 10.25, 19.14; Apollonius of Rhodes, *Argonautica*, 2.575; Plutarch, *Aemilius Paullus*, 17.8.

17. George Kazantzides, "Haunted Minds, Haunted Places: Topographies of Insanity in Greek and Roman Paradoxography," in *Landscapes of Dread in Classical Antiquity: Negative Emotion in Natural and Constructed Spaces*, ed. Debbie Felton (New York: Routledge, 2018), 226. In Mark 3:21 Jesus also is said to have been mad.

18. Death from grief was a literary motif. See, for example, 1 Maccabees 6.8–13 where *thambos* and death from grief are linked as they are in Mark 14:34. Galen

recognized the phenomenon and attributed it to weakness of soul and serious mental disease. See Caroline Petit, "Death, Posterity and the Vulnerable Self: Galen's Περὶ Ἀλυπίας in the Context of His Late Writings," in Caroline Petit, ed., *Galen's Treatise Περὶ Ἀλυπίας (De Indolentia) in Context: A Tale of Resilience* (Leiden: Brill, 2019), 56–58.

19. Plutarch, *Aemilius Paullus*, 34.1.

Chapter 14

The Sutures of Reason and the Short-Circuit of Faith

Belief in the Light of Contemporary Cognitive Theories

Guillermo Hansen

Since the seventeenth century, the Western world has witnessed a dichotomization of the relationship between *ratio* and *fides*. While scholasticism knew how to harmonize them, the Reformation knew how to hold them in paradoxical tension. The Enlightenment, however, reversed the first strategy by enthroning reason and dismantled the second by pushing faith to the realm of the private and the superstitious.

At the finish of World War I, a new scenario loomed. While not necessarily a vindication of faith, it fundamentally challenged the reach of reason—something already claimed by Kant more than a century before. The aftermath of the Great War—a conflict for imperial supremacy—opened a clearing for the diffusion of new ideas which questioned the nature and reach of "pure" reason by underscoring its mediations and limitations. There are three events that are seminal in this transition: quantum physics (Niels Bohr), the incompleteness theorem in mathematics (Kurt Gödel), and the re-discovery of the unconscious (Sigmund Freud, but above all, Carl G. Jung). These three movements, independent from each other, advanced a common daring vision, not just about the epistemological problem regarding the reach and function of reason, but about the *incompleteness* of reality as such.

This *ontological* questioning reveals the deep contradictions that reason itself has inadvertently unearthed. Put succinctly, reality as such presents contradictions that reason always has sought to amend, to *suture*, in order to present a smooth rendition of reality marked by continuities and logically apprehensible causalities. Reason must do that in order to "produce" a minimally hospitable world. Yet, when one considers the role of the observer in the measurement of quantum phenomena (physics), the assertion that no formal mathematical theory capable of describing the natural numbers can be both consistent and complete (mathematics), and the idea of consciousness as the tip of a deeper, unconscious mental dynamics (psychology), the old triumphalist and disingenuous account of reason begins to capsize.

Within Protestant European theology, the decades of the 1920s and 30s were characterized by the critique of liberal theology and an awakening to the fundamentals of Reformation theology's insights—as eventually expressed in the so-called neo-orthodox, dialectical, and kerygmatic theologies, as well as in the rise of phenomenological approaches to religion. Of the many important authors, perhaps the contributions of Rudolf Otto and Rudolf Bultmann best mirror this epochal change. These two Lutherans, in their own ways, relocate the problem of experiencing and articulating the sacred against the background of the crisis of reason, without thereby falling into simple fideisms, confessionalisms, or biblicisms. The question is this: how do their theological visions relate to the ontological (and not just epistemological) predicament that arises during these decades?

Both authors acknowledge openly Luther's influence. In the case of Otto, his awakening to the phenomenon of the Numen (*Mysterium tremendum et fascinans*) is dependent on his readings of the Reformer's *Servo Arbitrio*, several of his biblical commentaries, and Luther's own autobiographical references. The non-rational character of Luther's experience of God is expressed in the tension, even contradiction, which seems to exist between a "naked" or "hidden" God and the "preached" or "revealed" God.[1] In Otto's view Luther confronts a chasm that is indecipherable and therefore threatening to the creature. However, this tension is what awakens a new subjective orientation: faith.

In Bultmann's case his own demythologizing method was an enactment of the principle of justification by grace through faith.[2] His criticism of mythical thought is that it falls into a rationalization where God appears as a factor in a chain of causality.[3] As the case with science, mythical thought is objectivizing—though, unlike science, still open to external interventions. Indeed, mythical narratives are the first attempts of "science" to the extent that they express in reflective form one of the fundamental characteristics of the human mind: the intuitive search for *causalities*. What has changed in the scientific era, and which characterizes this as a turning point in human thinking, is the cessation of the projection of agential and/or personalized causes into the forces of nature, or the postulation of the necessity of a supernatural force.[4] For Bultmann, science (and myth) is the objectification of reality that presupposes a basic distinction between object and subject. However, should such a distinction be operative when we refer to God? How to approach this reality rationally, which by definition encompasses all the rest? According to Bultmann, it is not reason but faith—a mode of existence—which authorizes finite creatures to talk not so much about the *essence* of God but of the *act* of God as a new existential possibility.

THE ONTOLOGICAL QUESTION: LUTHER'S CASE

These two authors serve as illustrations of a new type of approach to the problematic posed a century ago. Both are critics of rationalism, without falling into irrationality. More important still, both relate the theme of faith (more mystically in Otto, more existentially in Bultmann) with the theme of God. The case is not that faith is in competition with reason; rather, reason and faith are different points of view or representational states. But how is this related to the alleged incompleteness of reality? Neither Otto nor Bultmann developed their theologies to address specifically this question, yet their theological commitments point us to Luther, and it is there that we may find a more appropriate engagement that moves from the mere cognitive and epistemological realm to the ontological and thereby theological plane.

In effect, behind both Otto and Bultmann, we hear an echo of Luther's theology in its critique of scholasticism and its location of the cross at the center of his theological perspective. We know that this controversy, especially in its early stages, acquired the stereotyped form of objective knowledge grounded on reason vs. knowledge gained through faith. Yet Luther's position relates both spheres not in a dichotomic relationship but in a *paradoxical* one, indicating an intrinsic unity between reason and faith that can be manifested in history only as a contradiction, even as a dispute. But what is of ultimate importance for us is that the dispute between Luther and scholastic theology discloses two different *ontologies* in their approach to the theological theme: one characterized by a Hellenistic metaphysics grounded on the positivity of *being*, the other by an *advenient* notion of *becoming* in the midst of negativity.

This paradoxical situation is seen in the different ways in which Luther refers to reason and faith. On the one hand—admittedly, in a typical misogynist way—he called reason a prostitute, *Frau Hulda, Domina Ratio*. On the other hand, reason is also valued as a gift, a creature that attends to humanity in the engagement with things relevant to this world.[5] In this latter sense, reason is a social, political, and cultural factor that is active in secular affairs but loses its footing when it stands as the foundation of a religious-metaphysical system—like an objective knowledge as the pre-condition for faith. Faith, however, involves a reorientation of life that necessarily reinscribes the subject in objects and, more radically, in God herself. From the standpoint of faith, then, a theological understanding unfolds which does not displace reason yet is critical of its presuppositions and reaches.[6]

When Luther speaks of faith, he frequently uses the metaphor of light or illumination.[7] Yet reason equally sheds light because through it creatures can both see and talk about the worldliness of the world. However, reason's luminosity dims when it aims to underscore issues pertaining to the divine. Here only faith can "see" because it consists of nothing more and nothing less than to gaze at the world with the eyes of Christ, to see things that are inhabited by a promise that is always manifested in its opposite. It is important to understand that faith does not look *elsewhere* (heavens, above, transcendence), but that it looks at the world from within through different eyes. In short, reason and faith look at the same but from different angles: one from the *past*, the other from the *future*.

Luther's rejection of the primacy of reason in theological and metaphysical matters has nothing to do with an anti-intellectual posture.[8] Rather, it is a protest against a way of doing theology that confuses primary and secondary issues, discursive strategies that make God an *object* of knowledge instead of a *subject* in knowing. Hence it is a rejection of a particular ontology of presence.[9] If philosophical reason occupies itself with the being or the essence of things assuming an ontology of presence, theological reasoning bases itself on an ontology of *absence*, or what is the same, *advenient presence*. For the Reformer, the being of things is located not in their *rerum quidditates* but in what makes something to become despite its inability to be in itself. Therefore, Luther's perspective rests on the openness inherent to things, pointing to an externality upon which things can lean in order to exist. This is the *relational* aspect of his ontology since things are to be considered in view of their future, as that which seeks or is oriented to what still does not exist.[10] Hence, the distinction between philosophy and theology is not simply the distinction between reason and faith, but the distinction between an ontology of *presence* based on objective knowledge and an ontology of the *future* based on faith alone. Depending on the ontological framework in which one moves, the epistemic frame will vary—and vice versa.

The sights set on the essence of things, the ontology of presence, is for Luther an indicator that the epistemic medium represented by philosophical reason is unable to perceive the cracks that traverse creation, the moaning and sighs spawned by nature, the suffering of creatures under the weight of their own "essence." In sum, unable to grapple with the fissures within the very web which sustain creatures in a string of hapless causalities. This is what characterizes a nature that in itself is incomplete, seemingly doomed to participate in a race leading nowhere.[11] What we call reality is no more than the sum of fragilities united by an incompleteness which reason desperately addresses in its suturing mode, repressing everything that seems to deny the illusion of living in a world of transparent totalities. However, there are fissures within this fabric, not so much as the result of a presence that breaks from the outside, but as the very impossibility of reality to transparently symbolize itself. There is a domain that neither the imaginary nor the symbolic can apprehend and represent.[12] This domain is, precisely, the holy, the numinous, the sacred.

This explains why for Luther the theology of the cross is actually inseparable from the *theologian* of the cross: its implicit ontology locates subjectivity as the meeting place (or rather, emergent place) between a nature that is incomplete, unfinished, and a God who is still coming.[13] Rather than transparency, in life the Christian experiences opacity: the opacity of things, the opacity of God, the opacity of one's self, even the opacity of faith.[14] This is the *anfechtung* into which the human mind and spirit fall when it jettisons the illusion that reality—including oneself—ultimately rests on immutable essences. The theology of the cross is the symptom of a vertigo, not only the vertigo of the theologian but the vertigo of God. The only way out of the vertigo is precisely to "fall"—the cross.[15]

The problem posed by Luther could be summarized as follows: if reason is a creature, belonging to the realm of the "worldly," its gift is to discriminate and thus order aspects concerning historical and finite existence. In principle, we can understand reason as a constitutive factor of our creatureliness, and here lies its grandeur. Faith, on the other hand, is not the "transcendent" complement of reason, for it does not seek to infer causalities and, even less, to apprehend God as an object. The Reformer's insistence that faith is the work of the Holy Spirit eschews a magical fideism and a bland sentimentality in order to underscore the process of becoming (truly human) as the coming of God to and in the creature. Faith, far from being a change made *to* the person, a perfection of previously existing qualities (moral, cognitive, etc.), is rather the change of the person herself who is now the site of an *advenient* becoming, Christ. In short, faith is the very "enfleshment" of a divinity-in-coming, and this begins in the flesh's fissures and contradictions.

CONSCIOUSNESS, KNOWLEDGE, AND REASON: AN EVOLUTIONARY APPROACH

Let us now approach the subject raised by Luther from a different angle. How should we understand reason and faith from an evolutionary point of view? How are they located amid the pressures of a world—both natural and social—subject to natural selection? I take the evolutionary framework[16] because it will give us clues for locating our theme in a post-metaphysical context, reminding us that both reason and faith are embodied in finite realities.[17] This will also allow us to advance beyond the state of the question as formulated in the sixteenth century, limited to a concept of reason mediated by Aristotelian philosophy and scholasticism. In what follows, two principles are assumed: In the first place, reason and faith presuppose the phenomenon of mind and consciousness, and therefore they are treated as "mental states" in relation to an environment—a past determined one and an *advenient* future one. In the second place, any approach to reality must include the subjective point of view.[18] Subjectivity is not a gloss on a reality previously given but a factor constituting that "reality." In other words, a contemporary ontology should consider both the virtual spaces of the subjective realm and the physical-temporal spaces of the material, not as in classical metaphysical dualism but as two aspects or dimensions of the same reality. Moreover, the realm of the virtual must be seen as a response to an incompleteness inscribed in the very ontology of things. In what follows, it will be clear the role played by reason, but what about faith?

The controversy between reason and faith epitomized by Luther's polemics with scholasticism can avoid a recalcitrant dualism only if we see them as two interfaces. Both are mental states, but their function, purpose, and origin are different. On the one hand, we have the virtuality enacted by reason whose central mission is to deal with adaptation to the natural and social environments. This reason is not "inscribed" in, nor does it hover over, reality. It is an expression of consciousness, which in turn is the result of a relationship with an environment by a species like ours capable of symbolic mapping or representation.[19] Its function is precisely to "stitch" phenomena which are disaggregated and which cannot be assimilated without placing them within a causal framework. This occurs both at the level of discursive strategy (widely analyzed by Michel Foucault) but even more so in the field of neuronal processes that were selected in the evolutionary history of a species that owes its adaptation and survival in large part to anatomical disadvantages and deficiencies. Precisely this deficiency is what must be completed by the enactment of a virtual world, a sort of a mental movie that seeks to express both the conditions of an environment as well as internal states of bodies and minds.

To understand reason, then, we must first approach the reality of mind. But rather than talk about the nature or essence of mind, it is important to consider the mental *phenomenon* and its biological basis. The neurobiologist Antonio Damasio is one of the main proponents of approaching the mind as an *embodied* process. Mental activity is preceded by events in the brain, especially by the peculiarity of the type of connections established by the nerve cells. These cells, through their fibrous extensions (axons), have the particularity of being highly excitable to the internal and external environment, being also able to send electrical signals to other neurons and muscle cells distant from the brain. Moreover, the mediation conferred by the body is what also allows for the signals sent by the central nervous system to be projected into a world.[20]

Thus, a mind emerges due to the activity of small circuits that make up large networks, establishing models or patterns with two different types of referents: On the one hand, mind represents events that are located beyond the primary scope of either the central nervous system, the body, or the world experienced as "objectivity." On the other hand, it also represents itself, i.e., the processes that occur in the brain in reference to its own state. In both cases Damasio uses the term "map" to refer to the representations of the world as well as to the very representations of mental processes. These maps are experienced as images, which are not limited to visual components but also encompass signals mediated by the auditory, tactile, and visceral senses.[21] In this view, then, what we call reason can thus be regarded as the formal patterns created by this process of mapping.

The cartographic metaphor also appears in the important contributions of the philosopher Thomas Metzinger, for whom mind mapping is linked primarily to the creation of a phenomenology of the body, i.e., the feeling of possession of a body, agency, and locality.[22] The conscious mental experience works as a sort of virtual interface, an invisible medium that enables the organism to flexibly interact with itself and with the environment. Mental activity is the creation of a virtual world, and conscious experience can be regarded as "nature's virtual reality."[23] Its function is the creation of a model of the world that, through their simulation in real time, allows the body to act and interact with both internal and external events and processes. Mind is always a process of interaction with an environment, yet the environment leaves deep imprints on what mind is all about. It is a two-way path.

The notion that the mind is a process of representation or mapping, i.e., an activity linked to a body in relation to its surroundings, places us squarely on the question of its relationship with the evolutionary dynamics and its demands. The cognitive scientist Donald Hoffman[24] argues that for every bit of information that one gets, there is a price to pay in the form of energy. In the case of biological organisms, this occurs in the form of calories: for every calorie spent in perceptual processes, one must ingest something to replace it. For this reason the dynamics associated with natural selection favor perceptual processes requiring fewer calories. Moreover, a way of saving energy is precisely the ability to perceive *less*, especially that which does not involve direct information for adaptive fitness. Reason is an efficient process of information, but not all information can be processed rationally. Most of it must remain hidden.

According to Hoffman, the icons that appear on the screen of a computer serve as an illustration of how human perception functions; its task is not to reflect the truth but to *hide* it. Most computer users are not interested in "seeing" the complexity of circuits, voltage, and magnetic fields that allow information to manifest itself virtually. If we had to deal with these levels of complexity, we could not act effectively. The icons are enough. Extrapolating this metaphor to the plane of human (virtual) representations, Hoffman argues that natural selection has not prepared us to perceive and deeply investigate the processes of our environment "objectively," for our perceptions are specific to the behaviors and provisions necessary to survive and reproduce. In a neo-Kantian twist inspired by the revolution of quantum mechanics, Hoffman concludes that both the categories of space and time, and the three-dimensionality of objects, are perceptual categories, not properties of reality as such.[25]

Hoffman's observations leave us in the place where we left our theologians. The problem that we face is not merely epistemological, nor concerning the evolutionary limits of mind and reason, but *ontological*. Hoffman intends to return to the subject of consciousness and subjectivity to explain how we build worlds, but the problem lies in the conditions of reality that elicit the construction of these virtual worlds in the first place. No one like Slavoj Žižek, in his neo-Hegelian vision, has given an account of this problem. In his vindication of Hegel over against Kant, the Slovenian philosopher argues that the genius of Hegel consisted in demonstrating that our epistemological limitations represent an *impotence* in nature. Quantum physics shows that: indeterminacy points to the weakness of nature in its function to determine itself.[26] For our author, Hegel outperforms the idealism that precedes him when he commits to a dialectical reversal that consists of transposing the epistemological obstacle to the very thing as such, as an *ontological incompleteness*. In other words, that which to us appears as an epistemological inability is actually a fracture in reality itself.[27]

If reason is seen as a reflective dimension of the conscious mind, it can then be said that it is both symptom and expression of an alienation. However, the main point here is to highlight the same contradiction that reason cannot solve because it rests on a process of estrangement that gives rise to the very phenomenon of subjectivity and self-consciousness. According to Žižek, the subject of reason germinates from an impediment, a gap that is the result of the failure of knowledge. In more Hegelian terms, subjectivity emerges when substance cannot achieve identity with itself. That is why the epistemological failure is simultaneously a lack in the substance as such, i.e., an ontological incompleteness.[28] With this we return to the ontological problem and the hypothesis that faith is an orientation inspired by a future, which cannot be based on the chain of reasoning provided by positive knowledge.[29]

In this breakdown of knowledge, in its gaps and fissures, is where faith appears as a new virtuality. This faith should not be regarded as standing in opposition to knowledge but as a reality that is immanent to the division that occurs within knowledge as the latter strives to apprehend an incomplete reality. Suffice it to recall that in the human evolutionary process, knowledge arose from discriminatory processes of objects and events that were concatenated at first in mythical constructions, which in turn gave rise to the self-referential consciousness, self-consciousness. It is curious that self-consciousness does not arise from the absorption of new content but arises by the *constraint* and restriction of areas previously undifferentiated and thus not "known." Consciousness implies saying "no" to the whole, the *uroboros*;[30] to discriminate, to distinguish, to mark out, that is what characterizes the operation of consciousness, and its outcome is what we call knowledge and reason.

The issue now is to see how faith, which presupposes an alienation in the emergence of consciousness, reason, and knowledge, is an existential possibility inscribed within an ontological incompleteness. In the end, there is no faith without the kenosis of God, without loss of the mythical suture of the primordial unity of things. Faith stands thus as a virtuality, and not only does it reconcile humanity with that which transcends it, but it reconciles God to herself by assuming her historical "incompleteness." At this point we must leave science and philosophy behind in order to rescue the glimpses provided by theology. Back to Luther.

THE "ANOMALY" OF FAITH

If reason and faith are both mental processes "mapping" environments, and if both are virtual processes imagining worlds dealing with the mechanisms of natural selection, what is the difference between them? On the one hand, we can postulate that the operations of reason, as a reflective state of the mind, objectifies the world in a network of causalities. This allows for a certain predictability for guiding behaviors facing the challenges of survival, thus mitigating (not canceling) the pressures of natural selection. Faith, on the other hand, is quite different: it not only imagines a world in which the effects of natural selection are mitigated but *challenges* its mechanisms and its effects. Both the narrative of the election of Israel, as well as stories about the resurrection—stories of faith—imagine worlds where the losers, the discarded, the marginal, and the condemned are vindicated. Faith, as a mental (spiritual) mapping, suggests something more than what reason is able to do, for it expresses a *revolt* against the very logic of natural and social selection.[31]

Faith is essential not just as a repositioning of the subject but also for imagining the reality of God—the ultimate symbol that constellates human psychic and behavioral energies. While Luther always defined faith as the act of trust that grounds the subject and frees her from the confinement to her own ego, we must inquire deeper into the effect of faith upon its paramount symbol, God. In order to do so, let us follow the paradigm that Žižek learned from Lacan, namely, to identify in what consists the rupture represented by an outstanding figure (Luther in our case); detect how a key dimension of the author's discovery is lost from view by the same author; and demonstrate that to be coherent with the rupture sketched by the seminal author, one must go beyond what he or she was prepared to recognize.[32] After all, what characterizes a great thinker is her *ignorance* about the radical dimension of her own discovery.

What is what the genius of Luther discovered as a rupture and yet lost from view to the point of suppressing it? We find an important clue in his exposition of the first commandment in the *Large Catechism*. There he writes, "As I have often said, it is the trust and faith of the heart alone that make both God and an idol. If your faith and trust are right, then your God is the true one. Conversely, where your trust is false and wrong, there you do not have the true God. For these two belong together, faith and God. Anything on which your heart relies and depends . . . that is really your God."[33] God and faith, therefore, are deeply intertwined, but what are the implications? Still more revealing is a paragraph in his lectures on Paul's letter to the Galatians (3:6, "So also Abraham 'believed God, and it was credited to him as righteousness'"), a showcase of the conflict unleashed within Luther between a deep discovery and its rational "correction." He contends that only faith, not reason, can attribute glory to God. In fact, faith is what carries the very attributes of God, as these attributes would not have existential space without the mediation of faith.[34] Luther concludes, "[Faith] consummates divinity; and, if I may put it this way, it is the creator of divinity [*ea consummat divininitatem et, ut ita dicam, creatrix est divinitatis*]."[35]

After such stunning assertions, however, he immediately corrects the "truth" that was hinted at: this creation is not "in the substance of God but in us [*non in substantia Dei, sed in nobis*]."[36] But it is already too late, for the genie is out of the bottle: Luther has stumbled upon a discovery whose consequences, from the point of view of faith's *reasoning*, must be initially repressed. Luther writes that through faith "God retains His divinity . . . He has whatever a believing heart is able to attribute to Him." Moreover, that "faith justifies because it renders to God what is due Him."[37] Does it mean that faith is constitutive of God? That without faith there is no "God," properly speaking? Would this not confirm Karl Barth's critique when he stated that one should trace the anthropological reductionism of modern theology to these statements of the Reformer?[38]

Three aspects must be considered. First, Luther's words should be taken at face value and be carried to the end: faith is the creator of *divinity*, enacting a constraint on the absolute and undifferentiated power of the *deity*. Divinity and deity should not be confused. To understand what deity is, we must bring up his numerous statements about the "naked God." This version of the *deus absconditus* cannot be positively comprehended by any symbol, idea, moral order, ontological principle, or agential will—unlike his other versions of the hidden God in creation, in Christ, and in faith, namely, the "revealed" or "preached" God, which is prone to symbolization.[39] In other words, deity is not "virtualizable." The territory of the deity is the abysmal, the undifferentiated. Would this perhaps not be what Lacan called the "Real," that which is beyond the capabilities of the imaginary and the symbolic?[40] That which refuses any representation because it is the breakdown of all symbolization? Can one even establish an analogy with what Jung called the unconscious, that because it is outside the reach of consciousness, it is completely unknown?[41] Is this not the *mysterium tremendum* of Otto? In sum, the *deus absconditus* is the deity without predicates or attributes, a true *monstrosity* from which we are to flee. Nonetheless, one cannot ignore its absential gravitational pull—as Luther was well aware.

If in Luther there is a great difference between the naked or hidden deity and the clothed or "preachable" God, one should read his comments in Galatians as a reference to the symbolization of God (divinity), not of the deity. This allows one to locate faith—that for Luther is not an anthropological a priori, but a divine "emerging" reality—as a symptom of a dispute between the (naked) deity and (clothed) God, between the Real and the virtual, between nudity and masking, in short, as the "collapse" of the undifferentiated deity by a new emergent property, i.e., faith. "Knowing" God (faith) has thus an effect on her divinity, for it makes it graspable, available, always coming.[42] This constraint of the undifferentiated (deity) by a symbolization (God and, more radically, Christ) is what faith mediates. Faith is thus an existential trust over against the apparently absurd, but it is also a perspectival stance in life that fully involves God deeply in the flesh. Hence, the believing subject is more than a different point of view on things, for she embodies a different ontological wager grounded not in a past determined by natural selection (nature) but in the *advenient* future (God). Through faith divinity is *less* than deity and therefore *more* for human beings caught in the riddles of their own becoming.

Secondly, and in response to Barth and his followers, we must appreciate the exquisite *kenotic* movement in Luther's theology. This appears in his theology of the cross, not simply as a re-formulation of the theory of atonement but as the manifestation of the divine in its contrary. The theology of the cross raises the issue of injustice, suffering, and the abandonment of Jesus as irreversible moments in the very emergence of a reliable God. Dietrich Bonhoeffer's statement that "only the suffering God can help"[43] could become a pious and sentimentalist message were it not that the cross is the perspective and the experience of the victim, which mediates God's own perspective and experience. The "distorted" perspective of suffering caused by natural, social, and political processes becomes the center for a new imaginary and symbolic world. On the cross God definitely appears as a discarded human for and to himself.

It is from the perspective of distorted humanity that it can be said that faith is not merely a projection upon "God" but the God who *emerges* from protest and hope. Recall that there is nothing that one can "project" onto an undifferentiated deity, a naked God. The deity can only return to the one that groans a representation of monstrosity, itself devoid of any hope. This is why the monotheistic idea first, followed by the Trinitarian representation of God later, emerged from distortion, exile, and persecution. It was and is a protest against the amoral character of evolution and the immoral nature of socio-political existence. It is from this distortion expressed as suffering that "God" begins to acquire "consciousness," experiencing what it means to be a finite creature subjected to grief.[44]

In other words, in the Trinitarian representation, the "fall" of the undifferentiated deity coincides with the "outbreak" of a human new consciousness and symbolization, eliciting thus new patterns of behavior. An immanent power (instinctual, archetypal) becomes thus transcendent, emergent, within the vicissitudes of human living. However, as anticipated in the book of Job, suffering is what operates as a constraint on the abyssal power of the deity, which must now contemplate the masks swept away and swallowed up by space and time from the point of view of the one who rebukes him, saying, "Why have you forsaken me?" (Mt. 27:46). The revelation of a "lack" in the deity is what prompts the deity to fall and God to emerge in creation—the coming of redemption. The fall of the unrepresentable and the emergence of the represented here coincide, and this takes place in a space that is no space, faith. This constitutes a bridge between unconscious energy and symbolic representation, unleashing a different mode of being and acting.

We come now to the third point, where faith emerges in the midst of the neurotic symptoms of the world—injustice, guilt, and death. In effect, faith can be regarded as an "ultra" or "counter" adaptation because it seeks to "adapt" not to our immediate niche but to an environment that is still coming, an *adventus*. After all, "faith is confidence in what we hope for and assurance about what we do not see" (Heb. 11:1). For Luther, faith creates a different world,[45] an "alchemical" environment where the discarded (i.e., sinner) is hypostatically assumed. The very incompleteness of reality is what opens up this possibility, namely, an adaptation to a world that we yet do not see but which (partially) releases us from the immediate adaptation to the constraints of our environment that constantly generates "waste."[46] Faith is what imagines minimally impossible worlds,[47] thus provoking a short circuit in the putative camouflage of reality that reason is determined to suture. Faith engenders a new virtuality that inscribes "God" as a reality that is not complete yet but is still coming. Faith in this God is thus a new perspective cast from the point of view of the distortion of rejected bodies and despairing souls.

In this vein faith appears not so much at the limits of reason (Kant) but within her womb (Hegel). It appears not in the liminalities (because these always are expanding) but in the cracks and incompleteness that reason wants to cover up. After all, the virtuality that reason creates arises because of the need to adjust to a world that does not forgive, which does not have any intrinsic telos, and which "progresses" just by a process of selection and elimination. Faith, on the other hand, "hallucinates" another possibility without which we cannot be fully human, since the question about humanity arises at the very heart of the incompleteness and failures of our mappings and historical trajectories. In sum, faith bridges a latent, unconscious energy with the dynamics of a world that is still coming. Its power comes from the future, and its medium is a new imagination that challenges what reason tends always to hide and normalize.

CONCLUSION

We return to the subject of reason with an appreciation for its power and scope but also aware of its limitations. Its origin and evolution, linked to the emergence of mind and consciousness in bodies subjected to the principles of natural selection, cannot but fill us with amazement. As Damasio rightly says, the human conscious mind has taken evolution in a new course, contributing significantly to the survival of the species by anticipating different scenarios and thus participating in life's regulation.[48] Or, as Deacon expresses, the experience of sentience is "what it feels like to be evolution."[49] In short, it is evolution dealing with itself, representing it, confining it, advancing it.

Since reason emerges by the very "ordering" and "mapping" of an incomplete reality, it is constrained to perform within the evolutionary imperative, which has no telos, no moral compass.[50] And when reason attempts to suture incompleteness, it usually conceives of a superior reality—either divine or secular—that ends up as the legitimizer of an order which clearly segregates winners and losers. It can be money, class, nation, or manifest destiny. It has only the past to hold on to, projecting into the future what is already known. No good news here, no promises uttered, only the suturing of the contradictions in order to provide the smoothest ideological picture possible and to legitimize forms of "adaptation." In the end, reason alone leads to a paralysis, for it lacks a perspective that is able to evoke the emotional energy that only another form of representation—faith—can provide.[51] Faith speaks about promises that are not contained in the natural course of events, for it holds fast to that which makes something become despite its inability to be in itself.

In the Christian tradition, promises are grounded at the point where incompleteness is not disguised or sutured but revealed as a short circuit that jolts the creature into a new mode of being. The Christian narrative that binds faith with a contingent historical event (Jesus) is the register of the very "christification" [*Verchristlichung*] of the reality of God.[52] To talk about the christification of God is to raise the underside of what Deacon pointed out: what does it feel like to be a discarded, maladapted creature? What can contain the perspective generated by the distortions of death and injustice? Faith comes from "what it feels like" to be evolution from the underside of the sutured "triumphant" story,[53] from Jesus's gaze that contains the many gazes of the "excrementals," the "waste" produced by natural selection, and the socio-political replications of this brutality. In sum, faith is a counterstrike within evolution, a short circuit within its own dynamics, the protest against terror. It does not seek to replace reason but seeks to elicit a different mind, one that holds fast to the "christification" of God—the event where our "hearts" hold tightly to Christ and where God holds steadfastly to us.

NOTES

1. See Rudolf Otto, *The Idea of the Holy* (New York: Oxford University Press, 1958), 97f.

2. See Rudolf Bultmann, "On the Problem of Demythologizing," in *New Testament and Mythology and Other Basic Writings*, ed. Schubert Ogden (Philadelphia: Fortress Press, 1984), 122. His demythologizing project was crystallized in the early 1940s but based on a program already outlined in the 20s and 30s.

3. Bultmann, "On the Problem," 97ff.

4. The cognitive science of religion, from Steward Guthrie to Pascal Boyer, argues that the detection of agentiality in search of establishing causal paradigms is one of the cognitive characteristics of the human being. This entailed an adaptive advantage to the environment, which soon projected invisible and counter-intuitive figures (gods) as the ultimate interpretation of those events without a direct causal relationship to immediately observable objects or situations. See Steward Guthrie, *Faces in the Clouds: A New Theory of Religion* (New York: Oxford University Press, 1993); Pascal Boyer, *Religion Explained: The Evolutionary Origin of Religious Thought* (New York: Basic Books, 2001).

5. See Martin Luther, "The Disputation Concerning Man," in *Luther's Works*, vol 34, ed. Lewis Spitz (Philadelphia: Muhlenberg Press, 1960), 127ff. For a systematic approach to Luther's view of reason, see Paul Althaus, *The Theology of Martin Luther* (Philadelphia: Fortress Press, 1966), 67; Walther von Löwenich, *Luther's Theology*

of the Cross (Minneapolis: Augsburg Publishing House, 1976), 68–70; Gerhard Ebeling, *Luther: An Introduction to His Thought* (Philadelphia: Fortress Press, 1970), 88.

6. See Martin Luther, *Lecture on Galatians*, in *Luther's Works*, vol. 26, ed. Jaroslav Pelikan (Saint Louis: Concordia Publishing House, 1963 [henceforth *LW*]), 284, 287.

7. See Eberhard Jüngel, *The Freedom of a Christian: Luther's Significance for Contemporary Theology* (Minneapolis: Augsburg, 1988), 39ff. Interestingly, the same metaphor of "light" will serve to characterize reason during the Enlightenment.

8. See von Löwenich, *Luther's Theology of the Cross*, 68.

9. As noted by the recent Finnish approach to Luther. See Tuomo Mannermaa, *Christ Present in Faith: Luther's View of Justification* (Minneapolis: Fortress Press, 2005); Tuomo Mannermaa, *Two Kinds of Love: Martin Luther's Religious World* (Minneapolis: Fortress Press, 2010).

10. See Ebeling, *Luther*, 88.

11. See von Löwenich, *Luther's Theology of the Cross*, 69.

12. These concepts were developed by the psychoanalyst Jacques Lacan. See Slavoj Žižek, *How to Read Lacan* (New York: Norton, 2006), 73; Christopher Hauke, *Jung and the Postmodern* (New York: Routledge, 2000), 217.

13. Regarding faith and subjectivity in Luther, see Guillermo Hansen, "Luther's Radical Conception of Faith: God, Christ and Personhood in a Post-Metaphysical Age," *Dialog: A Journal of Theology* (Fall 2013). As to the place of the subject in Luther's theology of the cross, see Vítor Westhelle, *The Scandalous God: The Use and Abuse of the Cross* (Minneapolis: Fortress Press, 2006), 53.

14. See Luther, *LW* 26:130.

15. We should not forget that this perspective emerges after Luther experiences God's and his own subjective opacity. Without finding answers there, he turns to God's promise in Christ. See Mark Taylor, *After God* (Chicago: University of Chicago Press, 2007), 62f.

16. Regarding evolutionary theory, see Terrence Deacon, *Incomplete Nature: How Mind Emerged from Matter* (New York: Norton, 2012); Davis Sloan Wilson, *Evolution for Everyone: How Darwin's Theory Can Change the Way We Think about Our Lives* (New York: Bantam, 2007); John W. Perry, *The Heart of History* (New York: SUNY Press, 1987); Ernst Mayr, *What Evolution Is* (New York: Basic Books, 2001).

17. Cf. Joseph O'Leary, *Questioning Back: The Overcoming of Metaphysics in Christian Tradition* (Minneapolis: Seabury, 1985), 117, 133.

18. See Thomas Nagel, *The View from Nowhere* (New York: Oxford University Press, 1986), 6.

19. I understand "reason" as the reflective state of the mind. It goes without saying that it depends on pre-reflective, intuitive, and unconscious cognitive processes. See Justin Barrett, *Cognitive Science, Religion, and Theology: From Human Minds to Divine Minds* (West Conshohocken, PA: Templeton Press, 2011).

20. See Antonio Damasio, *Self Comes to Mind: Constructing the Conscious Brain* (New York: Pantheon Books, 2010), Kindle edition, loc. 366.

21. Damasio, *Self Comes to Mind*, loc. 375.

22. See Thomas Metzinger, *The Ego Tunnel: The Science of the Mind and the Myth of the Self* (New York: Basic Books, 2009), Kindle edition, loc. 1206.

23. Metzinger, *The Ego Tunnel*, loc. 1613.
24. See Donald Hoffman and Chetan Prakash, "Objects of Consciousness," *Frontiers in Psychology* 5, art. 577 (June 2014): 1–22. See also Donald Hoffman, *The Case against Reality: Why Evolution Hid the Truth from Our Eyes* (New York: W. W. Norton & Co., 2019).
25. Theoretical physicists who subscribe to the theory of a holographic universe, such as Leonard Susskind, Gerard 't Hooft, and Stephen Hawking, would probably not disagree.
26. See Slavoj Žižek, *Absolute Recoil: Towards a New Foundation of Dialectical Materialism* (New York: Verso, 2014), Kindle edition, loc. 2230.
27. Id., *Less than Nothing: Hegel and the Shadow of Dialectical Materialism* (New York: Verso, 2012), Kindle edition, loc. 358–553.
28. Id., *Absolute Recoil*, loc. 430.
29. For example, we "believe" in human rights, not as a result of our rational knowledge of human nature, but by a wager (decision) that retroactively postulates a human nature with its inalienable rights.
30. See Erich Neumann, *The Origins and History of Consciousness* (New York: Routledge, 2002), 121.
31. See Gerd Theissen, *Biblical Faith: An Evolutionary Approach* (Fortress Press, 1985), 49.
32. Cf. Žižek, *Absolute Recoil*, loc. 686.
33. Martin Luther, "The Large Catechism," in Robert Kolb and Timothy Wengert, eds., *The Book of Concord: The Confessions of the Evangelical Lutheran Church* (Minneapolis: Fortress Press, 2000), 386.
34. Luther, *LW* 26:227; *WA* 40:360. As I will note below, Luther is referring to God's divinity, to be distinguished from deity as such.
35. It should be noted that the most accurate translation of *divinitatem* is divinity, not deity—as the American edition of *Luther's Works* renders. Since Augustine of Hippo, Latin had an expression for the undifferentiated essence of God, *deitas*. This was also part of Luther's lexical repertoire.
36. In the "Preface to the Complete Edition of Luther's Latin Writings" (1545), Luther strikes a similar note, emphasizing, however, that faith mediates to the believer God's own *attributes* (righteousness, power, wisdom, strength, salvation, etc.). In *Martin Luther's Basic Theological Writings*, ed. Timothy Lull (Minneapolis: Fortress, 2005), 9.
37. Ibid.
38. See Karl Barth, "An Introductory Essay," in Ludwig Feuerbach, *The Essence of Christianity*, trans. George Eliot (New York: Harper Torchbooks, 1957), xxiii.
39. See his dispute with Erasmus, "On the Bondage of the Will," in *Luther and Erasmus: Free Will and Salvation*, ed. E. Gordon Rupp (Philadelphia: Westminster Press, 1969), 200–201.
40. Cf. Žižek, *How to Read Lacan*, 72ff.
41. Cf. Carl G. Jung, "On the Nature of the Psyche," in *The Structure and Dynamics of the Psyche, Bollingen Series XX* (New York: Pantheon Books, 1960), 213.

42. See Heinz Zahrnt, *What Kind of God? A Question of Faith* (London: S.C.M. Press, 1971), 55ff.; Carl G. Jung, *Answer to Job* (Princeton: Princeton University Press, 1973), 28.

43. See Dietrich Bonhoeffer, "Letter to Eberhard Bethge (July 16, 1944)," in *A Testament to Freedom: The Essential Writings of Dietrich Bonhoeffer*, eds. Geffrey Kelly and Burton Nelson(San Francisco: Harper, 1995), 508.

44. Cf. Jung, *Answer to Job*, 46.

45. See Luther, *LW* 26:234.

46. See Slavoj Žižek, *The Parallax View* (Cambridge, Mass.: MIT Press, 2006), Kindle edition, loc. 4078.

47. Cf. Atran, loc. 582, 6716.

48. Damasio, *Self Comes to Mind*, loc. 657, 4068.

49. Deacon, *Incomplete Nature*, 502.

50. Cf. Steven Mithen, *The Prehistory of the Mind: Cognitive Origins of Art, Religion and Science* (London: Thames and Hudson, 1996), Kindle edition, loc. 29.

51. See Michael Shermer, *The Believing Brain: From Ghosts and Gods to Politics and Conspiracies* (New York: Times Books, 2011), Kindle edition, loc. 6188.

52. See Jürgen Moltmann, *Trinität und Reich Gottes: Zur Gotteslehre* (München: Ch. Kaiser Verlag, 1980), 147.

53. Cfr. Gustavo Gutiérrez, "Desde el reverso de la historia," in *La Fuerza Histórica de los Pobres: Selección de Trabajos* (Lima: CEP, 1980), 337ff.

Chapter 15

A Stranger God

Sketch of a Religionless Theology

Josh de Keijzer

PREAMBLE

Looking at the situation in Europe at the beginning of the second decade of the twenty-first century, one sometimes wonders if Christianity has not crossed the threshold toward extinction.[1] Christians who paid attention may have noticed but seem content to console themselves with their special calling to the martyrdom of irrelevance.

One of the main failures of Western Christianity, I believe, has been to make its religion about knowledge rather than being. Admittedly, with knowledge came a certain kind of being: a hierarchical ordering of the universe with at the center a divine authority that was imparted to the Church to rule the world. It is easy to find a culprit in that particular faction of Christianity we label fundamentalism, but the revelation-equals-information has held all of Christianity in its grip from the moment the gospel became something to be preached and announced, something that required cognitive consent. From there it was but a small step to the abuse of power. In the early Middle Ages, a unified power structure arose. The papal system not only was the guardian of knowledge but also became the conduit of salvation.

By challenging the internal corruption and destructive theology of this power structure, Martin Luther unwittingly set the stage for the demise of the political and cultural hegemony of Christianity. He no longer accepted clerical guardianship over divine knowledge and instead advocated the reading of Scripture by lay Christians in their own vernacular and in accordance with their conscience. The human being was coming of age. This did not quite work out as intended, however. Rival interpretations of divinely revealed knowledge (i.e., theologies) clashed in bloody feuds with political stakes at play that were similar to those in medieval times. New voices called for a stronger emphasis on reason and less so on the more speculative revealed things that did not seem to lead to a unity of interpretation. Faith was increasingly seen as unreasonable and relegated to the private sphere.

However, though the Enlightenment and the modern period brought tremendous advances in knowledge, science, and technology, these were invariably used for the same purposes of power, exploitation, and hoarding of wealth. Even though Christianity played an increasingly marginal and sometimes adversarial role in what was happening in the world at large, the tension between Church and world was mitigated by the fact that modernity and capitalism carried out the Christian ideals by simply secularizing them. The twilight of the gods, the *Götterdämmerung*, was a transformation of the gods of religion to the gods of ideology.

This is probably also what Bonhoeffer hinted at when he said that the world had come of age (*mündige Welt*).[2] Believers and the world aren't all that different from each other. They both push god[3] to the margin, Bonhoeffer suggested. Secularization is to the concept of god what the crucifixion is to the self-giving of god in Christ. That is to say, secularization and crucifixion marginalize god and Jesus, respectively. The crucifixion was merely more bloody. In both instances, however, god is rejected. The real difference between crucifixion and secularization is the context. By holding on to a religious concept of god and Christ during the process of secularization, Christianity was facing unprecedented challenges. Its discourse had become irrelevant because it held to claims that had lost their meaning both in terms of content and in terms of their plausibility.

Christianity, if it wants to escape utter irrelevance and avoid descending to the status of a cult, will have to think hard about where it is going. I believe Christianity needs to give up its concept of revelation as imparted knowledge and replace it with a concept of a hermeneutics of being. Bonhoeffer argues along similar lines in *Act and Being*,[4] the work that was the research subject of my Ph.D. under Gary Simpson.[5] While pursuing a similar objective in this essay, my understanding of the theology of the cross, deeply informed by my post-academic[6] location in late modernity and the European context, takes me into a different direction, namely that of radical theology.

THE ARGUMENT FOR A RELIGIONLESS THEOLOGY

Bonhoeffer advocated a religionless Christianity. In turn, I will argue for a religionless theology.[7] I'm not arguing for a well-defined concept derived from a precise understanding of Bonhoeffer's "religionless Christianity."

Rather, I use the term as a shorthand for a new way of thinking that I believe needs to emerge, among theologians and laypeople alike, if Christianity is to continue to retain some degree of relevance and prophetic efficacy.

Theology of the Cross

In this essay I want to chart a course from theology as religion-related discourse to a religionless theology. I will argue my way from a theology based on revelation as information to one that departs from and arrives at a concept of revelation as being. The latter is, as many will acknowledge, the true heart of the Christian movement. Yet the cognitive part still functions everywhere as a delimiter of what that being is. In the West, and especially in Europe, the age of organized religion providing a unified understanding of truth, aka the meaning of life, is over. This fact should compel us to crack the shell of the cognitive and let revelation as being present itself to us on its own terms. I will chart my course with a firm footing in Luther's theology of the cross. I do this with an eye toward the promise Luther's late medieval theology holds for late modernity. I'm also deeply informed by Bonhoeffer's journey from his idealist concept of the Church as the body of Christ (as developed in the two early dissertations, *Sanctorum Communio*[8] and *Act and Being*[9]) to the concept of the world come of age in the *Letters and Papers from Prison*.[10]

As deeply indebted as I may be to Bonhoeffer, however, I believe his proposal for a religionless Christianity does not go far enough. How could it, given his location and time? What Bonhoeffer did not yet grasp is what radical consequences flow from the actual possibility of living without god. My approach, moreover, is different than Bonhoeffer's in that I not only understand the secular theologically[11] but also attempt to understand the theological on secular terms. The god is truly superfluous, and the roles the god/s have played in our civilization in the past, we now realize, were always functions of political and economic power. Only through the death of Christianity and a most radical following after god's movement of embodiment in Jesus can its discourse become relevant again.

Two-fold Argument

My argument takes the concept of religionless Christianity beyond Bonhoeffer's territory where the irrelevance of god is still analogous to the same marginalization Christ suffered on the cross. For Bonhoeffer, god is still "up there, so to speak." I argue that god, in god's very nature, is irrelevant.[12] When we collapse god into his strange works of cross and suffering, we have the estranged god who is at the same time closer to the world than we are to ourselves. I want to bring Christian discourse out of the framework of organized religion to salvage its relevance and to let Christ speak today. The only way to arrive there, however, is to banish god from heaven. That is not god's place and never has been.

An important underlying assumption for my essay is that the secular is as religious as any religion that preceded it. Religiosity defines what it is to be human. For as long as we continue to use the word "religious" as something exclusively tethered to organized religion, Christianity will not be able to escape its clutches while the West continues to be ignorant of the deeply religious inclinations that pervade its destructive consumerism and capitalism. We never outgrow the religious (used here as a noun) even when we outgrow religions. The religious is what makes us human.[13]

THE HISTORICAL DIMENSION

There are two perspectives from which we may consider the need for a religionless theology, the historical and the theological. By way of preamble, I have already given a brief historical sketch above of how Christianity came to a point where its insistence on knowledge caused it to collapse in on itself. Its knowledge of salvation, the name of god, the number of extant angels, the origin of satan, various abodes and eternal states—in short, the entire array of metaphysical artifacts that populate the unseen world—was self-assuredly matched by its knowledge of more natural things, such as the age of the earth and the stages of creation. As the latter collapsed in the nineteenth century, the former became increasingly untenable and irrelevant.

However, it is not sufficient to merely have a historical perspective of loss. It may describe the experience from the vantage point of the adherents of Christianity, but it doesn't get at the heart of the matter. For the first time in history, the opening up of a secular space, a public marketplace of ideas, made it possible to see religion as optional amidst a panoply of other options. What is truly novel here, however, is that the secular is not just a new option next to religions; it is the discovery of the possibility of living without the gods. To put it even stronger, the secular is the condition of newfound freedom and sustains the continued existence of multiple religions as long as they operate in their assigned margin based on a mutual agreement of non-interference.

Instead of trying to argue for a place for religion or its continued relevance, I propose to back-engineer the secular condition, as it were, and apply it to the very beginnings of Christianity. Jesus out of necessity spoke from the framework of a religion, Second Temple Judaism. He couldn't envision a religionless perspective or cast his gospel in non-religious terms. Instead, he subverted most notions that were part of his religion: he presented god as our Father as well as our servant, promised hypocritical believers a destiny in hell, and claimed prostitutes and swindlers to be first in the Kingdom. I believe it is precisely in the subversion enacted in Jesus's life and teachings, however, that we find openings to an interpretation of Jesus beyond religion. Sadly, Jesus's followers did not do these teachings a service when they interpreted the connection between Jesus and god ontologically and made him the face and self-expression of the god. I will, however, make good use of the understanding of Jesus as god precisely for our religionless understanding of Jesus in the next section.

The last thing to be said under the historical perspective is that as long as Jesus's message and life are confined to the Christian religion qua religion, the discovery of the secular makes Jesus superfluous. I believe this is not sufficiently understood. In Europe Jesus has been hijacked by a religion that won't let him go. So he's no longer all that interesting. His only job is to purchase human souls, snatching them away from god's wrath with his blood . . . but god doesn't exist; not in Europe. Only if Jesus's religion is epiphenomenal, i.e., irrelevant or superfluous to his message and work, will his relevance be able to hold in the secular age. According to Christianity, to understand the message of Jesus, we first have to assume that god exists. With this the Christian religion has erected a barrier to the understanding of Jesus by insisting on invisible "thingies" and entities. But Jesus was never about insisting that people first believe that god(s) exist. He wanted them to have faith. Faith is never an assumption (belief) but a headlong leaping into the abyss of the risk, gods or no gods. This understanding particularly emerges in the Gospels in Jesus's interaction with non-Jews. I will now move on to a discussion of the theology of the cross.

THE THEOLOGICAL DIMENSION

The theological dimension takes us to the theology of the cross, a theological approach owned by no one and embraced by too few. The subversive tendency of this theology maintained as a paradox or even antithesis (instead of being grafted into human explanatory systems) is a constant threat to Christianity's desire to understand revelation as a body of information to be guarded and protected. The message of Christianity belongs to no one, and its center presents itself as an abyss that draws us deeper, not higher, to greater perplexity, not clarity, to self-involvement, not mastery. Let us look at the two main theological events that bookend the life of Christ, incarnation and cross, from the perspective of this theology as we seek an interpretation that supports my insistence on a religionless theology.

Incarnation

The main point of the incarnation, as is usually acknowledged, is that god is truly with humanity. Despite the never-ending warnings against lingering Docetism (god becomes human, but . . .), however, there have been many attempts to preserve a residue of the supposedly otherworldly "godness" of Christ. We even find such attempts in the Gospels. After his virgin birth, Jesus performs miracles, doves descend on him, heavenly voices are heard, and transfigurations happen on mountaintops. And there is, of course, the supernatural event of the resurrection. I do not want to dispute the historicity of the miraculous on historical grounds—many others have done that already. Rather, my argument is theological. If in Jesus god became human, then god is truly with humanity. Here is where I cash in on my earlier promise of the early church's crafting of an ontological connection between Jesus and god. We need to take the notion of the incarnation with utter seriousness. All we see in Jesus is humanity all the way down. There is no non-humanized divine remainder in Jesus, or else the incarnation is incomplete and thus fails in accomplishing its purpose. Any narrative supernaturalism is a form of Docetism, including the miraculous. In making Jesus god, the early Christians planted the seed of the demise of their supernatural view of the world as well as their supernatural understanding of god.

With the incarnation we run into a paradox, however. To the extent that the incarnation is complete, god is invisible. In his humanity Jesus is never divine proof but at best a divine incognito, a hidden god. This is the baffling realization that follows from a rigorous outworking of the incarnation. Incarnation, the embodiment of god into humanity, and incognito, the invisibility of god qua god as the necessary corollary of the incarnation, cancel each other out. The incarnation is not only the self-giving or self-revelation of god; it is also the hiding and thus erasure of god. To clarify this, I bring my earlier distinction between revelation as knowledge and revelation as being to bear. What claims there are as to what god is, what rules god needs to follow to qualify as a god, where god lives, and what god eats for breakfast, melt away like snow on a Minnesota sidewalk in late March with the reality of the incarnation. I have said nothing about God's being (capitalized here just once) because, like all the theologians I critique, all I have is interpretations of events and constructive efforts of the imagination. However, given the radical hermeneutical nature of theological discourse, we are free—no, we are compelled—to follow the alleged divine movement through Christ into the world with complete honesty and determination to its very end. When Jesus dies on the cross, this process is completed: god fully given and god fully gone. Exhaling his last breath in the depth of the sufferings of the world, god is no more.

Cross

Even though god disappears with the incarnation in terms of god's presupposed supernatural qualities, it is not contradictory to maintain that in Christ we see and encounter god. I can do so on account of my distinction between revelation as info and revelation as being. The alleged information about the god gets lost, but the being is present (whether or not recognizable and visible). So, let's continue in line with the insistence of the early church that Christ is the son of god, the second person of the trinity, etc. If god has indeed come in the flesh, then god participates in our human life. The paradox of givenness and erasure is itself the antithesis to the human expectation qua religion of god. The high and mighty god above, creator of the world, Pantocrator, king of all the earth, receives his antithesis in the given, embodied god who disappears in the crowd. This is Luther's "sub contrarium" of divine revelation. Maintaining that this is revelation, is at the same time saying that revelation disappears in the flesh of the Christ. The *deus revelatus* (the revealed god) is at the same time the *deus absconditus* (the hidden god). Please do note that the hiddenness is only hiddenness in terms of the human expectation, not necessarily in terms of the reality of god.

We are left with a double hiddenness: god in se and god in "revealed state." Luther understood this well; god is not only hidden in his eternal (pre-incarnation/revelation) state but also hidden in his revealed state (the babe in the manger). With the incarnation, hiddenness is even more complete. Before the incarnation god's hiddenness was shrouded by our speculations concerning the god, but now that the god is given in Christ and disappears in human flesh, we have nothing to work with anymore, so to speak. God's way in the Christ is that of an earthly human being who ends his life as a criminal on a cross. Sickness, humiliation, death, and dishonor all complicate the idea of revelation, the expectation of the god. Unless, of course, this worldly god is simply the true god, god's naked truth.

The question that lingers is this: to what extent is the hidden god truly hidden in the incarnation? To what extent is the paradox truly paradox? To what thesis are incarnation and cross the antithesis? To begin with the latter, the cross is the antithesis to our human expectations of god. The encounter with Christ as god offends the sensibilities of both philosophers of the Middle Ages and the ancient Greco-Roman world, but it is also an affront to the mythos of the god-king of the Judaic-Hebrew worldview. The paradox that consists in the disappearance of the god the moment he appears in the flesh of the Christ is a paradox only if we consider this god to come from an eternal abode above. It is a paradox only to the extent that the disappearance of the god in the flesh of Christ is anomalous to god, a temporary hiccup in god's unbounded eternal existence. In short, the hidden god is hidden only if what we see is not god or unlike god. But what if that *is* god? What if the world and all creaturely flesh and all suffering and death and sickness are exactly what god "is"? Then incarnation and cross are truly the revealing of god but just in a way that offends our religious sensibilities such that we call it a "sub contrarium," the opposite of god.

What I suggest is that the concept of revelation as knowledge will always run into the paradox, the antithesis, the refutation, and ultimately, in the secular age, the "irrelevantization" of Christianity. Revelation as knowledge leaves the prerogative of the definition of what god is in the hands of human beings and their religion. The concept of revelation as knowledge needs to make room for a concept of revelation as being, which is more in line with the Lutheran idea of revelation as god's self-revelation. Knowledge needs to be opposed to make way for being. With that I don't mean that nothing may be said but that all supposed knowledge with its supernatural claims and metaphysical imaginations must be given up for the sake of making Christ relevant by presenting him as a new form of being in the secular world. We must acknowledge that all our theology, doctrine, and knowledge of salvation is a mere figuring, a hermeneutical endeavor in response to the appearance of a certain being. And once the hermeneutics completes its work, the being is trapped in tradition and doctrine. There is nothing that prevents us from letting go of the framing of this so-called knowledge as religion, however. All we need to do is pay attention to what is at hand, i.e., the narrative of the flesh of Christ. Let us explore the notion of revelation as being in the following sections.

FROM HIDDEN GOD TO STRANGE GOD

We need to move from the hidden god to the estranged god; from *deus absconditus* to *deus alienus*. For Luther, god is hidden both in godself, *absconditus in se*, and in his revelation, *absconditus in revelatione*. His entire theological project hinges on god's "essence" not being epistemologically available both as god and as Jesus. Of course, in Jesus god is truly given but only as a hidden gift, as a paradox, as human flesh, in suffering, i.e., in ways that are contrary to god, according to Luther. Hence, whether god is actual or fiction, god disappears theologically speaking with Jesus, and the only way to get god back in any decent shape or form is to revive god in an Old Testament imagination as the supreme being, which is what Christianity has done in scholasticism and Calvinism. Though the Reformation has been flanked on both sides of history by systemic attempts to graft the god into the human system of a religion, there is nothing that prevents us from returning to Luther's discovery and radically pursuing it into a late modern, secular interpretation.

The Alien Work of god

To support my interpretation, and to illustrate where I want to go with the disappearance of god in the double hiddenness, we need to look at a related concept coined by Luther, that of the alien work of god, the *opus alienum*. In Luther's theology the concept of god's proper work versus god's alien work runs parallel to the *revelatus* (givenness) versus *absconditus* (hiddenness) of god. There is a work that is proper to god, namely through grace, blessing, and providence, and a work that is alien to god, namely through trials (*Anfechtungen*), the cross, suffering, and death. The latter is also referred to as the Left Hand of god.

The parallel, however, is rather ambiguous. The cross is presented as part of god's alien work. However, with regard to godself, the cross is the most intimate self-expression of compassionate being with creation. So we wonder to what extent the alien work, the *opus alienum*, is truly alien. Traditionally, incarnation and cross are both paradoxes in that they present to us the self-revelation of god but then in hiddenness. By implication god *in se*, the "real god" so to speak, is not very much like Christ. Could we interpret Luther as saying that the paradox consists not so much in the being of god but our expectation of god not being met in the babe in the manger and the mangled body on the cross?

As far as I can see, there is a good deal of wrestling with the concept of the god of the philosophers in Luther's theology, but perhaps even Luther doesn't completely overcome it. Perhaps he shrinks back from following through on the radical suggestions that emerge from his interpretation of the event of the cross. If god in the suffering Christ is still a hidden god, then behind Christ, the god of the human expectation, the god of the philosophers, the god of the mythos still stands tall. Interestingly, even for Luther, that hidden god is not the structured god at the apex of a theological system but something that opens up to the deep destabilizing dark groundlessness of the unknown. Dare we speak of a dangerous god who is an abyss? What if we follow through on this destabilization? Getting rid of the god of the philosophers and the mythical metaphysical reification of a supernatural deity "up there," what if we trace the coming of god in Christ and name it for what it is? We may start with what we observe. God is erased in the flesh of Jesus, and that flesh is erased on the cross. The incarnation is the great disappearing act of god in Christ but in a way that a gift is given, the gift of self-giving love. God is found as a gift to the world but simultaneously as reckless abandonment to the process of the world, i.e., suffering and death.

It is not difficult to connect incarnation and cross in which Jesus Christ suffers the worst sufferings a human being can undergo with Luther's *opus alienum*, the alien work of god: *Anfechtung*, suffering, sickness, and death. Perhaps god did not so much disappear in and through the flesh of Christ as god became before our eyes simply what it/she/he truly is: the world in its raw naked suffering and becoming. In other words, the *opus alienum*, the alien or strange work of god, is actually the *opus proprium*, the true work of god. This conclusion is not even that radical. We often talk about god's work in terms of loving us and blessing our lives. Looking at the reality of life, however, the *opus proprium dei* seems rather hidden from our view. The invisibility or absence of the *opus proprium* for most (if not all) of our lives leads us to suggest an *opus alienum* to make up for our perceived discrepancy between the reality of the world and our fantasy about god. It is done to harmonize the assumption of god being in control, providential, powerful, and good with the experience of the opposite. As much as we want to believe in and hope for the *opus proprium* (blessing), we get only the *opus alienum* (suffering). It is our true reality. We call it *alienum*, strange, only because we can't handle its abysmal character.

Why don't we bluntly say that god in Christ as the *deus revelatus* collapses into the *opus alienum* such that the hiddenness applies to the two things we never see, never have seen, and never will see: blessings and the beatific vision of god in god's otherworldly glory? The hidden god is not a hidden god but a fantasized one, just as the *opus proprium*, the work of god according to his nature, is a wonderful concept that is likewise never actualized. We still suffer and die, and that's the end of it. We need to connect the *opus alienum*, the strange work of god, with the *revelatus*, givenness of god in Christ. This may be a tough pill to swallow, but drawing on John Caputo's interpretation of the theology of the cross, I feel encouraged to say it is the only sensible and honest one.[14] It gives us a worldly god who is consonant with our experience of the world instead of a religion conforming to the metaphysical and mythical demands of our anxieties (as well as our traditions). In short, we have a god in and for the world.

This may not be very intuitive, but it is simply a radical interpretation of the theology of the cross. It does justice to our experience of the world. *Absconditus* (*in se*) and *opus proprium* belong together as they both function on the level of myth and metaphysical fantasy. No one has seen god, and no one has overcome death or experienced the goodness of the Lord in the land of the living. But Christ has come, and in Christ god suffered the sufferings of the world and was (and presumably is) with us till the bitter end. *Revelatus* (secondary hiddenness) and *alienum* belong together on the level of phenomenology in which we break through ("bracket") the bonds of the strictures and conceptions of Christianity as religion and let go of the invisible god.

The Estranged god

In all of this, it is perhaps tempting to see god disappear in the flesh of Christ and say, "Behold the *deus 'irrelevantus.'*" God is no longer a factor of significance. God is gone; we have overcome god as a concept in our society. This is the path our society has chosen. Christianity and the religions are over.

I suggest we take a different interpretation, one in which god and the world indeed become one after the incarnation but in which this event is understood to be meaningful beyond the disappearance of god. It is a two-step approach in which we move from an estranged god to a strange god. The first step is the estranged god. Rather than saying that *Anfechtung*, trial, suffering, sickness, and death belong to god's alien work, they must be seen as god's *proprium*. The incarnation was not the exception, anomaly, *contrarium*, or interruption of god. It is the true reality of god. The plane of the world with all its pain and misery is the true plane of god's existence, god's life.[15] Just as the experience of suffering is the true experience in this life, so the true god expressed in the flesh of Jesus is this alien god who without remainder surrenders to the process of the world, the evil of humanity, the sufferings of creaturely existence, and our common fate, death. In other words, the opus *alienum* is actually the opus *proprium*; it is the very life of god. God is not so much the deus *absconditus;* it is just that the *revelatus* is too strange for our eyes to behold. Instead of a *deus "irrelevantus,"* we speak of a god estranged from our expectations.

Before we can embrace this notion of *deus alienus*, the strange god, we need to pass through estrangement. We conflate the concept of god with the existential experience of mortality, the abyss of death, the nothingness, the gaping hole of blackness on the edge of which we barely maintain our balance. Luther's concept of the *deus absconditus* gets turned inside out. The revealed god may appear to us in the benign face of Jesus Christ, but what is really going on is that with the incarnation god reveals god's givenness, god's surrender, to the process of the world's becoming. This god is estranged from the comfort of religion. This god is stranger than fiction. Stranger, that is, than our religious fictions of the sky-god who dwells on high and possesses omnipotence, etc. We need to pass through the estrangement of letting go of our cherished religious assumptions and preconceptions of what, in our opinion, the god must be to qualify as god and then embrace the estranged god who comes in Christ only to die on the shores of history with a broken, mangled body on the cross. The estranged god who comes home, i.e., is no stranger to our suffering, angst, pain, sickness, and death. Ecce *deus alienum*!

The Strange god

Yet there is more to the strangeness of god. In Christ there is the turn to the other. With Christ god does not simply disappear into the abyss of the world. Phenomenologically speaking, there is an excess, a remainder that opens up new horizons and invitations. This functions not on the level of knowledge, however, but on the level of being. In the foregoing I made rhetorical use of the idea of Jesus as god because it worked in my favor to radically pursue the idea of the disappearance of god on behalf of a secular interpretation. On the level of revelation as being, however, the phenomenological obverse side of this disappearance is the being of revelation. Whatever we name it, we encounter it, without being able to erase it or ignore it.

With Jesus we encounter that form of being that doesn't pursue the preservation of the self at all costs. The very idea of incarnation entails a givenness, a being poured out for the sake of others. God becomes one with the world's fate, without a remainder in terms of origin but with a remainder in terms of address and invitation.[16] Jesus invites us to lose our lives for the sake of our neighbor. In Jesus we encounter the dual strangeness of a god who is completely worldly and entirely religionless. On the one side, there is the worldly strangeness of god being one with the world in all its suffering till the bitter end. On the other side, there is the religionless strangeness of god being the world's opposite in overcoming self-preservation through radical self-giving love for the other. Jesus is the never-ending subversion of the ubiquitous religious drive that pervades adherents of both religions and ideologies to become eternal gods in our own universe.

RELIGIONLESS THEOLOGY

What is religionless theology? A nothing. An idea, an ideal, a process, an invitation. I've tried to give reasons for the secularization of Christ out of historical necessity but especially because of, I believe, compelling theological arguments. The theological approach is what I have in common with Bonhoeffer even when our conclusions are not the same. Our projects are also driven by the same basic insight: revelation is not info but the kind of being, made manifest in Jesus. It is entirely worldly but at the same time entirely unworldly, not in a religious sense but in the sense that it sublates human existence through an exocentric self-giving that simultaneously embraces the abyss. Until the bitter end. Such is love, and love is divine.

NOTES

1. To say that Christianity is at a threshold is to state the obvious. When has Christianity not been at a threshold in its two thousand years of existence? When has it not been at the brink of collapse due to internal corruption, outside hostility, or maniacal revelry in worldly power?

2. Dietrich Bonhoeffer, "Letters and Papers from Prison," trans. Lisa E. Dahill et al., in *Dietrich Bonhoeffer Works, Vol. 8*, ed. John W. de Gruchy (Minneapolis: Fortress, 2010), 23ff, 426–31, 450–51.

3. I use "god" uncapitalized because in theological discourse the word is never more than mere concept. This is an important underlying assumption in this essay. All we ever have are speculations, interpretations, and constructs. The moment these get absolutized, god becomes a problem of our own making. If theologians actually meant God (capitalized), they would better remain silent.

4. Dietrich Bonhoeffer, "Act and Being: Transcendental Philosophy and Ontology in Systematic Theology," trans. H. Martin Rumscheidt, in *Dietrich Bonhoeffer Works, Vol. 2*, ed. Wayne Whitson Floyd (Minneapolis: Fortress, 2009), 95, 103–27.

5. J. I. de Keijzer, *Bonhoeffer's Theology of the Cross: The Influence of Luther in "Act and Being"* (Tübingen: Mohr Siebeck, 2019).

6. Everything I say in this essay is at the same time deeply personal. I realize it is not done in academic essays to deviate from the required academic attitude and mix personal details in with the academic subject matter. However, as a European theologian, I speak from a vantage point that is the direct result of the demise of Christianity in Europe. In a way the above is a long-winded attempt to say that as a theologian I've found myself without a job. My "Sitz im Leben" is therefore necessarily and consciously post-academic. I am a post-Christian theologian. Christianity in Europe has died because its god has evaporated. As a post-academic I am living the death of god. Although on a daily basis it is not quite so dramatic as it sounds, it still makes the urgency of the question concerning Christianity deeply personal.

7. Theology is not necessarily my objective. My call for a religionless theology is merely an attempt to draw attention to the fact that theological discourse needs to frame its subject matter in a way that is meaningful and relevant for a secular environment.

8. Dietrich Bonhoeffer, "Sanctorum Communio: A Theological Study of the Sociology of the Church," trans. Nancy Lukens Reinhard Krauss, in *Dietrich Bonhoeffer Works, Vol. 1*, ed. Clifford J. Green (Minneapolis: Fortress, 2009), 141, 147.

9. Bonhoeffer, "Act and Being," 95, 103–27.

10. Dietrich Bonhoeffer, "Letters and Papers from Prison," 23ff, 426–31, 450–51.

11. As explained earlier, Bonhoeffer interprets secularization as analogous to the cross. Both push god to the margins and out of the world.

12. Bonhoeffer wants to dispense with the idea of god as guardian ("Letters and Papers," 427), whereas I suggest we could do without the concept of god as such.

13. The ability to think about one's life as a thing to be considered and to make one's life about a project one comes up with all by oneself, a goal to be achieved, is

what sets us apart from all other known lifeforms. With it comes the desire for immortality and to be like the gods we ourselves erected in the first place.

14. John D. Caputo, *Cross and Cosmos: A Theology of Difficult Glory* (Bloomington: Indiana University Press, 2019), 142–50.

15. I don't mean this in the sense that god "does" these things in a sort of perverted providentialism. Rather, the suffering of the world is god's true life. God participates in the world's becoming right from the start.

16. Jesus overcomes the meaning paradox. The search for meaning is always tied up with the quest for self-preservation. But the only way to create meaning is to lose yourself on behalf of the other.

Epilogue I

Reflection about Professor Gary Simpson

Marie Y. Hayes

I started working at Luther Seminary on September 15, 1992, as a part-time secretary with the then Office of Cross-Cultural Education. My first encounter with Professor Gary Simpson was when I attended the Cross-Cultural Committee meeting at Luther Seminary; Gary was a part of that committee. He was also a part of the Global Mission Committee, serving on both committees for many years. I could tell from his engagements and through various discussions that this was someone who had the interest of the global church at heart.

At that time the Office of Cross-Cultural Education, among other things, handled the responsibilities of the admission processing, advising, and servicing of international students at Luther Seminary. The Global Mission Institute, in addition to building and developing global and local relations for the advancement of the church, also sought means by which international students at Luther Seminary could be supported financially, spiritually, and socially.

As the Office of International Student and Scholar Affairs was developed, Gary was one of the faculty members that supported the reason for having such an office. This way we could focus on the mandate of serving our global students and scholars without the challenges of also serving students from diverse communities and planning cross-cultural experiences. The establishment of this office also necessitated the formation of a faculty and staff committee through the academic dean's office. Gary was one of the faculty members who served on this committee. He again brought his experiences and foresight to the works of this committee, helping to identify qualified global perspectives within Luther Seminary. He was part of the committee that helped to reactivate the exchange of students with Norway and Sweden while speaking for the establishment of relationships with other institutions in the Global South.

In addition to serving on these and various other committees at Luther Seminary, Gary taught various courses as was expected of him as a professor. Gary is a very compassionate and caring teacher. While he imparted knowledge, he will tell you that he also learned a lot from his students, especially the global students. Gary was willing to listen to each student and to guide them when necessary. If at any time he needed an understanding of the perspectives of the student or challenges that each student faced, Gary would come to my office for clarity and/or advice. Often we would coordinate our efforts for the success of each global student that he felt especially responsible for.

Gary also served as advisor and reader for several international students' programs and thesis writing processes. Acknowledgments of his contributions are noted in several of the theses found in the seminary library.

Within the Luther Seminary community, I worked with Gary on the planning and execution of several diversity programs to include the Dismantling Racism for the Beloved Community (DRBC), MLK Jr. celebrations at Luther Seminary, and international students' events, among others. I am delighted to give this reflection for Gary.

Finally, I would like to thank Prof. Gary Simpson for his many contributions to academia, teaching and supporting the studies and research of international students from around the world. The impact of his teaching, instruction, and academic research is manifested in the lives and ministries of international students who have gone to serve in various capacities in the global church and even in the United States; his former students now serve as bishops, pastors, professors, presidents or leaders of theological institutions, and leaders within their communities.

Epilogue II

Gary M. Simpson: A Fruitful Vocation

David L. Tiede

Dear Reader:

You are holding a remarkable collection of essays written by the Rev. Dr. Gary Simpson's students and colleagues. The Germans would call this a *Festschrift* celebrating the career of an outstanding professor and scholar. And so it is. But many *Festschriften* are dry-as-dust essays that scholars first published elsewhere honoring themselves. So why has Fortress Press contracted to publish this groundbreaking collection? And why is this worthy of your attention?

The editors, Dr. Samuel Deressa and Dr. Mary Sue Dreier, speak for Professor Simpson's PhD students "and many others who have studied with him during the times that he taught at Luther Seminary (1990–2020). His love for the church, his dedication for engaging and raising scholars for the church worldwide, and his passion for teaching theology and how it translates to changing or transforming the lives of the community is what remained with us as we graduated from Luther and started serving in different capacities."

Yes, this project is worthy of your attention for reasons only you can best discern in the place you are leading and serving. Dr. Simpson is famous for paying attention to what he called "the participatory golden rule," giving priority to what matters to the recipients or "consequence takers" of an action or decision. My hunch is that you will grasp what is useful to you here by first attending to the pathways of Gary Simpson's Theological Calling and secondly exploring the fruits of his wisdom in his students' and colleagues' essays. First, the tree, then the fruit.

A Theological Calling

Invest some time in reviewing Dr. Simpson's remarkable resume, not so much to join his admiration society as to track the flow and disruptions of his vocation through the decades. His years of ministry display the constancy of God's call in the upheavals of the church and world. How lovely it would be to hear what you see in your review. Here are a couple of my glimpses:

1. In January of 1990, Dr. Simpson was interviewed at Luther Seminary for an appointment as an Associate Professor of Systematic Theology. The other candidates were also superb, perhaps as strong a field as we ever saw at Luther Seminary. We were not looking to call a middle-aged white male, born and bred in the Missouri Synod. But the faculty, president, and board votes were unanimous. You can spot the strengths in the education, religious leadership, and pastoral ministry sections of his resume.

   Here was an experienced pastor whose grandmother first announced his calling when he was a child singing at her side in worship. Blessed by the discipline of the Missouri Synod "system," in 1974 he "walked out" with Concordia Seminary's superb theological and biblical faculty and completed his ThD with distinction in 1983 at Christ Seminary—Seminex.

   His dissertation was on *Reciprocity and Political Theology*, signaling his enduring interest in civil society. You can also see this focus in his forthcoming monograph on the philosopher Cicero's influence on Martin Luther. But in 1990 he was already engaged with a host of public commissions, inter-faith associations, and ecumenical associations in Oregon. And Oregon was a mission context. His interest is both theological and practical.

   We needed faculty who could help us prepare our graduates for the disruptions that were coming to the "established church," grounded in the Lutheran confession of the gospel and alive to profoundly changing realities. The call went to Dr. Gary Simpson.

2. It was my privilege to be one of Dr. Simpson's colleagues for the next fifteen years as he and others inside and outside of the faculty struggled to re-form Luther Seminary to prepare our graduates to lead Christian communities in a new era of mission. We wrestled with every word in the seminary's mission statement and kept revising the curriculum to accomplish the mission effectively and faithfully. Luther Seminary had long been excellent at teaching, but could we learn to produce what our

graduates and the Church needed from us? These lessons will continue to be challenging.

As you can see in his list of publications from those years, Gary Simpson participated intensely in our learning. Drawing upon his love of pastoral ministry and listening to our graduates and their congregations, he testified to the public vocation of congregations.

Thus, when the United States attacked Iraq, we called on Gary Simpson to teach us the Just War Tradition, which he did with restraint to assure a disciplined conversation in a divided nation. See his book *War, Peace, and God*. Even as he reached an ecumenical audience, he kept close to the ground, teaching regularly in the Lay School of Ministry of the Northwest Synod of Wisconsin. With colleagues in and beyond Luther Seminary, his was a clear voice, identifying the calling of congregations as missional communities.

Many of you are better acquainted than I am with Dr. Simpson's remarkable global impact in his final fifteen years at Luther Seminary (2005–2020). But even to an outside observer, three generative aspects of his work stand out in his resume, and all three flourish in the vocations of his students: 1) his sustained witness to "Missional Congregations as Public Companions with God in Global Civil Society" (see his 2015 article in *Dialog*); 2) his awe in the revelation he shares with his students that "Africa is the Lord's and the fulness thereof, Praise be the Lord" (see his 2007 LWF essay); and 3) his continuing interest in Martin Luther's appreciation of Cicero's practical wisdom (see his forthcoming *Learn Cicero*).

So much could be said! Better read what he has written. Even a New Testament teacher who invested the last half of his Luther Seminary years in administration can hear the inspiring *coherence* of Dr. Simpson's work! Listen to three spectacular sentences from p. 147 of his piece on "Missional Congregations as Public Companions": "Social moral wisdom is a this-worldly matter of life and death. In the sapiential imagination there's a mutual love affair between moral wisdom and human life, indeed for the sake of planetary life. Furthermore, the Bible testifies that this affair is God's doing."

A Fruitful Vocation

Every pastor and teacher wonders if their work made any difference. It's not about justifying oneself before God. Jesus Christ took care of that. But did my work actually help anybody? Even the Apostle Paul claimed the Thessalonians as "our hope or crown of boasting . . . our glory and joy" (I Thess. 2:19–20).

Many of you who are reading this are Gary Simpson's "crown of boasting," although he would probably blush at the term. But you may be among the thousands who studied with him as a seminarian or a lay-school student or a reader of his scholarship. It's hard to imagine how much joy seminary faculty feel every year at Commencement or when the graduates return to campus. Thanks be to God!

To use another Pauline metaphor, this collection of essays is a harvest festival of Luther Seminary's students and colleagues who are prospering the work of one of its major professors, Dr. Gary Simpson. "I planted," says the Apostle, "Apollos watered, but God gave the growth" (1 Cor. 3:6). As you are nourished by the rich produce, make sure to appreciate the distinctive flavors of each of the contributions and the abundance of the whole project. As I am writing this reflection, I have not yet had access to the articles, but simply reviewing the titles and the authors is already a feast. And pay attention to all the places where these fruitful studies are planted. God is giving the growth in locations throughout the world. Thirty years ago who could have hoped for the theological and missional leadership in this list of contributors and essays?

Not to be cranky, but some of Gary Simpson's gifted colleagues abandoned the PhD program when its center of gravity moved from their academic comfort zones to the global context where Luther Seminary's strengths for a new time were most needed. The excellence of doctoral education can no longer be measured only by the eighteenth- to nineteenth-century standards of the University of Berlin. God's best is yet to be!

Professor Simpson understood this. So, dear reader: explore, play, appreciate the spectacular range of essays of Gary Simpson's students and colleagues. This is the future God is calling into being.

In gratitude and hope,
David L. Tiede

Afterword

Gary M. Simpson

ASTONISHING

"Oh my!" Grandma Klemm would say, her voice softening and breathy yet noticeably spirited when something so utterly astonishing, so purely amazing, was taking place in her presence. With her German Lutheran upbringing, Grandma had grown up far too pious to utter the G*d word out loud, in public, even in such a circumstance, lest she somehow violate the "do not take the name of the Lord your God in vain" commandment; or, more importantly to her, lest she somehow embolden even one of the many children in her care to speak God's name frivolously, without a thoughtful godly purpose.

In the presence of this volume, I can only echo through the ages my maternal grandmother's "Oh my!" Each essay in a volume like this, yes, in this very volume, appears as a fully clothed and accessorized labor of love, as the old saying goes. For you authors, I am so grateful—there really are no adequate words. And for you editors, Samuel and Mary Sue, "Oh my!" "Oh my!" again and again.

Based on my relationship with each of these authors, with each of you authors, I read these essays individually, indeed quite personally, with each author's unique identity, distinctive interests, and particular socio-political-cultural contexts shining forth. Yet I also read these essays constellationally, so to speak. That is, as multiple points of light traveling across a vast night sky, in reality positioned light years away from one another, nevertheless forming patterns of meaning and projecting actionable images that in their togetherness have an identifiable character. The editors have rightfully named this constellation of essays "a glimpse of emerging global public theology" with all of its thoroughgoing situational particularities matched by its overlapping narrative solidarities of pain, lamentation, and joy; of repentance, emancipation, and restoration; of justice, reconciliation, and the commonwealth of God.

Lynn Hunt, past president of the American Historical Association, has said about her book, *Writing History in the Global Era*, it's "a short book about a big subject." Teaching theology while attending to a quite vocal, purposefully disruptive, and superabundant world of Christianity, well, it's a big subject. I've surely been blessed in my thirty years at Luther Seminary to be at a place that, in addition to its thousands of domestic students from many Christian confessions, has drawn and welcomed a host of international students and scholars from across the globe. Even so, the Seminary's international makeup has remained a small treasure trove out of a very big world—small, yes, but in no way trivial!

A LUTHER SEMINARY JOURNEY

Before coming to Luther Seminary in 1990—at that time called Luther Northwestern Theological Seminary—I had been a parish pastor for fourteen years. Those formative years certainly influenced my theological attention as well as my teaching and scholarship. During my first call in the Bay Area of San Francisco, I became attentive to our congregation's public presence with and within its community. I also began reading essays from the Frankfurt School of Social Theory, which helped frame some of my curiosity about this public presence. In my doctoral studies, I worked on traditional subjects within the field-encompassing field of systematic theology but also immersed myself in emerging approaches to political theology, a North Atlantic movement sharing resonances with feminist theologies in the West and liberation theologies in the Global South. I also delved deeply into Critical Social Theory, an outgrowth of the Frankfurt School. This journey of theological studies in light of my interests and growing expertise in social theory bore fruit during my pastoral leadership in Portland, Oregon, a subject that was at the heart of my interview process at Luther Seminary on Martin Luther King Jr. Day, 1990.

When I arrived at Luther Seminary under the leadership of President David Tiede, the faculty was in the beginning stages of efforts to think transformationally about the traditional curriculum of Mainline Protestant theological schools. A key component of our wrestling was to more thoroughly center the entire curriculum around listening to and with living congregations and their leaders within their unique contexts, communities, and circumstances. To have the faculty and staff as co-learners with congregations contrasted with the conventional curricular thinking shaped by an American market mentality whereby we the faculty in our scholarship and teaching were to design theological products that congregations and their current and future leaders, as well as their members, would purchase and consume. Accomplishing this basic shift in attitude and perspective would change the nature not only of the discipline called "practical theology" but also that of biblical studies, church history, missiology, and yes, my own disciplines of systematic theology and social ethics.

What's more, we suspected that such a transformation in teaching and learning would expose not only *what* we taught but *how* we taught. Indeed, it would require a transformation of *who* we were as scholars, as teachers, as well as who we were as colleagues in our togetherness as a faculty. Like Lynn Hunt's "writing history in the global era," such transformations were "a big subject."

At Luther Seminary we of course were not alone in facing such challenges and opportunities. This was happening in many pockets throughout the Association of Theological Schools across North America. As a faculty and staff, we confronted unfamiliar agitations from our new learning and teaching partners, that is, from American congregations and their leaders and members who were facing on an everyday basis the swiftly coming crises of the Mainline denominations within a rapidly accelerating multicultural, multi-ethnic, and multi-religious America with its numerous ruptures in equality, civil rights, and social and economic justice. These phenomena were also accompanied by a deepening Enlightenment-style secularization that had befuddled European Christianity for decades, even centuries. As a faculty and staff, we also encountered new resistances from within our ranks to what we were learning and how we were responding, especially from certain prominent faculty. Such resistances occasionally broke out into little rebellions, too often quite petty ones, that reflected new power alignments, actually that reflected a number of new practices of collaborative power—what I like to call *perichoretic* power—that, yes, come with a cost for some, especially those invested in an old guard arrangement modeled largely on hierarchical familial and cultural relations. In this volume you can see various US-based authors responding to these crises in emancipatory, not reactive, ways.

Luther Seminary was a large enough institution that one could reinvent oneself, within limits, over the course of a long career. My stepped-up involvement in our two doctoral programs was part of my own reinvention in the early 2000s after a number of years in the mid to late 1990s when, in addition to teaching, I was engaged in administrative assignments and activities, such as serving on the Long Range Planning Committee; chairing the Board of our Seminary's journal, *Word & World*; and chairing our History/Theology Division of the faculty with its accompanying sub-committees.

Besides various standard topics within systematic theology, social ethics, and my own roots in Martin Luther's theology of the cross, communion

Christology, and the doctrines of justification by faith alone and of worldly vocation, four other fields of scholarly research emerged for me and combined with my years of experience as a congregational pastor. The first of these four fields listed below became for me a "disruptive find," to borrow a term used in the history of scientific advancement; indeed, it had already disrupted me while I was a working parish pastor. The four fields of research were a) the rising interest in and growing significance of the doctrine of the social trinity, traditionally underestimated within Western Christianity, with its focus on God's being as communion rooted in the ancient understanding of *perichoresis*; b) the burgeoning field of congregational studies ignited by the Congregational History Project at the University of Chicago; c) critiques of Christian colonialism and accompanying postcolonial approaches to missiology with pertinences for the renewal of congregations in North America; and d) the Civil Society turn in Critical Social Theory based in the communicative imagination and its implications for applying the Christian doctrine of vocation to the public life of missional congregations, thus moving the fruitful Reformation notion of vocation beyond its captivity to modern atomistic individualism and more in line with the down-to-earth realities of congregations called and sent in their communities with all their messy, sometimes quite traumatic, and yet still blessed particularities. In addition, the Civil Society turn in Critical Social Theory also helped me to ponder more thoroughly the crucial connections between the prophetic and the sapiential traditions and how these might play themselves out within the life of congregations in their communities. I also increased my teaching of public theology courses, featuring figures such as Dietrich Bonhoeffer, Martin Luther King Jr., and Eleanor Roosevelt. Finally, this vibrant constellation of factors helped me address the issues that were—and still are—interrogating, indeed agitating, Luther Seminary in its failures and its ventures toward a transformed and transformational curriculum.

In all of this, I too had to risk listening deeply and attending seriously to the agitations reverberating throughout this new era of World Christianity, what I acknowledge as the Holy Spirit's new apostolic era of public theology, with its many-faceted polycentricism and its multidirectional dimensions and dynamics. As you read these essays, you might spot traces of this constellation of themes that grabbed my own interests. Still, these authors do not merely go to places where I have already gone. Nor do they slavishly repristinate or simply reproduce formulations that I have previously honed. No, thankfully! Rather, they freely and regularly take a theme, or aspects of a theme, and run with it, combining it with dynamics and dimensions of their own particular contexts, of their own interests and necessities, of their own expertise and ways of going about things theologically and otherwise. New creations of theological agony and wonderment and joy are the results. Oh my!

ALLES IST GABE

Alles ist Gabe. So said a dear mentor of mine, and he said it more often as the years crept, and whizzed, by. "All is gift." In my own seminary and graduate school days, saying this only *auf Deutsch*—in German—was a kind of *last things* exclamation bursting out ahead of time with tinges of warning and promise all mixed up together. A kind of "this is most certainly true."

Especially for those of us who were Lutheran, *Alles ist Gabe* participated in Martin Luther's lifelong indebtedness to St. Augustine's *deus dare* theology, in literal Latin, "God [is] to give." God's very being and way of life is in giving. Of course, one didn't have to be either Augustinian or Lutheran, or even confessedly Christian for that matter, to experience this splendor of the giftedness of life and its continual surging into the gifting of life forward both temporally and socially.

Luther had promoted this *deus dare* theology across his oeuvre—he himself had been, after all, an Augustinian monk and even eventually the District Vicar over eleven monasteries of the Congregation of the Reformed Augustinians. With special poignancy he highlighted this Augustinian heritage of *deus dare* in his explanation of the Apostles' Creed in his *Large Catechism*. "Through this knowledge [of the triune God,] we come to love and delight in all the commandments of God because we see here in the Creed how God gives himself completely to us, with all his gifts and power, to help us keep the Ten Commandments: the Father gives us all creation, Christ all his works, the Holy Spirit all his gifts."[1] Do these three divine persons in communion really give themselves "completely," as Luther promulgates here? Or might he be merely exaggerating, perhaps rhetorically, as the saying goes? Every time I get to teach the Catechisms, which still happens month in and month out, I marvel at this assertion, at this promise. Oh my!

Luther supports and extends his trinitarian *deus dare* in various ways. Three continually catch my imagination. First is his biblical teaching of "the promising God." It erupts again and again but shows up prominently both in his robust sacramental theologies of Baptism and Holy Communion and in his centering theology of justification by faith alone. For example, he conspicuously elevated "the promising God" in his 1520 blockbuster *The Babylonian Captivity of the Church* during a deep dive into an array of biblical narratives, concluding, "It is plain therefore, that the beginning of our salvation is a faith which clings to the Word of the promising God, who without any effort on our part, in free and unmerited mercy takes the initiative and offers us his promise."[2] His "promising God" theology underlies the most enduring, and endearing, facets of Lutheran theology within *The Book of Concord*, the confessional documents of the Evangelical Lutheran Church globally. In point of fact, it is the Scriptures' promising God that engenders the pivotal teaching of justification by faith alone, as these confessional documents again and again testify. Once more, we arrive at a very "big subject."

Second, Luther distinctively cradles his *deus dare* heritage by way of his communion Christology, as I refer to it. I employ the term "communion Christology" as a synecdochal part for Luther's entire christological-soteriological redemptive whole, remembering that in his *Small Catechism*, he titled the Second Article of the Apostles' Creed "On Redemption," and in his *Large Catechism* he specifically names Jesus "Redeemer" among the numerous possible designations scripturally available.[3]

Luther's communion Christology, while remaining tethered to the trajectory of Augustine's *deus dare* tradition, nevertheless proffers a significant surpassing and transformation of Augustine's heritage. A constellation of three christological-soteriological tropes makes up this transformation. First, in his communion Christology, Luther promulgates "the joyous exchange" between Christ and his sinners/saints/friends/siblings, as he classically put it in "The Freedom of a Christian" and as he frequently employed it in his preaching.[4] Luther's favorite Scriptural precedent for "the joyous exchange" is the egalitarian marriage image in Song of Solomon 2:16 and 6:3, "My beloved is mine and I am my beloved's," with each beloved freely sharing with the other all things, indeed, freely sharing with the other one's very self.[5]

The dynamic of "bearing" is the second trope within Luther's communion Christology that proffers a transformation of Augustine's precedent-setting *deus dare* theology forged in the era of the Roman Empire. People today often presume that Rome had run its empire on the basis of its military supremacy. Rome, however, was quite aware that running a successful empire culturally, socially, economically, and politically could not be based on an army alone. Armies are far too expensive to maintain at full strength all the time everywhere, and armies, after all, produce nothing tangible beyond a forced peace and imposed concord. Rather, the most efficient and effective basis of Rome's empire was its hierarchical benefactor ethos with its archetypal patron-client pattern of sociality. Simply put, patrons were to give great gifts that the client could never match reciprocally that then permanently indebted the client to perpetual fealty. In fact, the greater the gift given by the patron, the greater the distance of superiority, and supremacy, the patron possessed over the client, with out-and-out exploitation merely a thin threshold away. This imperial benefactor ethos provided the basic, though hidden, background assumption for Augustine's *deus dare* theology as it took root in Western Christianity.

Luther's focus on Jesus's "bearing" dynamic bestows a decidedly different quality and character upon his communion Christology from Christologies shaped from within the imperial dynamics of the Western benefactor ethos. In Luther Jesus comes incarnationally bearing the flesh and blood finitude of human reality with all of its blessed connections together with its frail and fragile limitations, including life's vast array of different sufferings. Additionally, and crucially for Luther, Jesus also comes bearing the defects, faults, failures, and foibles of human sin and its divine accountability, as well as the notorious sufferings of being sinned against. In all of these senses, "bearing" is Jesus's prevenient work, so to speak, to "all his works" that he gives. In fact, bearing embodies a peculiarly patient, passionate, and perhaps ironically even a passive-like work that Christ gives. Furthermore, this bearing's prevenience often transpires temporally and always occurs ontologically, as philosophers would say, that is, in the order of significance and consequence.

Luther highlights Jesus's bearing as the all-embracing, prevenient precondition for divine redemptive giving, that is, for divine bequeathing, to employ the Scriptures' own customary metaphorical world of inheritance. Jesus's bearing of human reality, of real human beings in their essential sociality, shows up conspicuously in Luther's joyous-exchange discourses.[6] Jesus's prevenient way of bearing is the dynamic that surpasses and, in reality, overcomes the patron-client sociality rooted in the predominant Western traditions of gifting. Patrons in these traditions would never ever want to be caught dead actually bearing a client's reality in any deep, lasting, or meaningful way. In fact, the patron-client sociality of the West's benefactor ethos represents a general implicit bias of privileged groups in their supposed superiority and supremacy, even when that sociality may not be consciously intended. By contrast, Jesus's basic bearing reality, this solidarity of God in Christ with us through the perichoretic power of the Holy Spirit, fundamentally marks Luther's communion kind of theology of the cross. The outcome of Luther's communion Christology is the final coming of the Commonwealth of God, coming also to human reality already now ahead of time in Word and Sacrament. Once more we have a very big subject, several of them, introduced in quite a short essay.

I introduce the third trope within the constellation of Luther's communion Christology discourses by way of an irresistible example. Luther penned in Latin a July 5, 1537, letter to his own pastor, colleague, and friend, Johannes Bugenhagen. Bugenhagen had been invited to Denmark by King Christian III to bring Lutheran reforms there. He had cornered Luther to preach for him while he was gone, quite aware that Luther had almost died in February and March of that year, though he had been gradually gaining strength since. Luther then preached for Bugenhagen week after week on the Gospel of St. John, surely among the Christologically richest books in the Scriptures.

In the letter Luther noted, "Christ lives" and then continued, his Latin being, "*Christi sumus in nominativo et genitivo.*" No doubt, Luther's Christologically radical, Latin linguistic pun—*Christi sumus*—would not have been lost on his good friend, Johannes, also fluent in Latin. *Sumus* is simply the Latin for "we are." Luther's *Christi* is grammatically ambiguous, purposefully so. His suffix, the second *i*, can be either the genitive singular, "Christ's," or the nominative plural, "Christs." Or both simultaneously! Both, of course, being Luther's Christological point. We are Christ's. We belong with him in love, as married spouses belong together with one another. Again Luther's favorite: "My beloved is mine and I am my beloved's." Here we have *Christi in genitivo*, in the genitive singular.

We also have *Christi in nominativo*, in the nominative plural. "We are Christs." We are Christs to and with and for one another; to, with, and for our neighbors and neighborhoods; to, with, and for our communities and their infrastructures; to, with, and for Denmark and its form of Christianity; to, with, and for the world and all that that might bring. By the way, Luther, never the Christologically shy one, did not say, and indeed he never ever said, "little" Christs. As Christs, full-fledged Christs, we too belong to and with and for the world—here again we have a *short* aphorism about a *big subject*, fit for some other occasion. On the translation side of Luther's letter, there is nothing more virtuosic than a captivating translation. Remember, there were no apostrophes in Latin. Notably, nevertheless, Jaroslav Pelikan translated Luther's Latin punchline, "We are Christ's—with and without the apostrophe" (*LW* 22:x). Surely a short and pithy saying comprising, once more, a very big subject. In this way too, *Alles ist Gabe.*

The third way that Luther's communion Christology version of *deus dare* theology captures my imagination takes place in his theology of joy. Here again we can see that he was not a slavish follower of his great teacher, Augustine. In his blockbuster *The City of God*, Augustine unleashed a well-known adage of gloom that underlay a general and too-often this-worldly pessimism: "But the peace which we enjoy in this life, whether common to all or peculiar to ourselves, is rather the solace of our misery than the positive enjoyment of felicity" (Bk XIX, Ch 27). Go ahead, readers, try that one out with your friends, or your spouse, or your children, or your students and colleagues, or . . .[7]

Luther quite often, though not always, rejected such this-worldly pessimism with its well-known and popular *contemptus mundi*—contempt of the world—ramifications. Rather, as he urged his students in 1526, "Joyfully enjoy the joyful things when they are present" (*LW* 15:176), the theme of his lecture series the year following his *The Bondage of the Will*. He highlighted his theology of joy just a few years later in his *Large Catechism* explanation of the Fourth Petition of The Lord's Prayer, "Give us this day our daily bread." While not saying so explicitly to his lay audience, he again had Augustine, other influential theologians such as Jerome, and the conventions of this-worldly pessimism in his sights. "Here we consider the poor breadbasket—the needs of our body and our life on earth. It is a brief and simple word, but very comprehensive. When you say and ask for 'daily bread,' you ask for everything that is necessary in order to have and enjoy daily bread and, on the contrary, against everything that interferes with enjoying it."[8] Oh my! And say that again, Luther: "and, on the contrary, against everything that interferes with enjoying it."

Oh my! Our editors and authors have brought us all such a book of joy. *Alles ist Gabe.*

NOTES

1. Martin Luther, "The Apostles' Creed," *Large Catechism*, in *The Book of Concord: The Confessions of the Evangelical Lutheran Church*, eds. Robert Kolb & Timothy Wengert (Minneapolis: Fortress, 2000), 440. I have remained with Luther's own sixteenth-century usage of pronouns for God. Not only did Luther find this *deus dare* theology in Augustine and witnessed in the Holy Scriptures, but he also found it prominently displayed in his favorite philosopher, the Roman pagan Marcus Tullius Cicero, who argued that it was in the nature of the gods to be essentially giving and to freely share that giving nature with human beings—a big subject for another day.

2. Martin Luther, *The Babylonian Captivity of the Church*, in the American edition of *Luther's Works* (St. Louis and Philadelphia, 1955–1986), 36:39.

3. Luther, *The Book of Concord*, 355, 434.

4. Luther, *The Freedom of a Christian*, *Luther's Works*, 31:351. "*Der fröliche Wechsel*" is Luther's German for "the joyous exchange" and appears in Luther's own German version of *The Freedom of a Christian*. Further, take note, the German version is not at all a translation of the prior Latin version, written for Pope Leo X as a devotional digest of sorts of Luther's basic theology. Rather, the German version is directed at the German laity, particularly those not university educated. See Bertram Lee Woolf, *Reformation Writings of Martin Luther*, vol. 1 (London: Lutterworth Press, 1952), 363. Luther's prime scriptural reference for the joyous exchange in *The Freedom of a Christian* is Ephesians 5:30.

5. See, for example, Luther's well-known and much-beloved 1519 sermon, *Two Kinds of Righteousness*, *Luther's Works*, 31:300. Luther's communion Christology displayed in the joyous exchange and other subsequent tropes tears open, for instance, the modernist straitjacket that Gustav Aulen had famously fabricated with its three atonement options—objective, subjective, Christus Victor—into which Luther's approaches to Jesus's work of redemption had to be squashed and squeezed. See Gustav Aulen, *Christus Victor: An Historical Study of the Three Main Types of the Idea of Atonement* (New York: MacMillan, 1962). I find Ian Siggins's inductive approach to Luther's Jesus more accurate and more useful; see Ian D. Kingston Siggins,

Martin Luther's Doctrine of Christ (New Haven, CT: Yale University Press, 1970). Of course, I have also focused on certain ones of Siggins's findings.

6. See Luther's classic discussion of "What does it mean to bear?" within the encompassing redemptive field of his pathbreaking lecture on Galatians 3:13. See Martin Luther, *Lectures on Galatians*, 1531 (1535), vol. 1, *Luther's Works*, 26:276–91.

7. It is incumbent upon us to note that there were and remain numerous "Augustines," so to speak, sometimes even conflicting ones, that then garnered significant influence for centuries within Western Christianity. In this essay I have not attended to the complexity of St. Augustine's thinking and its consequences. See Bonnie Kent's essay, which clarifies certain aspects of this complexity: Bonnie Kent, "Augustine's Ethics," in *The Cambridge Companion to Augustine*, eds. Eleonore Stump and Norman Kretzmann (Cambridge, UK: Cambridge University Press, 2001), 205–33.

8. Luther, *The Book of Concord*, 449.

Select Bibliography

Adeyemo, Tokunboh. *Africa's Enigma and Leadership Solutions.* Nairobi, Kenya: WorldAlive Publishers, 2009.
Agang, Sunday Bobai, ed. *African Public Theology.* UK: Langham, 2020.
Bitrus, Ibrahim S. *Community and Trinity in Africa.* Routledge Studies on Religion in Africa and the Diaspora 1. New York: Routledge, 2017.
Bloomquist, Karen L. and Musa Panti Filibus, eds. *So the Poor Have Hope, and Injustice Shuts Its Mouth: Poverty and the Mission of the Church in Africa.* Geneva: Lutheran World Federation, 2007.
Bonhoeffer, Dietrich. *Act and Being: Transcendental Philosophy and Ontology in Systematic Theology.* Translated by H. Martin Rumscheidt. Vol. 2 of Dietrich Bonhoeffer Works. Edited by Jr. Wayne Whitson Floyd. Minneapolis: Fortress, 2009.
———. *Letters and Papers from Prison.* Translated by Lisa E. Dahill, et al., Vol. 8 of Dietrich Bonhoeffer Works. Edited by John W. de Gruchy. Minneapolis: Fortress, 2010.
———. *Sanctorum Communio: A Theological Study of the Sociology of the Church.* Translated by Nancy Lukens Reinhard Krauss. Vol. 1 of Dietrich Bonhoeffer Works. Edited by Clifford J. Green. Minneapolis: Fortress, 2009.
Burns, James MacGregor. *Leadership.* New York: Harper & Row, 1979.
Bvumbwe, Joseph. "Can the Pulpit Also Be Used? A Handbook for Pastors and Lay Leaders: On Breaking the Silence on HIV/AIDS." D.Min Diss., Luther Seminary, 2004.
Caputo, John D. *Cross and Cosmos: A Theology of Difficult Glory.* Bloomington: Indiana University Press, 2019.
Crosby, Barbara C., and John M. Bryson. *Leadership for the Common Good: Tackling Public Problems in a Shared-Power World.* San Francisco: Jossey-Bass, 2005.
de Keijzer, J. I. *Bonhoeffer's Theology of the Cross: The Influence of Luther in "Act and Being."* Tübingen: Mohr Siebeck, 2019.
Deacon, Terrence. *Incomplete Nature: How Mind Emerged from Matter.* New York: Norton, 2012.
Deressa, Samuel Yonas, and Sarah Hinlickey Wilson, eds. *The Life, Works, and Witness of Tsehay Tolessa and Gudina Tumsa, The Ethiopian Bonhoeffer.* Minneapolis: Fortress, 2017.

DiAngelo, Robin. *White Fragility: Why It's So Hard for White People to Talk About Racism.* Boston: Beacon Press, 2018.
Ebeling, Gerhard. *Luther: An Introduction to His Thought.* Philadelphia: Fortress Press, 1970.
Fredrickson, David E. *The Promise of Not-Knowing: A* New *New Testament Reading.* Minneapolis: Fortress, 2022.
Guder, Darrell L., et al., eds., *Missional Church: A Vision for the Sending of the Church in North America.* Grand Rapids: William B. Eerdmans, 1998.
Hansen, Guillermo. "Luther's Radical Conception of Faith: God, Christ and Personhood in a Post-Metaphysical Age," *Dialog: A Journal of Theology* (Fall 2013): 212–21.
Heifetz, Ronald A., and Martin Linsky. *Leadership on the Line: Staying Alive through the Dangers of Leading.* Boston: Harvard Business School Press, 2002.
Kolb, Robert, and Timothy J. Wengert, eds. *The Book of Concord.* Minneapolis: Fortress, 2000.
Kolb, Robert. *Bound Choice, Election, and Wittenberg Theological Method: From Martin Luther to the Formula of Concord.* Grand Rapids: Eerdmans, 2005.
———. *Luther's Treatise on Christian Freedom and Its Legacy.* Lanham, MD: Fortress Academic/Lexington, 2019.
López, Ian Haney. *White by Law: The Legal Construction of Race.* New York: New York University Press, 2006.
Luther, Martin. *D. Martin Luthers Werke.* Weimar: Böhlau, 1883–1993. (WA)
———. *Heidelberg Disputation 1518.* In *Martin Luther's Basic Theological Writings*, ed. Timothy F. Lull, 2nd edition ed. William R. Russell. Minneapolis: Fortress Press, 2005.
———. *Luther's Works.* Saint Louis/Philadelphia: Concordia/Fortress, 1958–1986. (LW)
Moltmann, Jürgen. *God in Creation: A New Theology of Creation and the Spirit of God.* Minneapolis: Fortress Press, 1993.
———. *The Church in the Power of the Spirit: A Contribution of Messianic Ecclesiology.* Minneapolis: Fortress Press, 1993.
———. *The Trinity and the Kingdom: The Doctrine of God.* Minneapolis: Fortress Press, 1993.
———. *Trinität und Reich Gottes: Zur Gotteslehre.* München: Ch. Kaiser Verlag, 1980.
Neumann, Erich. *The Origins and History of Consciousness.* New York: Routledge, 2002.
Newbigin, Lesslie. "Activating the Christian Vision." In *Faith and Power: Christianity and Islam in 'Secular' Britain*, eds. Lesslie Newbigin, Lamin Sanneh, and Jenny Taylor. London: SPCK, 1998.
———. "Can a Modern Society Be Christian?" In *Christian Witness in Society: A Tribute to M. M. Thomas*, ed. K. C. Abraham. Bangalore: Board of Theological Education—Senate of Serampore College, 1998.
———. "What Kind of Society?" *Trinity Journal for Theology and Ministry* IV, no. 2 (Fall 2010): 49–61.

Nordstokke, Kjell, ed. *Transformation, Reconciliation, Empowerment: The LWF Contribution to the Understanding and Practice of Diakonia*. Geneva: Lutheran World Federation, 2009.

Nygren, Anders. *Agape and Eros*, Parts I and II. Translated by Philip S. Watson. Philadelphia: The Westminster Press, 1953.

Oduyoye, Mercy Amba. "Be a Woman and Africa Will Be Strong." In *Inheriting Our Mothers' Gardens: Feminist Theology in Third World Perspective*, eds. Letty M. Russel et al. Philadelphia, PA: John Knox Press, 1988.

Roth, Brad. *God's Country: Faith, Hope and the Future of the Rural Church*. Harrisonburg: Herald Press, 2017.

Roxburgh, Alan J., and Fred Romanuk. *The Missional Leader: Equipping Your Church to Reach a Changing World*. San Francisco, CA: Jossey-Bass, 2006.

Sanneh, Lamin. *Translating the Message: The Missionary Impact on Culture*. Maryknoll, NY: Orbis, 2009.

Simpson, Gary M. "Africa Is the Lord's and the Fullness Thereof." In *So the Poor Have Hope, and Injustice Shuts Its Mouth: Poverty and the Mission of the Church in Africa*, eds. Karen L. Bloomquist and Musa Panti Filibus. Geneva: Lutheran World Federation, 2007.

———. "Changing the Face of the Enemy: Martin Luther King, Jr., and the Beloved Community." *Word & World* 28, no. 1 (Winter 2008): 57–65.

———. *Critical Social Theory: Prophetic Reason, Civil Society, and Christian Imagination*. Minneapolis: Augsburg Fortress, 2002.

———. "'God is a God Who Bears': Bonhoeffer for a Flat World," *Word and World* 26, no. 4 (Fall 2006): 419–28.

———. "A Reformation Is a Terrible Thing to Waste: A Promising Theology for an Emerging Missional Church." In *The Missional Church in Context: Helping Congregations Develop Contextual Ministry*, ed. Craig Van Gelder, 65–93. Grand Rapids, MI: Eerdmans, 2007.

———. "African Realities Today through Lutheran Lenses." https://crossings.org/african-realities-today-through-lutheran-lenses/?print=pdf (accessed September 22, 2021).

———. "Civil Society and Congregations as Public Moral Companions," *Word & World* 15, no. 4 (Fall, 1995): 420–427.

———. "Congregational Strategies for Invigorating Lutheranism's Just Peacemaking Tradition," *Journal of Lutheran Ethics* 3, no. 7 (July, 2003), http://www.elca.org/scriptlib/dcs/jle/search.asp.

———. "Fruit of the Spirit." In *The New Testament and Ethics: A Book-by-Book Survey*, ed. Joel B. Green. Grand Rapids, Michigan: Baker Academic, 2013.

———. "God against Empire: Implicit Imperialism, Deliberative Democracy and Global Civil Society," *Consensus* 29, no. 2 (2004): 9–60.

———. "God, Civil Society, and Congregations as Public Moral Companions." In *Testing the Spirits*, ed. Patrick R. Keifert, 67–88. Grand Rapids, MI: Eerdmans, 2009.

———. "Missional Congregations as Public Companions with God in Global Civil Society: Vocational Imagination and Spiritual Presence," *Dialog: A Journal of Theology* 54, no. 2 (Summer 2015): 135–50.

———. "No Trinity, No Mission: The Apostolic Difference of Revisioning the Trinity," *Word & World* 18, no. 3 (1998): 264–71.

———. "Our Pacific Mandate: Orienting Just Peacemaking as Lutherans," *Journal of Lutheran Ethics* 5, no. 7 (June 2005). http://www.elca.org/scriptlib/dcs/jle/search.asp.

———. "Puckering Up for Postmodern Kissing: Civil Society and the Lutheran Entwinement of Just Peace/Just War." *Journal of Lutheran Ethics* 2, no. 12 (December 2002). https://learn.elca.org/jle/puckering-up-for-postmodern-kissing-civil-society-and-the-lutheran-entwinement-of-just-peace-just-war/ (accessed August 29, 2022).

———. "*Theologia Crucis* and the Forensically Fraught World: Engaging Helmut Peukert and Jürgen Habermas." In *Habermas, Modernity and Public Theology*, eds. Don S. Browning and Francis Schüssler Fiorenza. New York, NY: The Crossroad Publishing Company, 1992.

———. "Toward a Lutheran 'Delight in the Law of the Lord': Church and State in the Context of Civil Society." In *Church and State: Lutheran Perspectives*, eds. John R. Stumme and Robert W. Tuttle, 20–50. Minneapolis: Augsburg Fortress: 2003.

Smith, Robert O. "Let Them Die: COVID-19, Civil Society and the Market Economy." *An Okie Abroad*, Wordpress, March 24, 2020. https://robertowensmith.wordpress.com/2020/03/24/let-them-die-covid-19-civil-society-and-the-market-economy/.

———. "Societal Chaplaincy: Preparing for the Storm to Come." Northern Texas–Northern Louisiana Synod of the ELCA, April 4, 2020. https://www.ntnl.org/societal-chaplaincy-preparing-for-the-storm-to-come/.

Van Gelder, Craig, and Dwight J. Zscheile. *The Missional Church in Perspective: Mapping Trends and Shaping the Conversation.* Grand Rapids, MI: Baker Academic, 2011.

von Löwenich, Walther. *Luther's Theology of the Cross.* Minneapolis: Augsburg Publishing House, 1976.

Walter, Gregory. *Being Promised: Theology, Gift, and Practice.* Grand Rapids, MI: Eerdmans, 2013.

Index

abundance, 5–22, 83, 256
abundant human relationships, 15, 19
abundant life, 14–15, 22
ACS (American Community Survey), 98
Africa, 5, 7–10, 12, 16–22, 25–30, 34–37, 71, 76–77, 79–83, 93, 267–69; abundance, 7, 16; Christianity, 5, 7, 25, 29; churches, 28, 36–37, 76–77, 81, 91, 93; communal life, 19; communities, 12, 26, 36; context, 25, 34, 37, 71–83; culture, 72; diaspora, 25; economies, 21 leadership, 27–28, 35; leadership crisis, 26, 28; maladies, 8; mineral fortune, 27; national economies, 17; patriarchy, 79; philosophy on life, 78; population, 18–19; problems, 25, 27–28; public theology, 8, 12, 20; public theology of abundance, 22; scholar on African women's theology, 79; traditions, 77; women, 79; women's theology, 79
Africans, 6, 8, 16, 18–19, 25, 27, 37, 79
AIDS orphans, 159
America, 1, 25, 27, 47, 51, 97, 109, 157–59, 172, 174, 178; congregations, 259; society, 177, 180, 182

American Community Survey (ACS), 98
American Historical Association, 258
Americans, 88, 130, 158, 173–74, 176–79
ancient Greco-Roman world, 243
Anglo-Saxon world, 117
Apollonius, 211
Aristotle, 112, 143, 146, 151
art, 11, 50
Association of Member Episcopal Conference of Eastern Africa (AMECEA), 36–37
Athanasius, 146
Augsburg Confession, 110
Augustine, 141, 143, 145, 262, 264–66
Australia, 110, 117

Barth, Karl, 229
BCC (British Council of Churches), 125
Benjamin, Walter, 196
Berg, Bishop Robert, 88
Bethesda, 101
Bethesda Lutheran Church in Bayfield, 101
Beza, Theodore, 110
Bible, 82, 88, 93, 99–100, 129, 206
Birx, Deborah, 173, 178
Bitrus, Ibrahim S., 5–22

Black America, 51
Bohr, Niels, 219
Bonhoeffer, Dietrich, 111, 181, 260
Book of Acts, 206
Bretherton, Luke, 164
Briarwood Leadership Center, 171
Britain, 124, 130, 132–33, 136, 138
British Council of Churches (BCC), 125
Bultmann, Rudolf, 197, 220
Burundi Leadership Training Program, 167–68
Burns's transformational leadership, 34
Burundi Leadership Training Program (BLTP), 167–68
Burundi National Police, 168
Burundian educators, 167
Bvumbwe, Bishop Joseph, 88–90, 92, 102

Calvin, John, 117
Carpenter, Joel, 26
Census Bureau, 96
challenges facing rural public churches, 96
Christ Seminary, 254
Christians, 7, 25–26, 28, 74, 89–90, 107–8, 124–28, 132–37, 141–42, 146–51, 161, 163, 165–66, 237, 261–62; anthropology, 160, 163; callings, 115; churches, 5, 26, 34, 135; church in Africa, 28–29; community, 10, 33–34, 36, 127, 133, 135, 137, 163, 254; democrats, 111; dogmatics, 160; early Christians, 242; ethics, xi–xii, 107–8, 141–42, 144, 149, 151–52; faith, 9–11, 26, 110, 115, 124, 126, 129–30, 132–34, 136, 212; gospel, 129; leaders, 26; love, 74, 141, 143–44, 146, 148–49; ministry, 87; mission, 1, 31, 134; missionaries, 129; mission movements, 26; organizations and leaders, 6; society, 107, 123–38; society thesis, 127, 129; state, 126; theology, 9–11, 26; tradition, 143, 147, 152, 187,
196, 232; values of leadership, 36; vision for society, 133, 136; witness, 75–76, 126
Christianity, 25–26, 28–29, 136, 206–8, 212, 237–41, 244, 246–47;
Christologies, 165, 260, 262
church, xi–6, 28–29, 31–33, 36–38, 71–83, 88–94, 96–97, 99–102, 115–16, 124–29, 131–37, 141–42, 159–60, 162–68, 237–39, 253–55; Africa, 36, 71; district, 72, 76; governance, 71, 76; governance and diakonia, 71, 74; leaders, 1, 97–98, 108, 172, 180; Malawi, 88–90, 92; and society, 72, 75; and state, 270
civil society, xi, 2, 36, 99, 172–77, 180–81; critical social theory, 260
co-creators, 108, 146, 159–65, 167–68
colonization, 174, 176
concord, 148, 261–62
confessional documents, 261–62
Congolese Lutheran, 28
congregations, 1–2, 72–76, 78–79, 82, 88–90, 94–98, 100–102, 128, 179, 255, 258–61; mission and leadership, 271; study/missional church, xi
context, 1, 3, 45, 71–72, 115–16, 124
country coordinating mechanisms (CCMs), 93
COVID-19, 173–74, 179–80
crisis in democracy, 159
critical social theory, xi, 3, 171, 173, 175–76, 181–82, 258, 260
cross, 189–202, 239, 243
Cross-Cultural Committee meeting, 251
Cross-Cultural Education, 251
culture, 28, 31, 34, 37, 45–48, 111, 114, 124, 127

democracy, 20, 116–17, 157–60, 167–68
democrats, 158
Democritus, 210
demographic dividend, 18
Denmark, 61, 263–64
dependency syndrome, 75

Index

Derrida, Jacques, 207
development, 8, 18, 27, 36, 50, 79, 112, 130, 174; holistic, 36
diaconal ministry, 71, 80, 82
diakonia, 71–77, 79–83, 268; contextual, 6, 72; department, 72, 77–78; and justice 71–83; work, 72, 79, 81, 82
dictators, 92
dimensions of missional church, 32
Dismantling Racism for the Beloved Community (DRBC), 252
divine love, 141–44, 147–49
divine persons, 12–13, 15–16, 27, 261
Docetism, 242
doctrine of creation, 107, 141, 147, 151, 160
Domina Ratio, 221
Duke George of Saxony, 116
Duke University, 123, 125, 130, 132–33

ecclesia, 35, 115
economic cooperation, 27
economic growth, 18, 21, 27
education, 19, 21, 27, 39n20, 60, 77–78, 93, 166, 254, 272
Egypt, 88
ekklesia, 43
Elert, Werner, 111
Ellison, Ralph, 50
empowerment, 31, 35, 80–81, 268
Enegho, Felix E., 28
Eucharist, 33, 199
Eucharistic fellowship, 34–35
Europe, 25, 109, 237, 239, 241
Evangelical Lutheran Church: in America, 88, 94, 171, 180; in Malawi, 6, 87–91, 94–95, 102
ever-dominating African patriarchy and diakonia, 74

Faith Based Community Organizing, 96
faith in action, 74
feminist theologies, 258

First Commandment, 228
Floyd, George, 51, 92, 181
forensically fraught world, 187, 191, 193, 195–96, 198–200
Foucault, Michel, 224

Galatians, 150, 228–29
gross domestic product (GDP), 8, 17, 21, 27, 158
German Lutheran, 257
Germany, 92, 111
Gethsemane, 209, 214–15
global churches, xii, 251–52
Global Civil Society, 102, 255
Global Mission Committee, 251
Global Mission Institute, 251
Global North, 1, 3
global pathway, 87, 94
Global South, xii, 1, 3, 109, 157, 252, 258
global theologians, 1
Gnesio-Lutherans, 110; Magdeburg, 111
Gospel and Our Culture (GOC), 125, 130
Gospel and Our Culture Network, 31
Gospel of Mark, 187, 205–7, 211–13, 215; contests, 214
gospels in Jesus's interaction, 241
governance, 21, 73, 76, 173–74
Great Commission, 81
Greeks, 127–28, 142, 212
Gronberg, Bishop Erik, 171

Habermas, Jürgen, xi, 172, 173, 192, 194–95, 270
Hankinson, Robert, 210
Hayes, Marie Y., 251–52
Heidelberg Disputation, 107, 141–42, 151–53, 200
Hendriks, H. Jurgens, 8
hints, 124–25, 131, 134, 147
HIV-AIDS crisis, 93
holy ground, 88, 95, 97, 99, 102
Holy Spirit, 13, 15, 88, 91, 94, 102, 148, 161–62, 166, 260–61, 263

Horkheimer, Max, 196
Hoyme, Bishop Richard, 88
Hungary, 111, 157
Hunsberger, George R., 43, 107, 123–38
Hunt, Lynn, 258–59

Ibsen, Henrik, 196
image of God, 146, 160–61, 163
Immanuel, 101
inclusiveness, 48
India Lutheran, 112
injustice, 6, 9, 75, 77–78, 80–82, 88, 91, 98, 109, 112, 230, 232
Islam, 123, 130, 136

James, 206, 208, 210, 213, 215
Jesus's mission, 195
Judaic-Hebrew worldview, 243
Jung, Carl G., 219
justice, 2, 6, 51, 71–83, 88, 90–91, 94, 101, 114
justification, 82, 163, 189, 192–94, 196, 199–200, 260–62; by faith, 260–62

Kaufmann, Greg, 99
Kenya Evangelical Lutheran Church (KELC), 6, 72–73, 76–80, 82; gender policy, 80
King Henry VIII, 116
King's College, 130
Kinoti, George, 26, 28
Kossuth, Louis, 111
Kotter, John P., 45

Large Catechism, 228, 261–62, 264
Latin, 142, 263–64
Lay School of Ministry (LSM), 87, 99, 101–2, 255
leaders and followers, 29–30, 35
leadership, 5–6, 25–27, 29–31, 33–37, 44–47, 76, 79–80; crisis, 5, 28; formation, 33, 35; national, 174, 179; shared, 35, 45
Lectures on Galatians, 150

lifeworld, 2, 82, 175–76, 181; and civil society, 176; political state/market economy, 175; regular people, 176
Luther, 107–17, 141–52, 200, 220–24, 227–29, 243–45, 261–65; Christologically, 263; Christological point, 264; communion Christology, 262–63; communion kind of theology, 263; concept of faith, 187; doctrine, 111; seminary colleagues, 3; seminary journey, 258; experience, 220; Heidelberg Disputation, 191; theology, 109–17, 239, 245; thesis, 143–44, 149; writings, 107
Luther Northwestern Theological Seminary, 258
Lutherans, 82, 89–90, 109–11, 117, 220, 261; church, 6, 71, 73, 111; confessions, 111, 254; diaconal work, 71; families, 111; immigrant churches, 109; leadership, 110; in Malawi, 90; in Nordic lands, 111; theologian, 3; theology, 261; traditions, xi–xii

Magdalene, Mary, 206, 208, 210, 213
Malawi, 87–90, 92–95, 97, 102; church, 89
market economy, 173–77
Mark's Gospel, 187, 210, 213–14
Martin Luther King, 47, 50, 78, 258, 260
Martin Luther King Jr, 77, 82
Matthew, 52n7, 74, 115, 138, 205–7, 212, 215
Matthew's Jesus, 207
Meierotto, Mary, 101–2
missiology, 44, 138, 259–60
mission, 31, 33, 37, 74–75, 82–83, 87–88, 137, 197, 254; churches, 109, 112
missional church, xii, 5, 31–37; conversation, 31–33; congregations, 102, 255, 260; leaders, 31, 34–36; leadership, 33–37, 100, 256

missionary encounter, 31, 125, 127, 135
Missouri Synod, 254
Moltmann, Jürgen, 108
Multi-Party Democracy, 167

National Socialism, 109, 111
National Socialist, 111
National Socialist ideology, 111
Newbigin, Leslie, 31
New Testament, 43, 94, 100, 151, 162, 255
Nigeria, 17–18, 20–21
North Africa, 34
North America, 31, 110, 117, 259–60

Obaga, Margaret Kemunto, 6, 71–82
Obeizu, Emeka Xris, 25
Oduyoye, Mercy, 79
Ordass, Bishop Lajos, 112
Otto, Rudolf, 220

Pearl Harbor, 178
Pederson, Bishop Duane, 88–89
Pew Research Center, 25; report, 96
Princeton Theological Seminary, 125
public theology in Africa, 9
public theology of abundance, 5–21
public vocation, 11, 136, 255

racism, 5, 8, 44, 47–48, 51, 92, 100, 165, 168
radical theology, 238
revelation, 7, 15, 188, 230, 238–39, 241–44, 248, 255

Sanneh, Lamin, 130
Ström, Marie-Louise, 108, 157–68
systematic theology, xi, 1, 254, 258–59

theological discourse, 194, 242
transformational leaders, 28–31, 35–36; leadership, 5, 28–30, 34–37; leadership theory, 30–31, 35
Trump, Donald J., 8, 173–74, 177–78, 181

ubuntu, 78
Uganda, 28
United States of America, 157

vocation, 14–15, 22, 36, 78, 81, 102, 120n33, 180, 254–55, 260; baptismal, 102

Wesley, John, 51
Western Theological Seminary, 129
William James, 201
World Council of Churches (WCC), 125

About the Contributors

THE EDITORS

Rev. Samuel Yonas Deressa, PhD, is assistant professor of Theology and the Global South and Fiechtner Chair for Christian Outreach at Concordia University, St. Paul, Minnesota. In addition to these two volumes, Deressa's published works include *Leadership Formation in the African Context: Missional Leadership Revisited* (Eugene, Origen: Wipf and Stock, 2022); *A Church for the World: A Church's Role in Fostering Democracy and Sustainable Development* (London: Lexington/Fortress Academic, 2020), which he co-edited with Josh de Keijzer; and *The Life, Works, and Witness of Tsehay Tolessa and Gudina Tumsa, the Ethiopian Bonhoeffer* (Minneapolis: Fortress Press, 2017), which he co-edited with Sarah Wilson; and he is the editor of *Christian Theology in African Context: Essential Writings of Esthetu Abate* (Minneapolis: Lutheran University Press, 2015).

Rev. Mary Sue Dreier, PhD, is retired professor of pastoral care and missional leadership at Lutheran Theological Southern Seminary of Lenoir-Rhyne University (Columbia, South Carolina). She previously taught congregational mission and leadership at Luther Seminary (Saint Paul, Minnesota) and before that served as a Lutheran pastor for twenty-five years in rural, large multi-staff, and new church development congregations. She is author of a book of sermons, editor of *Created and Led by the Spirit: Planting Missional Congregations*, and co-editor with Samuel Deressa of these two volumes on global public theology. She has spoken widely and written various book chapters, journal articles, and church resources. In retirement she has become a certified spiritual director.

THE CONTRIBUTORS

Ibrahim S. Bitrus, PhD, is Lecturer of Christian Doctrine and Ethics at Federal College of Education Yola, Nigeria. He is author of *Community and Trinity in Africa* and the co-editor *of The History of the Boys' Brigade Nigeria, LCCN Fellowship*. He has published a variety of book chapters and journal articles within and outside Nigeria.

Josh de Keijzer, PhD, lives in the Netherlands where he owns a copywriting and a content marketing business. His published works include *Bonhoeffer's Theology of the Cross: The Influence of Luther in "Act and Being"* (Tübingen: Mohr Siebeck, 2019) and *A Church for the World: A Church's Role in Fostering Democracy and Sustainable Development* (London: Lexington/ Fortress Academic, 2020), which he co-edited with Samuel Deressa.

David L. Everett, PhD, currently serves as the associate vice president of Inclusive Excellence at Hamline University. He previously served as an Equity Consultant for the State of Minnesota, and his published works include "A Model for Institutional Equity," in *Challenges to Integrating Diversity, Equity, and Inclusion Programs in Organizations*; "An Institutional Model for Tolerance and Peace Using a Formulaic Integration of Equity, Diversity, and Inclusion," in *Paths to a Culture of Tolerance and Peace*; and *The Future Horizon for a Prophetic Tradition: A Missiological, Hermeneutical and Leadership Approach to Education and Black Church Civic Engagement*.

David E. Fredrickson, PhD, is professor of New Testament at Luther Seminary in Saint Paul, Minnesota. He has written on ancient Greek and Roman philosophy and poetry and their influences on the writings of Paul and the Pauline tradition. *Eros and the Christ: Longing and Envy in Paul's Christology* was published by Fortress in 2013, and his *Reading the New Testament in the 21st Century* (also Fortress) is forthcoming. His essay "Hellenistic Philosophy and Literature" in *The Oxford Handbook of New Testament, Gender, and Sexuality* (ed. B. Dunning, Oxford, 2019) signals his interest in the human relation.

Guillermo Hansen, PhD, is professor of Theology and Global Christianity at Luther Seminary, Saint Paul, Minnesota. From 1994 to 2008 he was professor of Systematic Theology at Instituto Universitario ISEDET, a major ecumenical seminary in Buenos Aires, Argentina. He has been a member of the Council of the Lutheran World Federation (LWF) as a theological advisor in the Department of Theology and Studies, and he has participated in numerous global research projects and conferences of the LWF. He is author of many theological essays and articles, both in Spanish and English, as well as editor of several books. His main publications are *En las fisuras: esbozos luteranos para nuestro tiempo* (Buenos Aires: ISEDET/VELKD, 2010) and, jointly with Nancy Bedford, *Nuestra Fe: Una introducción a la teología* (Buenos Aires: ISEDET, 2008).

Marie Y. Hayes, MBA, has worked at Luther Seminary, St. Paul, Minnesota, since 1992 in Student Services and Enrollment Management, with special emphasis on international education. Currently, she is the director of International Student and Scholar Affairs at Luther Seminary, as well as Principal Designated School Officer (PDSO) and Responsible Officer (RO) for the F and J visa status programs, respectively. Marie has served on various Luther Seminary committees, especially relating to diversity and equity. She has been a member, workshop leader, and trainer with NAFSA: Association of International Educators, and has served in leadership positions for Minnesota International Educators (MIE), the Organization of Liberians in Minnesota (OLM), and her home congregation.

Rev. George R. Hunsberger, PhD, taught New Testament and Christian Ministry at Belhaven University (Mississippi) and Missiology at Western Theological Seminary (Michigan, where he continues to reside in retirement). Previously, he served as a pastor for twelve years in various contexts. He completed the PhD in Missiology and Ecumenics at Princeton Theological Seminary (New Jersey), focusing on Lesslie Newbigin's theology of cultural plurality. He is the author of *Bearing the Witness of the Spirit* and *The Story That Chooses Us*, the co-author of *Missional Church* and *Treasure in Clay Jars*, and the co-editor of *The Church Between Gospel and Culture*, *A Scandalous Prophet*, and *Christian Ethics in Ecumenical Context*. He was the founding coordinator of The Gospel and Our Culture Network in North America.

Rev. Robert Kolb, PhD, professor of systematic theology emeritus, Concordia Seminary, Saint Louis, Missouri, is editor with Timothy J. Wengert of *The Book of Concord* translation (2002) and with Irene Dingel and L'ubomír Batka of *The Oxford Handbook of Martin Luther's Theology* (2014). He wrote *Luther's Treatise on Christian Freedom and Its Legacy* (2019), *Luther's Wittenberg World* (2018), *Martin Luther and the Enduring Word of God* (2016), *Luther and the Stories of God* (2012), *Martin Luther, Confessor of the Faith* (2009), and with Carl Trueman *Between Wittenberg and Geneva* (2017), among other works.

Rev. Hak Joon Lee, PhD, has been professor of theology and ethics at Fuller Theological Seminary, Pasadena, California, since 2011 and was named Lewis B. Smedes Professor of Christian Ethics in September 2015. He is an ordained Minister of Word and Sacrament in the Presbyterian Church (USA). Dr. Lee's research focuses on covenant, public theology, global ethics, Asian American theology and ethics, and the ethics and spirituality of Dr. Martin Luther King Jr. With more than seventeen years of experience in pastoral ministry, Lee's passion has been the renewal of the church in the globalizing, digitized world through the deeper integration of ecclesia and academia. He has written numerous books, articles, and curriculum materials in both English and Korean.

Pum Za Mang, PhD, is associate professor of World Christianity at Myanmar Institute of Theology. His articles have appeared in *Asia Journal of Theology, Church History, Church History and Religious Culture, Dialog, Independent Journal of Burmese Scholarship, International Bulletin of Mission Research, International Journal of Public Theology, International Review of Mission, Journal of Church and State, Studies in World Christianity, The Journal of World Christianity, The Review of Faith & International Affairs, The Expository Times, Theology Today,* and *World Christianity and Interfaith Relations.* His special interests include religion, politics, and ethnicity in his native country of Burma.

Rev. Margaret Kemunto Obaga, PhD, is head of the Diakonia department at the Kenya Evangelical Lutheran Church (KELC). She has previously worked and taught in Germany as an ecumenical staffer in intercultural theology with the Mission EineWelt, the center for mission and development department of the Evangelical Lutheran Church in Bavaria. She also taught intercultural theology at the Evangelical University in Nuremberg, Germany. Dr. Obaga has given numerous presentations and published book chapters and journal essays on, among others, church partnerships, overcoming violence against women, *Ubuntu* as an African way of seeing the world, and intercultural understanding.

Rev. Gary M. Simpson, ThD, is professor of Systematic Theology, Emeritus, and The Northwestern Lutheran Theological Seminary Chair of Theology, Emeritus, at Luther Seminary, St. Paul, Minnesota. In 1990 Luther Seminary called him as associate professor of Systematic Theology, and in 1997 he attained the rank of professor. In 2014 Luther Seminary appointed him The Northwestern Lutheran Theological Seminary Chair of Theology. In 2020 Simpson attained the rank of Emeritus. Prior to Luther Seminary, Simpson held pastorates and chaplaincy appointments as Worker-Priest Associate

Pastor, Immanuel Lutheran Church, Alameda, CA (1976–1983); Protestant Chaplain, Highland-Alameda County Hospital, Oakland, CA (1976–1978); Minister of Youth and Adult Education, St. Charles Christian Church, St. Charles, MO (1981–1983); and Associate Pastor, The Lutheran Church of the Resurrection, Portland, OR (1983–1990).

Rev. Laurie Skow-Anderson, DMin, was elected in 2018 to serve as the Bishop of the Northwest Synod of Wisconsin (NWSWI), one of the most rural synods in the Evangelical Lutheran Church in America. She teaches the missional leadership course at the synod's lay school of ministry and has taught at the Pastor's Academy in Lilongwe, Malawi. Bishop Skow-Anderson previously served four years as the director of Evangelical Mission in the NWSWI and for twenty-five years as pastor in small-town rural congregations in Minnesota. Her 2010 Doctor of Ministry thesis, *Pentecost on the Prairie*, focused on multiracial ministries in rural communities.

Rev. Robert O. Smith, PhD, is assistant professor of history at the University of North Texas (Denton, Texas). Previously, he directed the Briarwood Leadership Center (Argyle, Texas), served as an Associate to the Bishop for the Northern Texas-Northern Louisiana Synod of the ELCA, and directed the University of Notre Dame's Jerusalem Global Gateway, where he was affiliated with both the Department of Theology and the Keough School of Global Affairs. He has served in parish ministry, campus ministry, and churchwide administrative posts for the ELCA. Among other publications he is the author of *More Desired than Our Owne Salvation: The Roots of Christian Zionism* (Oxford, 2013).

Marie-Louise Ström, MA, is originally from South Africa where for twenty years she directed the democracy education program at the Institute for Democracy in South Africa (Idasa). She designed and conducted citizen leadership training programs across the continent of Africa and elsewhere. Now based in Saint Paul, Minnesota, she is assisting with the establishment of the Institute for Public Life and Work. In 2016 she graduated from Luther Seminary with an MA in systematic theology focused on an exploration of how God can, does, and might work in the world through efforts to build more democratic societies.

Rev. John R. Stumme, PhD, is a retired Lutheran pastor. He was Director for Studies in the Church in Society unit of the Evangelical Lutheran Church in America where he was the lead staff person for several social statements and social messages, co-edited books on Lutheran ethics and church and state, helped initiate an annual meeting of Lutheran ethicists, and founded the online *Journal of Lutheran Ethics*. He taught theology and ethics at the ecumenical seminary Instituto Superior Evangélico de Estudios Teológicos (ISEDET) in Buenos Aires, Argentina, and was elected vice president of the Iglesia Evangélica Luterana Unida. He is the author of *Socialism in Theological Perspective: A Study of Paul Tillich, 1918–1933* and of numerous articles in English and Spanish.

Rev. David L. Tiede, PhD, joined Luther Seminary's New Testament faculty in 1971 and served as president from 1987 to 2005. He later became the Bernhard Christensen Professor of Vocation at Augsburg University, then an interim President, first at Wartburg Seminary and then at Luther College. His scholarship focuses on interpreting Luke-Acts in the world of the first century. David reports that reading Scripture with seminary students is a joy and privilege, and he is awed by the competence, creativity, and hope in which Luther Seminary continues to educate leaders for twenty-first-century Christian communities.

Gregory Walter, PhD, is professor of Religion and Harold H. Ditmanson Chair of Religion at Saint Olaf College, Northfield, Minnesota. He is author of *Being Promised: Theology, Gift, and Practice* (Grand Rapids, MI: Wm. B. Eerdmans Publishing, 2013), as well as numerous chapters in books and journals on topics and methodological questions in Christian systematic theology.

Milton Keynes UK
Ingram Content Group UK Ltd.
UKHW011415211223
434786UK00006B/55